Valuation of Regulating Services of Ecosystems

T0330685

Policy and management decisions are often made on financial grounds. However, the economic value of the benefits that people derive from ecosystems, that is, ecosystem services, may not be fully recognised and hence ecosystem considerations may not be incorporated adequately into decision-making processes. This is particularly true for regulating services, the benefits obtained from the regulation of ecosystem processes, the valuation of which requires an interdisciplinary approach. In essence, valuation is a problem-solving strategy and a problem is a problem, it does not respect the boundary of any particular discipline.

The valuation of regulating services is an evolving field of ecological economics. In this book, Dr Pushpam Kumar and Dr Michael D. Wood have invited some of the foremost international experts in the field of ecosystem services valuation to contribute chapters on the valuation of regulating services and highlight some of the main obstacles to the implementation and acceptance of these methodologies in the context of decision-making. The contributors explore the theoretical underpinning of valuation of ecosystem services and demonstrate ways in which these theories can be applied to case-specific problems in order to inform decision-making processes.

This collection clarifies some of the doubt and uncertainty regarding the valuation of regulating services. Innovative methodologies in this field have started to emerge and in coming years there may be much further discussion on this topic as methodologies and understanding continue to evolve. This is a highly active area of interdisciplinary research with far reaching social and environmental implications, and this book should be of interest to those who are new to the field, as well as established experts, in moving both theory and practice forward.

Pushpam Kumar is Reader in Environmental Economics, School of Environmental Sciences, University of Liverpool, UK. His research interests include valuation and accounting of ecosystem services, policies and response options for ecosystem management. He is Scientific Coordinator of the Economics of Ecosystems and Biodiversity (TEEB) and was Coordinating Lead Author and Coordinator, Responses Working Group for the Millennium Ecosystem Assessment and Lead Author for the Fourth Assessment of the IPCC. **Michael D. Wood** is an environmental scientist at the University of Liverpool, UK. His research interests include ecosystem processes, poverty–ecosystem linkages and the development of assessment and decision-making tools for use in ecosystem management.

Routledge explorations in environmental economics
Edited by Nick Hanley
University of Stirling, UK

Valuation of Regulating Services of Ecosystems

Methodology and applications

Edited by Pushpam Kumar and Michael D. Wood

Routledge
Taylor & Francis Group

LONDON AND NEW YORK

First published 2010
by Routledge
2 Park Square, Milton Park, Abingdon, Oxon OX14 4RN

Simultaneously published in the USA and Canada
by Routledge
711 Third Avenue, New York, NY 10017

Routledge is an imprint of the Taylor & Francis Group, an informa business

First issued in paperback 2012

© 2010 Selection and editorial matter, Pushpam Kumar and Michael D.
Wood; individual chapters, the contributors

Typeset in Times by Wearset Ltd, Boldon, Tyne and Wear

British Library Cataloguing in Publication Data
A catalogue record for this book is available from the British Library

Library of Congress Cataloging in Publication Data
A catalog record for this book has been requested

ISBN13: 978-0-415-56987-3 (hbk)
ISBN13: 978-0-415-53982-1 (pbk)
ISBN13: 978-0-203-84760-2 (ebk)

Contents

Contributors

Sara Aniyar, Beijer International Institute of Ecological Economics, The Royal Swedish Academy of Sciences, Stockholm, Sweden.

Ian Bateman, Centre for Social and Economic Research on the Global Environment, School of Environmental Sciences, University of East Anglia, UK.

Saudamini Das, SSN College, University of New Delhi, India.

Helen Ding, Center for Environmental Economics and Management, Department of Economics, Ca' Foscari University of Venice/Fondazione Eni Enrico Mattei, Italy.

Arun M. Dixit, Centre for Environment and Social Concerns (CESC), Ahmedabad, India.

Anantha Duraiappah, Ecosystem Services Economics Unit, Division of Environmental Policy Implementation, United Nations Environment Programme, Kenya.

Thomas Elmqvist, Stockholm Resilience Centre/Department of Systems Ecology, Stockholm University, Sweden.

Brendan Fisher, Woodrow Wilson School of Public and International Affairs, Princeton University, USA.

John M. Gowdy, Department of Economics, Rensselaer Polytechnic Institute, New York, USA.

Laura A. Hildreth, Department of Statistics, Iowa State University, USA.

Kristoffer Hylander, Department of Botany, Stockholm University, Sweden.

Åsa Jansson, Beijer International Institute of Ecological Economics, The Royal Swedish Academy of Sciences, Stockholm, Sweden.

Nicolas Kosoy, Ecosystem Services Economics Unit, Division of Environmental Policy Implementation, United Nations Environment Programme, Kenya.

Jagdish Krishnaswamy, Ashoka Trust for Research in Ecology and the Environment (ATREE), Bangalore, India.

Lalit Kumar, Bhimrao Ambedkari College, University of Delhi, India.

Pushpam Kumar, School of Environmental Sciences, University of Liverpool, UK.

Karl-Göran Mäler, Beijer International Institute of Ecological Economics, The Royal Swedish Academy of Sciences, Stockholm, Sweden.

Carlota Molinero, Ecosystem Services Economics Unit, Division of Environmental Policy Implementation, United Nations Environment Programme, Kenya.

Paulo A.L.D. Nunes, Center for Environmental Economics and Management, Department of Economics, Ca' Foscari University of Venice/Fondazione Eni Enrico Mattei, Italy.

Kinjal Pathak, Centre for Environment and Social Concerns (CESC), Ahmedabad, India.

Aneel Salman, Centre for Public Policy and Governance, Forman Christian University, Lahore, Pakistan.

Kimsey Savadago, Faculty of Economics, University of Ouagadougou, Burkina Faso.

R. David Simpson, National Center for Environmental Economics, United States Environmental Protection Agency, USA.

Rodney B.W. Smith, University of Minnesota, USA.

Sonja Teelucksingh, University of the West Indies, Trinidad and Tobago/Fondazione Eni Enrico Mattei, Italy.

R. Kerry Turner, Centre for Social and Economic Research on the Global Environment, School of Environmental Sciences, University of East Anglia, UK.

Magnus Tuvendal, Stockholm Resilience Centre/Department of Systems Ecology, Stockholm University, Sweden.

Premachandra Wattage, Centre for the Economics and Management of Aquatic Resources (CEMARE), University of Portsmouth, UK.

Michael D. Wood, School of Environmental Sciences, University of Liverpool, UK.

Makiko Yashiro, Ecosystem Services Economics Unit, Division of Environmental Policy Implementation, United Nations Environment Programme, Kenya.

Acknowledgements

The editors wish to acknowledge the support of the United Nations Environment Programme (UNEP) and the Ecosystem Services for Poverty Alleviation (ESPA) programme in the development of this book. The ESPA programme is an initiative developed by three organisations in the United Kingdom, namely the Department for International Development (DfID), the Economic and Social Research Council (ESRC) and the Natural Environment Research Council (NERC). The editors have taken lead roles in two major interdisciplinary projects funded under the ESPA programme: *Ecosystem Services and Poverty Alleviation in South Asia: A Situation Analysis for India and the Hindu Kush Himalayan Region (ESPASSA)* and *Strengthening Capacity to Alleviate Poverty through Ecosystem Services: Putting Methodological Developments into Practice (SCAPES)*. We wish to thank the members of the ESPASSA and SCAPES project teams for the interactions and discussions within those projects which have both directly and indirectly helped to enrich the contents of this book.

1 An introduction to the valuation of regulating services

Pushpam Kumar and Michael D. Wood

1.1 Development of ecosystem services valuation

Valuation of the goods and services people care about is a central issue for decision-makers and, in particular, for economists. Decision-makers look to economists to provide methods to resolve some of the hard and conflicting choices that people face in everyday life. The structured debate on economic value and valuation methodology dates back to the early nineteenth century, beginning with Dupuit (1844) and subsequently Smith (1961), Marshall (1890), Hicks (1946) and many others. The economic value of a resource usually shuttles between 'value for use' and 'value for exchange' through the famous 'water–diamond paradox' described by Adam Smith (1961).

Until the mid-twentieth century, economic value was measured through consumer surplus as propagated by Marshall (1890) and Hicks (1946). The gradual reliance on market price to measure the economic value also became popular (and it still is), as it combines demand (something that has worth to people) and supply (costs incurred to obtain it). Although valuation should be based on demand, economists tend to use the cost of supply due to ease in estimation.

The term 'economic value' invariably gets misconstrued when addressing the problem of ecosystems and natural environment, where interdisciplinary and methodological pluralism take the centre stage – for legitimate reasons. Benefits appropriated from the services that arise as a result of ecosystem structure and processes are popularly termed 'ecosystem services'. These ecosystem services interact with, enrich and enhance various constituents of human well-being (Millennium Ecosystem Assessment, 2003). One popular taxonomy of ecosystem services was presented by the Millennium Ecosystem Assessment (MA), which recognized four categories of service: provisioning (e.g. food, timber), regulating (e.g. climate regulation, waste minimization), cultural (e.g. education and aesthetics) and supporting (e.g. soil formation, nutrient cycling) (Millennium Ecosystem Assessment, 2003, 2005). There are other equally useful ways to categorize ecosystem services, but the appropriate categorization depends upon the purpose for which the analysis is being done. While a standard and unitary classification of ecosystem services may be appealing, it might not prove helpful across the broad range of different decision-making contexts (Wallace, 2007; Fisher and Turner, 2008).

Sustainable ecosystem service delivery depends on the health, integrity and resilience of the ecosystem. For economic valuation, the services flowing from ecosystems must be amenable to economic analysis in that they should serve the consumptive or productive purposes of the humans. Most of the provisioning and cultural services like timber, fish and recreation are services that the economics profession has long been adept at estimating the economic value of. However, regulating services present much greater challenges. Regulating services are the benefits obtained from the regulation of ecosystem processes, including, for example, the regulation of climate, water and some human diseases (Millennium Ecosystem Assessment, 2005). One area of confusion in the valuation of regulating services has been the difficulties faced in deciding on what should be valued – the ecosystem processes or the service. Actually, benefits are the end element of an ecosystem process–service–benefit chain, and only these benefits enter into the domain of well-being that is likely to be analysed for policy and decision-making discourse. Regulating services of ecosystems can be both final and intermediate services. Economic science uses the taxonomy of final and intermediate good, stock and flow for accounting and valuation purposes, so adopting the final and intermediate classification of regulating services enables a more direct alignment and application of classical valuation methodologies to estimating the value of regulating services. A lack of clear understanding about this distinction might lead to double counting and mix income with wealth – not a good way to practise meaningful economics!

As long as the final goods and services produced with the intermediate services as inputs are measurable and enter the domain of the market, valuation can be done. However, difficulties can arise when the role of the regulating service is scale-dependent, with services being intermediate in nature at larger spatial scales, but with final services at smaller scales. In this instance, the valuation approach depends on the decision-making context. For example, maintenance of hydrological flow in a small catchment by forest in the upstream area would be an intermediate product for the economy-wide national income accounting process, but if a payment mechanism is designed between the lowland people (beneficiary) and upland people (provider of services), valuation of the hydrological flow would be required to enable an efficient and credible payments for ecosystem services system to be designed and implemented.

1.2 Applying economic theory to the valuation of ecosystem services

The economic value of ecosystem services is instrumental, anthropocentric, individual-based, subjective, context-dependent, marginal and state-dependent (Goulder and Kennedy, 1997; Baumgartner *et al.*, 2006; Barbier *et al.*, 2009). The marginal value of one unit of ecosystem service – water, for example – does not depend on the total value. Some of the studies done in the past have been criticized on the grounds that marginal value has been added to get the total value (Brauman *et al.*, 2007). In fact, valuation of ecosystem services or ecosystems as natural capital should be done in the range where its demand is inelastic (region II in Figure 1.1). In the range where the demand for natural capital or the flow of ecosystem services from it is perfectly elastic (region I in Figure 1.1) or inelastic (region III in Figure 1.1), valuation is of little benefit because demand is either too sensitive or insensitive to price.

The economic value of any asset, including a natural asset like an ecosystem, is only perceived and revealed where the flow of services proves to be beneficial to people. People would be willing to pay for services when they have to use resources to get these services from alternate sources. Alternatively, the value of ecosystem services is essentially a marginal concept arising out of scarcity and the value would jointly depend upon the condition of the ecosystem and the social cultural context in which people make choices and face conflicting goals for consumption and production. Essentially, the valuation process should consider the effects on ecosystems that are socially important, the prediction of ecological responses must be evaluated in economic value-relevant terms, and finally, the process must consider the possible use of a broad range of valuation methodologies to estimate values (Environmental Protection Agency, 2009). Another important insight on valuation is that the value of ecosystem services would refer to the impact of a small change in the state of the world, and not the state of the world itself (Barbier *et al.*, 2009).

The valuation of ecosystem services is essentially an interdisciplinary effort where economic theory is applied to obtain the relative worth of ecosystem services arising out of scarcity. However, it must adopt and integrate the information on the initial condition of the ecosystem and the resultant change in the flow of services after a change is applied to the system. Information on the initial condition of the ecosystem and then the changed condition due to various drivers of

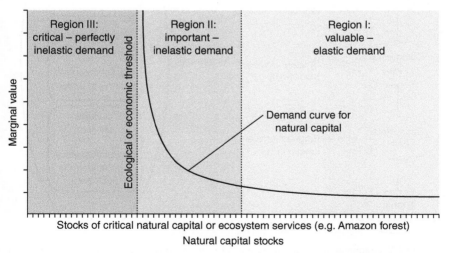

Figure 1.1 Theoretical demand curve for ecosystem services (source: Farley, 2008).

change would help in identifying the ecological production function central to a valuation exercise.

The Scientific Committee of the United States Environmental Protection Agency (EPA) (2009) suggests that ecological models at various levels are responsible for ecological productivity and they in turn map into 'ecological services' (Figure 1.2). These 'ecological services' can easily be mapped into classifications of ecosystem services, such as that presented by MA. In Figure 1.2, ecotourism, water and harvest would fall under provisioning services, flood control under regulating services, and spiritual and aesthetics under cultural services. Accurate mapping of these ecological production functions is a key step in performing reliable estimation of the economic value of regulating services.

There have been numerous studies in recent years, either advocating the need for interdisciplinarity in economic valuation or actually demonstrating how the joint effort of ecology and economics can yield credible and acceptable estimates

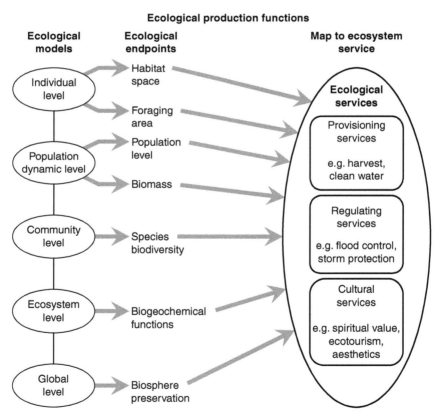

Figure 1.2 Graphical depiction of ecological production functions (source: adapted from EPA, 2009).

of the economic value of ecosystem services (Daily, 1997; Chichilnisky and Heal, 1998; Bjorklud *et al.*, 1999; Heal, 2000; Balmford *et al.*, 2002; Freeman, 2003; Millennium Ecosystem Assessment, 2003, 2005; Rickets *et al.*, 2004; Barbier and Heal, 2006; Johnston *et al.*, 2006; Barbier, 2007; Hanley and Barbier, 2009; Maler and Jansson, 2009; Naeem *et al.*, 2009).

Valuation of regulating services is an evolving field of ecological economics, and although the decision-makers and conservation practitioners recognize the need for valuation, there are few reliable studies (based on sound ecological economic foundations and using credible datasets) that are acceptable to policy-makers. In some case, the ability of ecosystems to sustain biodiversity has been treated as one of its regulating services, though there are few studies where the regulating services of an ecosystem are correlated with biodiversity, especially functional biodiversity. Finally, people's willingness to pay for a reduced risk to ecosystem stability is taken as a regulating service (Tilman *et al.*, 1996). There are other types of regulating services where the benefits have been estimated directly. The role of mangroves in storm protection has been estimated by Barbier (2007), and the value of watershed services has been estimated by Pattanayak and Cramer (2001). Pollination benefits have been evaluated by others (Rickets *et al.*, 2004; Maler *et al.*, 2008, 2009). The emerging challenges to valuation are bound to motivate economists and ecologists to come out with more studies in the near future.

For any ecosystem service, its social value must be equated with the discounted net present value of the flow of that service (Hanley and Barbier, 2009). Decision-makers tasked with making choices would like to see that the marginal benefit – for example, of conservation of urban or coastal wetlands – equates with the marginal costs of conservation. Typically, regulating services like bioremediation and nutrient cycling by wetlands are ignored as they are outside of the conventional market. As a result, the marginal cost of conservation exceeds the marginal benefit of conservation, which sends the wrong signal to policy-makers. Social choice becomes sub-optimal and inefficient. In this context, incorporating valuation of regulating services into the analysis would make the decision-making efficient and optimal (Kumar *et al.*, 2001). There are many other decision contexts where valuation of regulating services would also help the distribution and conservation goal worthy and attractive on the basis of economic arguments. The contexts could be public policy (cost–benefit analysis), evaluation of damage to ecosystems and resource allocation for a conservation goal, to name a few.

1.3 Book overview

In this book, we have invited some of the foremost international experts in the field of ecosystem services valuation to contribute chapters on the current state-of-the-art in the valuation of regulating services. These contributions highlight some of the main obstacles in the implementation and acceptance of regulating services valuation methodologies in the context of decision-making. The contributors have explored the theoretical underpinning of valuation of ecosystem services and demonstrated ways in which these theories can be applied to case-specific problems in order to provide information for decision-makers. Given that this field of ecological economics is still in its infancy, there is still much debate and discourse on the topic of valuation of regulating services. This is reflected in some of the opposing views presented by the different contributors. We make no value judgment regarding the views expressed by the contributing authors, leaving the reader to draw their own conclusions.

Readers will note that there is some overlap in the material presented in the different chapters, especially in terms of theoretical discussion. This is intentional and necessary as each chapter is intended to be self-contained and comprehensive in its consideration of the topic. It is envisaged that, in addition to being of interest to conservation managers and development practitioners, this book will be an important reference text for students of environmental/ecological economics. The self-contained nature of individual chapters will enable students to readily access material without the need to refer to previous chapters (although reading the chapters in order will improve the reader's overall understanding of the topic).

The book has been divided into three main parts: concepts (Part I), methodological applications (Part II) and synthesis (Part III). The following paragraphs provide an overview of the purpose and content of these parts.

Part I discusses some of the philosophical arguments and theoretical considerations underpinning the ecosystem services concept, with a specific focus on regulating services.

In Chapter 2, Fischer *et al.* open the theoretical discourse with an analysis of some of the important issues practitioners must consider prior to attempting to link ecological and economic models via valuation approaches. The analysis is centred on three major themes: 'services versus benefits', 'price versus value' and 'here and now versus there and then'. Through consideration of the distinction between services and benefits, Fisher *et al.* present a mechanism by which the concept of ecosystem services, *sensu* the MA, can be operationalized in the context of economic valuation. The authors go on to demonstrate the difference between price and value, the latter being the focus for decision-making. Finally, they discuss the temporal and spatial consideration pertaining to the development and implementation of valuation exercises.

In Chapter 3, Elmqvist *et al.* present a more ecological perspective on regulating services. They demonstrate the role of economics in developing methodologies to manage trade-offs between provisioning and regulating services. Building on the analysis presented, Elmqvist *et al.* propose a general framework for managing these trade-offs using a landscape-based approach.

The theoretical discussion is continued by Simpson (Chapter 4), with a critique of the 'ecosystem services framework'. He questions both the justification for adopting an 'ecosystem services framework' and the extent to which some prominent examples of valuation of regulating services can withstand detailed scrutiny. The views expressed in the chapter may be seen as controversial by many readers, but they highlight some of the fundamental theoretical and methodological considerations that underpin this field of ecological economics.

Part II builds on the theoretical discussion presented in Part I, considering various methodological approaches for estimating the economic value of regulating services and, through a range of case studies, demonstrates some of the ways in which these methodologies have been applied in practice.

In Chapter 5, Smith *et al.* estimate both a quadratic production function and a directional output distance function for agricultural crops in order to evaluate the role of water inputs on crop yield. The study is centred on Burkina Faso in West Africa. The two principal crops under consideration are white sorghum and millet. Based on the results of the analysis presented, the authors conclude that water harvesting (e.g. using mulch to increase soil moisture retention) could be a valuable poverty reduction strategy in the region.

Through consideration of economic and ecological theory, Mäler *et al.* (Chapter 6) describe methodologies that can be used to estimate the accounting prices for regulating services. Their methodological analysis demonstrates the importance of defining the purpose behind valuation prior to selecting and applying a valuation methodology, as well as the requirement for adequate interdisciplinary understanding of the ecosystem services to be valued.

In Chapter 7, Wattage analyses the application of stated-preference methods for valuing coastal ecosystem services in two case studies. The contingent valuation method (CVM) is used to estimate the total economic value of wetland conservation in Mutharajawela Marsh and Negombo Lagoon in Sri Lanka. In the second case study, choice experiments, which are often regarded as both an evolution of and alternative to CVM, are used to demonstrate the process of marine protected area decision-making in the context of the deep-water Lophelia reefs of the Republic of Ireland. Both approaches are shown to be effective in capturing the non-use values of ecosystems.

Das (Chapter 8) continues the coastal ecosystem theme with a demonstration of the application of valuation methodology to regulating services in an analysis of the storm protection value of mangroves in the Kendrapada District of the Indian state of Orissa. Das takes a highly interdisciplinary approach, drawing on both biophysical and economic methodologies to estimate a cyclone damage function. The analysis reveals that the storm protection value of mangroves is high, the presence of mangrove forests having been shown to significantly reduce the extent of cyclone damage on the leeward side of the forests.

Ding *et al.* (Chapter 9) consider another regulating service of forests – carbon sequestration. They present an economic valuation of the impact of climate change on forest regulating services in Europe. As with other chapters in Part II, Chapter 9 demonstrates the interdisciplinary nature of estimating the economic value of regulating services. Using global circulation models and integrated assessment models, an economic assessment of the carbon sequestration in European forests is presented and future projections are made based on the four climate change scenarios that have been presented by the Intergovernmental Panel on Climate Change.

In Chapter 10, Dixit *et al.* apply the benefit transfer method to estimate the economic value of coral reef systems in the Gulf of Kachchh in the Indian state of Gujarat. The estimated net present value of the total benefits arising from coral reef ecosystem services in the case study region demonstrate the very high value of the coral reefs and their importance for the local economy.

Part III provides three synthesis chapters.

In Chapter 11, Gowdy and Salman discuss various ways to value ecosystem functions in terms of the hierarchies of services provided and the complex relationship between economic and ecological systems. The interrelated problems of ecosystem integrity, human institutions and climate change are explored using data from the village of Keti Bunder in Pakistan's Sindh province. The analysis demonstrates the dependence of the poor on ecosystem services and, more specifically, confirms that, in the case of Keti Bunder, the gross domestic product of the poor is largely dependent on ecosystem services. The analysis also demonstrates the extent to which coastal ecosystems are under threat from both environmental changes and institutional failures.

Kosoy *et al.* (Chapter 12) review recent research on the valuation of regulating services. Through comparison of orthodox and heterodox valuation methodologies, the authors identify some of the key underlying assumptions of the methods and implications of these assumptions for policy design and implementation. The authors reflect on the various valuation approaches that have been applied within the sub-global assessments of the MA and discuss the role of valuation in decision-making.

The chapters described above guide the reader through the development of the theory, methodology and application of valuation methodologies in the context of regulating services. However, as noted previously, this is a developing field of ecological economics and there are many areas of research that need to be addressed, both in terms of the socioeconomic and biophysical aspects of valuing regulating services. In the final chapter (Chapter 13), we consider some of the emerging research priorities and the likely future directions and applications of valuation methodologies for incorporating regulating services into the domain of decision-making.

References

Balmford, A., Bruner, A., Cooper, P., Costanza, R., Farber, S. Green, R.E., Jenkins, M., Jefferiss, P., Jessamy, V., Madden, J., Munro, K., Myers, N., Naeem, N., Paavola, J., Rayment, M., Rosendo, R., Roughgarden, J., Trumper, K. and Turner, R.K. (2002) Economic reasons for conserving the wild nature. *Science* 397, 950–953.

Barbier, E.B. (2007) Valuing ecosystem services as productive inputs. *Economic Policy* 22 (49), 177–229.

Barbier, E.B. and Heal, Geoffrey M. (2006) Valuing ecosystem services. *The Economists' Voice* 3 (3), Art. 2.

Barbier, E.B., Baumgärtner, S., Chopra, K., Costello, C., Duraiappah, A., Hassan, R., Kinzig, A., Lehman, M., Pascual, U., Polasky, S. and Perrings, C. (2009) The valuation of ecosystem services. In Naeem, S.D., Bunker, E., Hector, A., Loreau, M. and Perrings, C. (2009) *Biodiversity, Ecosystem Functioning, and Human Well-being*, Oxford University Press, Oxford.

Baumgartner, S., Becker, C., Manstetten, R. and Faber, M. (2006) Relative and absolute scarcity of nature: assessing the roles of economics and ecology for biodiversity conservation. *Ecological Economics*, 59, 487–498.

Bjorklud, J., Limburg, K.E. and Rydberg, T. (1999) Impact of production intensity on the ability of the agricultural landscape to generate ecosystem services: an example from Sweden. *Ecological Economics* 29, 269–291.

Brauman, Kate A., Daily, G.C., Duarte, T.K. and Mooney, H. (2007) The nature and value of ecosystem services: an overview highlighting hydrological services. *Annual Review of Environmental Resources* 32, 67–98.

Chichilnisky, G. and Heal, G. (1998) Economic return from the biosphere. *Nature* 391, 629–630.

Costanza, R., D'Arge, R., DeGroot R., Farber, S., Grasso, M., Hannon B., Limburg, K., Naeem, S., O'Neill, R., Paruelo, J., Raskin, R., Sutton, P. and van den Belt, M. (1997) The value of the world's ecosystem services and natural capital. *Nature*, 387, 253–260.

Daily, G.C. (1997) (ed.) *Nature's Services: Societal Dependence on Natural Ecosystems*, Island Press, Washington, DC.

Daily, G.C., Soderqvist, T., Anyar, S., Arrow, K.J., Dasgupta, P., Ehrlich, P.R., Folke, C., Jansson, A., Jansson, B.-O., Kautsky, N., Levin, S., Lubchenco, J., Maler, K.-G., Simpson, D., Starrett, D., Tilman, D. and Walker, B. (2000) The value of nature and the nature of value. *Science* 289, 395–396.

Dupuit, J.J. (1844) De la measure de l'utilite de travaux publics, *Annales des Ponts et Chaussees*, 8 (2), 332–375.

EPA (2009) Valuing the protection of ecological systems and services, a report of the EPA Science Advisory Committee, EPA-SAB-09-012, May. Available at: www.epa.gov/sab.

Farley, J. (2008). The role of prices in conserving critical natural capital. *Conservation Biology* 22 (6), 1399–1408.

Fisher, B. and Turner, K. (2008) Ecosystem services: classification for valuation. *Biological Conservation* 141, 1167–1169.

Freeman, A.M. (2003) *The Measurement of Environmental and Resource Values: Theory and Methods*, Resource for the Future, Washington, DC.

Goulder, L.H. and Kennedy, J. (1997) Valuing ecosystem services: philosophical bases and empirical methods. In Daily, G.C. (ed.) *Nature's Services: Societal Dependence on Natural Ecosystems*, Island Press, Washington, DC.

Hanley, N. and Barbier, E.B. (2009) *Pricing Nature: Cost Benefit Analysis and Environmental Policy*, Edward Elgar, Cheltenham.

Heal, G. (2000) Valuing ecosystem services. *Ecosystems* 3, 24–30.

Hicks, J. (1946) *Value and Capital*, Clarendon Press, Oxford.

Johnston, R.J., Ranson, M.H., Basedin, E.Y. and Helm, E.C. (2006) What determines willingness to pay per fish? A meta analysis of recreational fishing values. *Marine Resource Economics* 21, 1–31.

Kumar, P., Babu, C.R., Sharma, R.S. and Love, A. (2001) Valuation of ecological services of wetland ecosystems: a case study of Yamuna floodplain in the corridors of Delhi, Mimeograph, IEG, Delhi.

Maler, K.G., Aniyar, S. and Jansson, A. (2008) Accounting for ecosystem services as a way to understand the requirements for sustainable development. *Proceedings of the National Academy of Sciences* 105, 9501–9506.

Maler, K.G., Anyar, S. and Jansson, A. (2009) Accounting for ecosystems. *Environment and Resource Economics* 42, 39–51.

Marshall, A. (1890*) Principles of Economics*, McMillan, New York.

Millennium Ecosystem Assessment (MA) (2003) *People and Ecosystems: A Framework for Assessment*, Island Press, Washington, DC.

Millennium Ecosystem Assessment (MA) (2005) *Findings from Responses Working Group*, Island Press: Washington, DC.

Naeem, S.D., Bunker, E., Hector, A., Loreau, M. and Perrings, C. (2009) *Biodiversity, Ecosystem Functioning, and Human Well-being*, Oxford University Press, Oxford.

Pattanayak, S.K. (2004) Valuing watershed services: concepts and empirics from southeast Asia. *Agriculture, Ecosystems & Environment* 104: 171–184.

Pattanayak, Subhrendu K. and Kramer, Randall A. (2001). Worth of watersheds: A producer surplus approach for valuing drought mitigation in Eastern Indonesia. *Environment and Development Economics* 6 (1), 123–146.

Rickets, T.H., Daily, G.C., Ehrlic, P.R. and Michener, C.D. (2004) Economic value of tropical forest to coffee production, *Proceedings of the National Academy of Sciences* 101, 12579–12582.

Smith, A. (1961) *An Inquiry into the Nature and Causes of the Wealth of Nations*, edited by Edwin Cannan, Methuen, London.

Tilman, D., Wedin, D. and Knops, J. (1996) Productivity and sustainability influenced by biodiversity in grassland ecosystems. *Nature* 379, 718–720.

Wallace, K.J. (2007) Classification of ecosystem services: problems and solutions. *Biological Conservation* 139, 235–246.

Part I
Concepts

2 Valuing ecosystem services

Benefits, values, space and time

Brendan Fisher, Ian Bateman and R. Kerry Turner

2.1 Introduction

A growing body of evidence suggests that in the twenty-first century we will face a number of pressing and interrelated problems, including large-scale conversion of ecosystems and the subsequent loss of biodiversity (Millennium Ecosystem Assessment, 2005); increasing poverty and water scarcity (Rosegrant *et al.*, 2003); potentially dangerous alteration in the climate system (Schneider, 2001; Mastrandrea and Schneider, 2004); and global fisheries collapse (Myers and Worm, 2003). These problems are occurring on an unprecedented scale and are inherently connected to growing societal demands. The mitigation of these problems requires a deeper comprehension of the environmental infrastructure upon which human existence and welfare depends (Schroter *et al.*, 2005; Sachs and Reid, 2006).

The concepts of ecosystem services and 'natural capital' have recently been developed to make explicit this connection between human welfare and ecological sustainability for policy, development and conservation initiatives (Daily, 1997; Millennium Ecosystem Assessment, 2005). Recent efforts have shown that incorporating ecosystem services into land use decisions typically favours conservation activities or sustainable management over the conversion of intact ecosystems (Balmford *et al.*, 2002; Turner *et al.*, 2003). Although much ecosystem service research is still at an early stage, systematic approaches to measuring, modelling and mapping of ecosystem services, governance analysis and valuation are needed urgently. In order to make progress in these areas it must be transparent what is being considered an ecosystem service versus other concepts in the literature, such as ecosystem processes, functions, goods and benefits. This delineation is of particular import to any valuation exercises that might accompany ecosystem service research. There are important economic concepts that need to be made transparent for meaningful estimates to be made. These concepts include the distinction between prices and values, and acknowledgment that values are context specific – meaning they change across space and time. This chapter discusses these issues with the aim of informing valuation exercises from an economic perspective.

2.2 Services versus benefits

In 2005 the Millennium Ecosystem Assessment (MA) defined a framework for relating ecosystem services to the larger scientific and policy communities. It proved to be an important development and excellent heuristic. The MA divided ecosystem services into a few very understandable categories – supporting services, regulating services, provisioning services and cultural services. This in turn makes the classification scheme readily accessible as a heuristic to decision-makers and non-scientists. The MA delivered a broad definition (by design) of ecosystem services as 'the benefits humans obtain from ecosystems'. However, this definition has not been shown to be operational for all research purposes (Boyd and Banzhaf, 2007; Wallace, 2007; Fisher and Turner, 2008; Maeler *et al.*, 2008), and efforts have been made to more carefully classify and understand ecosystem services to make their analysis more operational (see Fisher *et al.*, 2009 for review).

We have argued elsewhere (Fisher and Turner, 2008; Fisher *et al.*, 2009) that a simpler delineation of intermediate services, final services and benefits is more useful for valuation. There are multiple relationships between ecosystem processes and human benefits (see Boyd and Banzhaf, 2007 for a description of the benefit-dependence aspect of ecosystem services), but what is important for valuation exercises is that you value the endpoints that have a direct effect on human welfare – in economics these are considered through the use of the term 'benefits'. Both intermediate and final services are ecological phenomena (as opposed to things like cultural fulfilment). The term 'intermediate services' here is similar to the MA's 'supporting services', and these intermediate services combine in complex ways to provide final services, which have direct effects on human welfare. Benefits, which include things like wood, food and cultural aspects and recreation, are related but different to the services that provide them. For example, water regulation and drinking water are not the same thing. Benefits also typically require other forms of capital to affect human welfare. For example, clean drinking water for consumption is a *benefit* of the final service of water provision. In turn, water provision by an ecosystem is a function of the intermediate services, including nutrient cycling and soil retention. The end benefit typically requires some built capital to be realized, whether it is a well or an urban water distribution system.

In this scheme we avoid the double counting flaws acknowledged in earlier ecosystem service valuation exercises. This is not the case for the MA classification, which could lead to double counting the value of some ecosystem services. For example, in the MA, nutrient cycling is a supporting service, water flow regulation is a regulating service, and recreation is a cultural service. However, if you were a decision-maker contemplating the conversion of a wetland, and you utilized a cost–benefit analysis including these three services, you would commit the error of double counting. This is because nutrient cycling and water regulation both help to provide the same service under consideration, providing usable water. The MA's recreation service is actually a human benefit of that water pro-

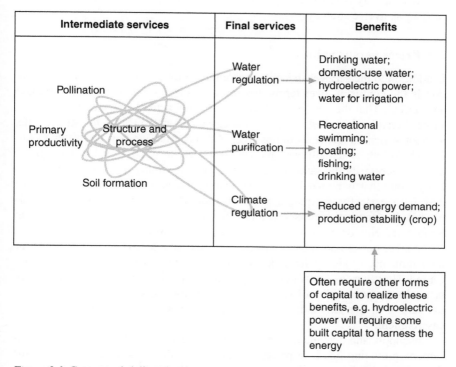

Intermediate services	Final services	Benefits
Pollination Primary productivity Structure and process Soil formation	Water regulation	Drinking water; domestic-use water; hydroelectric power; water for irrigation
	Water purification	Recreational swimming; boating; fishing; drinking water
	Climate regulation	Reduced energy demand; production stability (crop)

Often require other forms of capital to realize these benefits, e.g. hydroelectric power will require some built capital to harness the energy

Figure 2.1 Conceptual delineation between ecosystem services and the benefits derived from them (source: Fisher *et al.* 2009).

vision. An analogy is that when buying a live chicken you do not pay for the price of a full chicken, plus the price of two legs, two wings, head, neck and other body parts, you simply pay the price of a whole chicken.

Figure 2.1 provides a conceptual example of our schema, where complex ecosystem processes and functions give rise to ecosystem services (final and intermediate), which then interface with direct human usage and provide benefits. Again, some benefits require other forms of capital in order to be realized. For example, hydroelectric power requires water provision and regulation from ecosystems, but also requires dams and transmission infrastructure.

This line of argument, however, is not meant to imply that intermediate services have no value. Without a sufficient configuration of structure and processes, ecosystems will not function (or will function less well) and will not provide the diverse range of final services and benefits that they could potentially deliver (Turner, 1999; Gren *et al.*, 1994). Regulating services that provide the capacity to respond to environmental stresses and shocks are encompassed by the concepts of infrastructure or primary value associated with the role that functional diversity can play in certain contexts, providing increased ecological stability and resilience. The conservation and protection of regulating and support services capacity is in some ways a decision about reducing risk and the costs of such a risk averse strategy.

2.3 Prices versus values

In addition to the services–benefits problem regarding ecosystem services valuation is the confusion over terms that most people use interchangeably: 'value' and 'price'. That they are not in fact equivalent is actually very easy to demonstrate. Consider that most basic of all necessities, water. This is the stuff of life, without which existence is impossible. Yet the price we pay for water in our household bills is actually very modest. It is clear to see that 'value' and 'price' are not necessarily the same thing. In fact, price is simply that portion of underlying value that is realized within the market place. Now, in many cases price may be a perfectly acceptable approximation of value, particularly for goods produced in competitive markets and where there is not large-scale intervention by governments or other authorities. Indeed, even when these latter distortions (i.e. market power and subsidy effects) do arise, economists can often adjust for their influence to yield what is known as the 'shadow value' of the goods concerned. However, as the water example shows, market price can in some cases be a poor approximation of value. Indeed, this divergence can often be substantial and is a characteristic of many of the goods produced by the natural environment.

So, supply and demand can interact in ways that are highly beneficial to consumers, providing goods at prices that are below the value consumers have for those goods. This excess between price and value is known as the 'consumer surplus'.[1] Of course decision-makers should be interested in the value different goods provide rather than their price. Indeed, this constitutes the fundamental difference between accountants and economists. While the former are interested in price, the latter are (or at least should be) interested in value.

Here the fundamental problem facing any economic analysis is one of measurement – i.e. how do we measure the value or utility provided by any given good? The economist's solution is to use a surrogate measure that is highly compatible with the decision-making process and is transparent and amenable to subsequent adjustment if we wish to allow for different circumstances across individuals. That measure is to assess the amount that individuals are prepared to pay for changes in the provision of goods. Note immediately that we are relating value to willingness to pay (WTP) rather than what actually has to be paid. A simple example serves to illustrate the importance of this difference. Consider the value of walking in a woodland. This generates benefits including exercise, appreciation of nature, perhaps entertainment of one's children and inner calm. Yet if the woodland is publicly owned, the amount paid to enter such a wood is likely to be zero. Clearly, here, price paid is a highly misleading indicator of value.

Arguably, there is no perfect way in which to estimate the value of any good. However, several decades of research have resulted in the development of a variety of valuation methods, including the following:

- Adjusted market prices. For goods that are traded in markets and have prices we can estimate WTP by examining the reaction of demand to observed variations in prices. Adjustments need to be made for distortions arising from factors such as imperfect (non-competitive) markets and policy interventions (e.g. taxes and subsidies). This allows the analyst to estimate consumer surplus and hence values. For example, one can estimate part of the value of improved water quality by examining the increased value of commercial fishing catches.
- Productivity methods. Ecosystem services often provide the factors of production required to produce marketed goods. Production functions relating inputs to the output of goods can be estimated and the contribution of individual services assessed. Continuing the water quality improvement example, one could also estimate the value generated by greater agricultural productivity, or the decreased costs of providing clean drinking water.
- Revealed preference methods. Many goods that capture environmental services can only be enjoyed through money purchases. For example, individuals may pay extra for homes in quiet neighbourhoods or incur substantial costs to visit areas of natural beauty. By relating behaviour to the characteristics of those goods, one can observe the money–environment trade-off and so reveal the values held by individuals for the environmental good.
- Stated-preference methods. The most direct of all approaches is to ask individuals to state their willingness to pay for some change in the provision of an environmental good.

In practice, the costs of conducting novel valuation research across the multitude of potential decision situations often means that analysts are forced to rely on value transfer methods, which transfer existing benefit estimates from studies already completed for another location or issue.

In addition to the various valuation methods described above, many studies adopt simpler 'pricing methods', such as avoided damage or expected damage approaches, which examine the costs of avoiding damages due to lost or at-risk services (e.g. the loss of coastal wetlands and subsequent changes in the impact of storm events).

The damage-cost-avoided approach is also used by the IPCC to underpin the economic analysis of their climate change assessments (Pearce *et al.*, 1996). Here the process, in situations as complex as climate regulation, is typically an agglomeration of valuation techniques such as revealed preference approaches for market goods and WTP in hypothetical markets for non-market goods.

With this approach again, the focus is on the benefits, or technically the avoided costs – the damages that are the results of climate change impacts on individual and societal welfare. Ecological and atmospheric modelling are at the cornerstone of this approach, as these underpin any valuation estimates. Table 2.1 shows some of the key damages that could be valued as a result of a doubling of CO_2 concentration in the atmosphere. Here we see that there are both market and non-market effects of CO_2 increases. Major market consequences will be felt in the agricultural sector. The impacts of climate change will be manifested in agricultural production through process effects such as heat stress, soil moisture loss, pest/disease increases, shorter growing season (where temperatures rise too high) and precipitation decrease. Conversely, these same effects might produce benefits, such as increased precipitation in some regions, longer growing seasons in higher latitudes and carbon fertilization effects. This shows exactly why damage and value estimates are spatially heterogeneous and need to be evaluated at scales appropriate to capture these distinctions.

We can see both market and non-market damages from a sector like forestry. Where climate change may negatively affect forest cover and therefore timber values in a region, but also elicit losses in recreational and cultural significance. Several of the impacts in Table 2.1 are easy to estimate and several are rather difficult. Examples of the latter include the values of species loss, and damages due to increases in hot and colds spells, which will be both spatially and temporally heterogeneous.

Table 2.1 Potential damages from CO_2 doubling in market and non-market sectors

	Market impacts	*Non-market impacts*
Primary economic sector	Other sectors Property loss Extreme event damage Ecosystem damage	Human impacts Extreme events
Agriculture	Water supply Dryland lost Hurrican damage Wetland loss	Human life Hurricane damage
Forestry	Energy demand Coastal protection Damage from drought Forest loss	Air pollution Damage from drought
Fisheries	Leisure activities Urban infrastructure Non-tropical storms Species loss	Water pollution Non-tropical storms
Insurance	River floods Other ecosystem loss	Migration River floods
Construction	Hot/cold spells	Morbidity Hot/cold spells
Transport		Physical comfort
Energy supply		Political stability Human hardship

Source: adapted from Pearce *et al.* 1996.

We can see that estimating these damages is heavily reliant on the ecological and atmospheric models that predict how changes in greenhouse gas emissions will affect land cover, seascapes and ecosystem functions and responses. Even with sophisticated, spatially explicit models there are still a number caveats and assumptions that need to be highlighted. On the biophysical side, damages will be a function of the rate of change, as well as the degree to which different eco-systems are linked. For example, how exactly does the evapotranspiration from the Amazon affect agricultural productivity in North America – i.e. how tightly linked are regions and ecosystems?

Another approach has been to use replacement costs as a proxy for the loss of existing ecosystem services. This is not a true valuation method as it is not based on WTP, but can be an effective approach demonstrating the importance of eco-system services to policy-makers. In this context, the 'cost versus value' distinc-tion raises similar concerns to the 'price versus value' distinction. It is easy to make the error of assuming that the replacement cost is the true value (benefit) of the service under assessment. It is also the case that the method can result in unrealistically high estimates.

2.4 'Here and now' versus 'there and then'

As intimated above, the value of an ecosystem service is dependant on where the service is delivered and the time at which the value is being assessed. The fact that valuation is temporally and spatially contextual is what we mean by 'here and now' versus 'there and then'.

Let us first deal with the spatial aspects. First, there are several spatial rela-tionships between where an ecosystem service is produced and where the benefit is felt. Some ecosystem services are produced in the same area where the benefit is realized. For example, soil formation occurs in a given spot and may be uti-lized as an ecosystem service when a farmer plants a crop in that locale. Some ecosystem services are produced in one place, but the benefit is felt elsewhere. Water regulation is a good example of this, where an up-slope vegetated land-scape may attenuate rain runoff and conduct surface water into the ground, which then returns to the surface as part of a river that flows down-slope. Here a downstream user benefits from the upstream landscape. Another such relation-ship is where a service is produced in a particular spot, but the entire world may receive benefits from it. Carbon storage is one example, where it does not matter where the carbon is being stored – all of humanity benefits from it (if we desire our current, relatively stable climate regime). In essence, ecosystem services 'flow' from a point of production to a point of use.

This 'flow' of service changes through space in at least three ways:

1   The biophysical process itself varies across the landscape or seascape. This is obvious in the above example, pointing to how carbon storage or net primary productivity is going to vary based on things like slope, aspect, ele-vation, species and structural diversity.

2   The benefits and beneficiaries change across a landscape. Water regulation might be an important service for providing the irrigation potential to farmers abutting a forest or woodland – the same service might provide the benefit of hydroelectric power to beneficiaries far downstream. These user groups will hold different values and preferences for this water regulation, report different WTP, and hold different information about how the system works. All of these will affect an aggregate valuation assessment.
3   The costs of provision of the ecosystem service will likely vary across space. Consider forest protection for the sake of regulating water flows. To local people habituated to utilize forest resources for non-timber forest products (NTFP) collection, their opportunity cost is the lost availability to collect such resources. To local livestock keepers the cost might be the increased predation or disease transmission to livestock. To urban water users the cost might only be a small additional fee on water bills.

The reality that ecosystem service provision changes in its ecological processes, magnitude, beneficiaries and costs across space is critical for any valuation process. This demands that spatially explicit ecological models, a detailed understanding of benefit stakeholders and knowledge of all costs (including opportunity costs) be incorporated for robust ecosystem service valuation exercises.

The *now* and *then* of ecosystem service research implies that just as services and benefits change across space, they also change across time. Let us consider three reasons why ecosystem services or the value of their benefits change across time and why this is important for valuation.

First, the ecological conditions or processes themselves change over time. For example, a restored wetland attenuates larger storm surges, assimilates more heavy metals and houses more breeding waders. Conversely, a shrinking woodland may produce less NTFPs, store less carbon and house fewer pollinator species. Any ecosystem service assessment occurs at a point in time. Future changes in ecosystem condition or function can be modelled based on past changes, forecasted based on predicted future drivers of change, or perhaps instigated through scenario building and analysis. The very fact that ecosystem service research has risen to such prominence in science and policy circles is based on an acknowledgement that over the past few decades we have seen precipitous declines in the provision of some services in certain locales.

Second, over time societies' preferences change. For example, wetlands were once more commonly and derisorily termed 'bogs' and 'swamps'. They were often considered to be wasteland to be improved by drainage. Now, in many places, such wetlands are highly valued for their ability to provide superb wildlife habitat, store carbon and assimilate pollutants such as nitrogen and heavy metals. To some degree this change in preferences can be explained by the dwindling supply of such natural resources (it is noticeable that in countries where such resources are still common, they are often less prized). However, increasing real incomes and leisure time, and better transportation and a growing appreciation of the services of such areas, all play a part in the transformation of such values. This causes considerable difficulty for economic analyses as it is difficult to assess changes in future preferences.

The sustainability literature offers a strategy based on the maintenance of a set of 'opportunities' carried across intergenerational timescales. The core idea is that future generations should possess at least the equivalent set of economic, social, cultural and other opportunities as previous generations. Natural capital (ecosystems and their relationships) should be conserved as a store of wealth and wealth creation opportunities. Taking a weak sustainability position, natural capital can be extensively substituted for by human and physical capital. From a strong sustainability perspective, important components of the natural capital stock are 'critical' to life support and other services, and cannot be substituted – their loss is effectively irreversible. So-called social capital also needs to be nurtured in a strong sustainability policy world (Neumayer, 2003; Pearce and Turner, 1990).

Third, and linked to this second point, is the complexity that individuals tend to prefer benefits to be provided sooner rather than later (and the opposite for costs). For example, people typically prefer $100 today rather than $105 a year from now. This seemingly innocuous facet of preferences leads to the problem of discounting – that the present-day value of future benefits (and costs) falls the further into the future those values occur. Determining the nature and rate of this decline is important as it can radically alter present-day assessments of the value of different options. For ecosystem service assessments it is clear that the economist should not adopt the discount preferences of the individual, but rather use a social discount function (Pearce *et al.*, 2003). It is also becoming more obvious from a strong sustainability viewpoint that the discount function (particularly for non-market benefits – for example, from ecosystem services) should be declining in nature for large-scale societal decisions (Turner, 2007). This means that in each time period the rate at which a benefit (or cost) is discounted should itself decline. This reflects the longevity of society and the greater weight placed upon delayed benefits and costs relative to the preferences of individuals. That said, the choice of discount function can have massive impacts upon the economic assessment of long-term concerns such as ecosystem services – sensitivity analyses of the impact of different discounting strategies are advisable. In the end, ethics plays as important a part as economics in the discounting debate.

2.5 Conclusion

The importance of providing policy-makers with timely and robust estimates of the value and benefits of well-functioning ecosystems has never been more critical. As Professor Jeffrey Sachs said in his 2007 Reith Lectures, the world is 'bursting at the seams'. While there is still much ignorance with regards to how ecosystems function to provide benefits to human, how humans behave and value such benefits, and how these two interact in the face of diminishing natural capital, we are beginning to make some progress, both conceptually and analytically, so that we can deliver estimates and recommendations to decision-makers. In this chapter, we discussed casually a few of the conclusions that natural scientists and economists are coming to regarding this literature, including the importance of delineating between goods and services, the understanding that market prices may serve as a poor proxy for individual or societal values, and that ecosystem service assessment needs to include spatial and temporal aspects to be truly policy relevant. While these are just three small conceptual steps in the typical long journey of an ecosystem service assessment, they are critical steps, in each journey.

Note

1 Of course, where either demand or supply changes, so does price. Consider, for example, the long-standing drought in Australia and how this affects water prices.

References

Balmford, A., A. Bruner, P. Cooper, R. Costanza, S. Farber, R.E. Green, M. Jenkins, P. Jefferiss, V. Jessamy, J. Madden, K. Munro, N. Myers, S. Naeem, J. Paavola, M. Rayment, S. Rosendo, J. Roughgarden, K. Trumper and R.K. Turner. 2002. Ecology: Economic reasons for conserving wild nature. *Science* 297: 950–953.

Boyd, J. and S. Banzhaf. 2007. What are ecosystem services? *Ecological Economics* 63: 616–626.

Daily, G.C. 1997. *Nature's Services: Societal Dependence on Natural Ecosystems*. Island Press, Washington, DC.

Fisher, B. and R.K. Turner. 2008. Ecosystem services: Classification for valuation. *Biological Conservation* 141: 1167–1169.

Fisher, B., R.K. Turner and P. Morling. 2009. Defining and classifying ecosystem services for decision making. *Ecological Economics* 68: 643–653.

Gren, I.M., C. Folke, K. Turner and I. Batemen. 1994. Primary and secondary values of wetland ecosystems. *Environmental and Resource Economics* 4 (1): 55–74.

Maeler, K.G., S. Aniyar and A. Jansson. 2008. Accounting for ecosystem services as a way to understand the requirements for sustainable development. *Proceedings of the National Academy of Sciences* 105 (28): 9501–9506.

Mastrandrea, M.D. and S.H. Schneider. 2004. Probabilistic integrated assessment of 'dangerous' climate change. *Science* 304: 571–575.

Millennium Ecosystem Assessment. 2005. Island Press, Washington, DC.

Myers, R.A. and B. Worm. 2003. Rapid worldwide depletion of predatory fish communities. *Nature* 423: 280–283.

Nuemayer, E. 2003. *Weak Versus Strong Sustainability*. Edward Elgar, Cheltenham.

Pearce, D. and R.K. Turner. 1990. *Economics of Natural Resources and the Environment*. Harvester Wheatsheaf, Hemel Hempstead.

Pearce, D., W. Cline, A. Achanta, S. Fankhauser, R. Pachauri, R.S.J. Tol and P. Vellinga. 1996. The social costs of climate change: Greenhouse damage and the benefits of control. In IPCC, ed., *Economic and Social Dimensions of Climate Change*. Cambridge University Press, Cambridge.

Pearce, D.W., B. Groom, C. Hepburn and C. Koundouri. 2003. Valuing the future: Recent advances in social discounting. *World Economics* 4: 121–141.

Rosegrant, M.W., X.M. Cai and S.A. Cline. 2003. Will the world run dry? Global water and food security. *Environment* 45: 24–36.

Sachs, J.D. and W.V. Reid. 2006. Environment: Investments toward sustainable development. *Science* 312: 1002–1002.

Schneider, S.H. 2001. What is 'dangerous' climate change? *Nature* 411: 17–19.

Schroter, D., W. Cramer, R. Leemans, I.C. Prentice, M.B. Araujo, N.W. Arnell, A. Bondeau, H. Bugmann, T.R.Carter, C.A. Gracia, A.C. de la Vega-Leinert, M. Erhard, F. Ewert, M. Glendining, J.I. House, S. Kankaanpaa, R.J.T. Klein, S. Lavorel, M. Lindner, M.J. Metzger, J. Meyer, T.D. Mitchell, I. Reginster, M. Rounsevell, S. Sabate, S. Sitch, B. Smith, J. Smith, P. Smith, M.T. Sykes, K. Thonicke, W. Thuiller, G. Tuck, S. Zaehle and B. Zierl. 2005. Ecosystem service supply and vulnerability to global change in Europe. *Science* 310 (5752): 1333–1337.

Turner, R.K. 1999. The place of economic values in environmental valuation. In I.J. Bateman and K.G. Willis, eds, *Valuing Environmental Preferences*. Oxford University Press, Oxford.

Turner, R.K. 2007. Limits to CBA in the UK and European environmental policy: Retrospects and future prospects. *Environmental and Resource Economics* 37: 253–269.

Turner, R.K., J. Paavola, P. Cooper, S. Farber, V. Jessamy and S. Georgiou. 2003. Valuing nature: Lessons learned and future research directions. *Ecological Economics* 46: 493–510.

Wallace, K.J. 2007. Classification of ecosystem services: Problems and solutions. *Biological Conservation* 139: 235–246.

3 Ecosystem services

Managing trade-offs between provisioning and regulating services

Thomas Elmqvist, Magnus Tuvendal, Jagdish Krishnaswamy and Kristoffer Hylander

3.1 Introduction

The concept of ecosystem services was successfully introduced into the global policy arena by the Millennium Ecosystem Assessment (MA) (2005) and has been welcomed by both the conservation and development communities as a potential bridge between the biodiversity and sustainable development discourses (e.g. Tallis *et al.*, 2008). Ecosystem services are here defined following the recent perspectives developed within The Economics of Ecosystems and Biodiversity (TEEB) report as "the direct and indirect contributions of ecosystems to human well-being" (TEEB, 2009). Despite the apparent success of the concept of ecosystem services, the progress in the practical application in land-use planning and local decision-making has been slow (e.g. Naidoo *et al.*, 2008; Daily *et al.*, 2009). This stems not only from failures of markets to capture values of ecosystem services, but also from our limited understanding of: (1) how different services are interlinked with each other and to various components of biodiversity; (2) the influence of differences in temporal and spatial scales of demand for and supply of services; and (3) the potential trade-offs among services and, in particular, the lack of knowledge of the relationship between provisioning and regulating services (TEEB, 2009). We here define provisioning services as "fluxes of nutrients, soil, water and biomass (food, wood, fibre, medicine, etc.) that are generated by ecosystems and harvested and used by people" and regulating services as "eco-physiological functions and ecosystem processes necessary for maintaining functioning ecosystems and which directly and indirectly regulate the production of provisioning services".

Functioning ecosystems produce multiple services and these interact in complex ways – different services being interlinked. They are therefore affected negatively or positively as one service (e.g. food) increases. Some ecosystem services co-vary positively (more of one means more of another), e.g. maintaining soil quality may promote nutrient cycling and primary production, enhance carbon storage and hence climate regulation, help regulate water flows and water quality and improve most provisioning services, notably food, fibre and other chemicals. Other services co-vary negatively (more of one means less of another), such as when increasing provisioning services may reduce many regulating services, e.g. increased provision of agricultural crops may reduce soil quality, climate regulation and water regulation.

Most studies so far have focused on one or a few services, such as pollination or food versus water quality and quantity. Attempts to characterize multiple eco-system services across regions have only recently emerged (e.g. Schroter *et al.*, 2005), and the little quantitative evidence available to date has led to mixed con-clusions (e.g. Bohensky *et al.*, 2006). The spatial correlation among different services varies widely (Naidoo *et al.*, 2008), with quantification and mapping of services being challenging (Meyerson *et al.*, 2005). Assessing how multiple eco-system services are scaled and coupled in "bundles" represents a major research gap (Carpenter *et al.*, 2009). Attempts at quantifying spatial aspects of multiple services include that of the service-providing unit (SPU), defined by Luck *et al.* (2003) as ecosystem structures and processes that provide specific services at a particular spatial scale. For example, an SPU might comprise all those organisms contributing to pollination of a single orchard, or all those organisms contribut-ing to water purification in a given catchment area (Luck *et al.*, 2003, 2009). One of the major challenges in applying the SPU concept is to translate the unit into tangible, and ideally map-able, units of ecosystems and landscape/seascape. The concept potentially offers an approach that focuses on multiple services and can be used where changes to key species or population characteristics have direct implications for service provision.

Focusing on single provisioning ecosystem services in isolation from regulat-ing services has frequently resulted in policy failures. Perhaps the best recent example of this is the new European biofuel policy. The European target of 10 per cent of motor fuel derived from biofuel has resulted in management of eco-systems for a single provisioning service, but other services of importance for climate regulation, such as carbon storage and trace gas regulation performed by the same or other organisms in the same system, have been completely ignored. By ignoring regulating services, the capacity to fulfil long-term goals of sustain-able landscape management – e.g. maintaining agricultural productivity, conser-vation of biodiversity and reducing the rate of climate change – may be seriously jeopardized.

Today 35 per cent of the earth's land surface is used for agriculture – growing crops or rearing livestock (MA, 2005). Grazing land alone accounts for 26 per cent of the earth's surface, and animal-feed crops account for one-third of all cul-tivated land (FAO, 2006). The extensive use of the earth's surface for agriculture severely affects the generation of many regulating ecosystem services that under-lie human well-being (MA, 2005). Adding to the existing pressure, global food production will need to increase by more than 50 per cent within the next four decades to meet the demands of a growing human population (FAO, 2009). In addition, the development of biofuels is placing massive and rapid demands on land. Biofuels accounted for almost half of the increase in consumption of major food crops in 2006–2007 (TEEB, 2008). Given these rapid global trends, we need to understand how trade-offs among services can be addressed and to what extent new insights in ecology and innovations in institutions and governance may help to reduce some of the most undesirable trade-offs. Here we outline the possibility of moving towards "winning more and losing less" by developing a framework that could deepen our understanding of how losses of regulating services may be reduced under various scenarios of development of provisioning services.

3.2 Trade-offs among provisioning and regulating services

It has been suggested that major ecosystem degradation tends to occur as simultaneous failures in multiple ecosystem services (Carpenter *et al.*, 2006). The dry lands of sub-Saharan Africa provides one of the clearest examples of these multiple failures, causing a combination of failing crops and grazing, declining quality and quantity of fresh water, and loss of tree cover. However, on the other hand, a synthesis of over 200 cases of investments in organic agriculture in developing countries around the world (both dry lands and non-dry lands) showed that the implementation of various novel agricultural techniques and practices could result in a reduction of ecosystem service trade-offs, even as crop yields increased (Pretty *et al.*, 2006). In other words, multiple failures can be avoided with the appropriate knowledge, incentives and institutions at hand. In Figure 3.1 we illustrate a range of possible trade-offs between provisioning and regulating ecosystem services. In response type A there is a steep decline in regulating services, even with a moderate increase in provisioning services production. In response type B there is a linear relationship, and in response type C provisioning services may increase to very high levels before there is a decline in regulating services. Depending on the type of response, the supply of regulating services can be low, intermediate or high for a similar level of provisioning services.

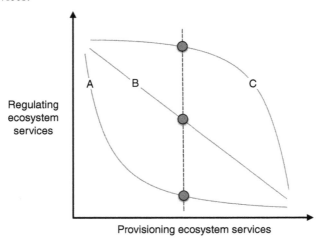

Figure 3.1 The potential trade-offs between provisioning services (e.g. food and timber) and regulating services (e.g. soil quality maintenance, pollination, biological control and water regulation).

A major task for forestry and agricultural research during the next decade is to design studies that generate information on how current production with often strongly negative effects on regulating services – response type A – can be transformed into type B or even type C.

3.2.1 Regulating ecosystem services

Regulating services represent the role ecosystems have in: climate regulation, water regulation, biological control, pollination, maintenance of soil quality and erosion prevention and hazard control (see classification in TEEB, 2009). These services are based on complex processes and interactions in ecosystems and may exhibit different thresholds in response to, for example, land cover change. Here follows a short review of current knowledge about the dynamics of these services (based on TEEB, 2009):

Climate regulation: All soils store carbon, but to widely varying extents. Forests are the only major ecosystems where the amount of carbon stored in the biomass of the plants exceeds that in the soil; deforestation therefore also affects climate regulation. Agricultural ecosystems currently have low soil carbon stores owing to intensive production methods, and there is scope for enhancing those stores. There are major uncertainties associated with this service, particularly related to large time lags in the feedback between changes in ecosystem processes and the atmosphere. The complex interactions and long time lags make it very difficult to forecast eventual outcomes or whether important thresholds have already been passed (Rockström *et al.*, 2009).

Water regulation: Vegetation is a major determinant of water flows and quality, and micro-organisms play an important role in the quality of groundwater. Ecosystems such as forest and wetlands with intact ground cover and root systems are considered very effective at regulating water flow and improving water quality. Water reaches freshwater stores (lakes, rivers, aquifers) by a variety of routes, including direct precipitation, surface and sub-surface flows and human intervention. In all but the first case, the water quality is altered by the addition and removal of organisms and substances. Ecosystems therefore play a major role in determining water quality. In particular, the passage of water through soil has a profound impact, both through the dissolution of inorganic (for example, nitrate or phosphate) and organic (dissolved organic carbon compounds, pesticides) compounds and the modification of many of these by soil organisms. Most changes to the capacity of ecosystems to regulate and provide freshwater seem to derive from, and be generally proportional to, land-use change. There are, however, situations in which a relatively small additional change may trigger a disproportionate – and sometimes difficult to reverse – response from an ecosystem's hydrological function (Gordon *et al.*, 2008). For example, human-induced eutrophication can lead to sudden shifts in water quality from clear to turbid conditions (Scheffer *et al.*, 2001) which affect freshwater fisheries and recreational use of water bodies. Reduction of nutrient concentrations is usually insufficient to restore the original state, with restoration necessitating very substantially lower nutrient levels than those at which the regime shift occurred. In addition, climate change can potentially trigger sudden changes, particularly in regions where ecosystems are already highly water-stressed.

Biological control: The relationship between densities of natural enemies and the biological control services they provide is unlikely to be linear (Losey and Vaughan, 2006) and biological control functions may decline disproportionately when a tipping point in natural enemy diversity is passed. The importance of natural enemy assemblage composition in some instances of biological control (Shennan, 2008) indicates that changes in composition can lead to disproportionately large, irreversible and often negative shifts in ecosystem services (Díaz *et al.*, 2006).

Pollination: It is possible that a threshold in pollinator species/functional diversity exists below which pollination services become too scarce or too unstable (Klein *et al.*, 2007). Such a tipping point might occur when, in a landscape context, sufficient habitat is destroyed that the next marginal change causes a population crash in multiple pollinators. Alternatively, a threshold in habitat loss may lead to the collapse of particularly important pollinators, leading to a broader collapse in pollination services. Supporting this prediction, Larsen *et al.* (2005) found that large-bodied pollinators tended to be both most extinction-prone and most functionally efficient, contributing to rapid functional loss with habitat loss.

Maintenance of soil quality: The process of soil formation is governed by the nature of the parent materials, biological processes, topography and climate. The progressive accumulation of organic materials is characteristic of the development of most soils and depends on the activity of a wide range of microbes, plants and associated organisms (Brussaard *et al.*, 1997; Lavelle and Spain, 2001). Soil quality is underpinned by nutrient cycling, which occurs in all ecosystems and is strongly linked to productivity. A key element is nitrogen, which occurs in enormous quantities in the atmosphere and is converted to a biologically useable form (ammonium) by bacteria. Nitrogen fertilizer is becoming ever more expensive, with about 90 per cent of the cost directly related to the use of energy (typically from gas), which means supplies are therefore not sustainable. Nitrogen fixation by organisms accounts for around half of all nitrogen fixation worldwide, and sustainable agricultural systems will have to rely on this process increasingly in the future. Soil formation is a continuous process in all terrestrial ecosystems, but is particularly important and active in the early stages after land surfaces are exposed. Agricultural expansion into new areas often occupies terrains that are not particularly suitable for agriculture, and soil fertility may decline very quickly as crops effectively mine the soil nutrients (Carr *et al.*, 2006).

Erosion prevention and hazard control: Vegetation cover is the key factor preventing soil erosion. Landslide frequency seems to be increasing, and it has been suggested that land-use change, particularly deforestation, is one of the causes. In steep terrain, forests protect against landslides by modifying the soil moisture regime (Sidle *et al.*, 2006). The ecosystem service is generally not species-specific or dependent on biodiversity in general, though in areas of high rainfall or extreme runoff events, forests may be more effective than grassland or herb-dominated communities. The effect of ecosystems on natural hazard mitigation is still poorly understood and it is uncertain to what extent abrupt changes in this service may be associated with abrupt changes in ecosystem extension and condition, such as the degradation of forests due to climate change.

We may conclude from this review that, even though uncertainty is high, to varying degrees these regulating services may respond along the A, B or C response curves in Figure 3.1 as provisioning services increase (corresponding to a specific land-use/cover change), depending on the specific spatial and temporal context. The question is, are there strategies in designing production of provisioning services and landscape management that can reduce the likelihood of response type A and increase the likelihood of type B or even type C? We will illustrate the potential of such management with an example of one important provisioning service: coffee.

3.2.2 *Coffee-production and regulating services*

The montane rainforest of south-western Ethiopia is widely considered to be the centre of origin of *arabica* coffee, *Coffea arabica* (Sylvain, 1955; Meyer, 1965). Still, more or less wild coffee can be found throughout these forests (Woldemariam, 2003; Schmitt, 2006). People living in agricultural areas surrounding these forests and forest fragments utilize this coffee by picking the berries from scattered shrubs, but also by managing certain areas within the forests to increase coffee productivity. A widespread activity is to clear some forest under-story and increase coffee density below the canopy of indigenous trees by planting or by allowing natural regeneration. There is thus a gradient in coffee density within the forest ecosystem from true forest coffee to semi-forest coffee systems, where most small trees and shrubs have been removed in favour of coffee (Senbeta and Denich, 2006). Besides these systems with continuous canopy cover, farmers also cultivate coffee in home gardens below single shade trees (Hylander and Nemomissa, 2008). This practice promotes a tree-rich matrix and decreases the dependency on forests for many forest plants and animals (ibid.; Gove *et al.*, 2008).

Arabica coffee is nowadays grown in similar climatic contexts (rather humid climates at intermediate elevations) throughout the tropics (Klein *et al.*, 2008). Moguel and Toledo (1999) have summarized the large variety of coffee systems found in Latin America as a gradient from coffee grown without any shade – sun-coffee – to coffee planted in the under-story of indigenous forests (rustic systems) with several intermediate steps showing a variety in density and diversity of tree species. In India there is a clear distinction between systems that are shaded by monocultures of exotic species, e.g. *Grevilliea* and systems that utilize indigenous species. Shade-coffee in the Western Ghats biodiversity hotspot in India is grown in close proximity to remaining (protected) forests and has replaced medium elevation evergreen and deciduous forests. Shade-coffee's intrinsic biodiversity values are a complex function of both local shade practices and landscape factors, and are within proximity of biodiversity-rich protected forests or in a corridor that can be a major driver of patterns of biodiversity (mammals, birds and butterflies) in coffee plantations (Bali *et al.*, 2007; Dolia *et al.*, 2008; Anand *et al.*, 2008).

In the Western Ghats in India, coffee is regarded as one of the most biodiversity-friendly agro-ecosystems (Das *et al.*, 2006). Similarly, many studies from Latin America have shown the superiority of various shaded coffee systems compared to sun-coffee in terms of providing habitats and enhancing biodiversity (Moguel and Toledo, 1999; Gordon *et al.*, 2007; Anand *et al.*, 2008). Less is known regarding the capacity of various coffee systems to regulate water balance (infiltration, groundwater production), erosion control, local climate, pollination, soil productivity, etc., but the general view is that high tree cover with a variety of tree species would increase the capacity to generate these functions (cf. Steffan-Dewenter *et al.*, 2007). For example, in coffee agro-ecosystems, ants, birds and bats can control important coffee pests (Borkhataria *et al.*, 2006; Philpott and Armbrecht, 2006; but see Philpott *et al.*, 2008) and pollinator activity could increase close to natural forest fragments (Rickets, 2004; Klein *et al.*, 2008). Coffee in the Western Ghats and elsewhere straddles a gradient of carbon storage, sequestration and evapotranspiration levels depending on shade practices and management. In general, areas with shade-coffee are expected to have similar hydrologic functions (green water and blue water flux) and carbon sequestration services relative to native forest types that it has replaced (Krishnaswamy *et al.*, 2009; Olchev *et al.*, 2008; Kumar and Nair, 2006). However, it may have severe detrimental effects on water quality due to discharge of coffee pulp effluent into streams. In addition, biodiversity values are often more strongly a function of proximity to remnant forest rather than management practices or shade type (Anand *et al.*, 2008; Dolia *et al.*, 2008; Bali *et al.*, 2007).

From these examples it is clear that the various land uses with coffee production vary in terms of both provisioning ecosystem services and regulating ecosystem services ranging from low yield per hectare in forested landscapes to very high yields in areas of intense inputs of fertilizer and pesticide, and with regulating services showing responses from type A to type C (Figure 3.2).

In Figure 3.2, we analyse production using yield per hectare and assume a strong relationship between yield and intensity of cultivation (sun-coffee produces more per hectare than forest and shade-coffee) (Perfecto *et al.*, 2005). Sun-grown coffee is often dependent on an intensive use of pesticides and fertilizers (cf. Soto-Pinto, 2002). A shift towards a less intensive way of cultivating could be expected if the price for pesticides, fertilizers and energy (i.e. fossil fuels) increases. Then, regulating ecosystem services such as biological pest control and natural fertilizing through nitrogen fixing organisms, become more attractive.

In the centre of Figure 3.2 we illustrate that for shade-grown coffee, the level of regulating services may be high, low or intermediate at the same yield per

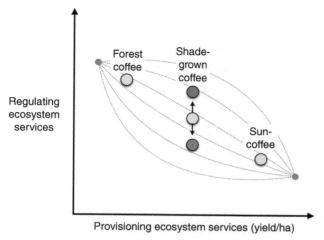

Figure 3.2 A model of trade-offs in coffee production.

hectare. This represents an opportunity to introduce the right incentives for farmers to move from the lower to the higher levels of regulating service without sacrificing yield (see further discussion below in relation to Figure 3.3).

However, regulating ecosystem services are complex and the specific relationship will look different for different services. The difference in response to a conversion of an ecosystem can be illustrated by the different responses of different taxa along the gradient from rustic to sun-coffee, where butterflies may have an A-type response (i.e. lower curve in Figure 3.2) and ants a C-type response (i.e. like the upper curve in Figure 3.2) (Perfecto *et al.*, 2003).

If, instead, income per hectare is used to analyse production of the provisioning service (Figure 3.3), the pattern is slightly different since the price per volume can vary widely depending on quality. Wild-harvested coffee can have a very high price on the global market (hatched arrow to the right)[1] and the high costs of input in sun-coffee often reduces net revenues (hatched arrow to the left). For example, in a recent study from Mexico, Gordon *et al.* (2007) showed that there was small or no differences in net profitability between "rustic" coffee plantations and more intensively cultivated farms.

Another mechanism that can increase revenues of more low-intensive production is represented by certification schemes with price premiums for certain cultivation techniques (Philpott *et al.*, 2007). Figure 3.3 illustrates that there are potentially many levels of regulatory ecosystem services for the same income level, especially at intermediate incomes. There is some empirical evidence of this and Perfecto *et al.* (2005) predicted a range of relationships between coffee production and biodiversity/shade complexity and proposed that certain small changes in, for example, species composition of trees which do not affect shade or productivity, may significantly enhance regulating ecosystem services such as

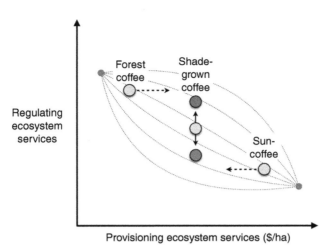

Figure 3.3 A model of trade-offs in coffee production with income per hectare as
the variable.

pest control, pollination and functional groups of taxa. Benefits may also include
the possibility of utilizing other provisioning services than coffee from the same
area. In Ethiopia both timber and non-timber products are used from the same
areas as coffee is cultivated, e.g. harvesting of honey from bee-hives put in the
shade trees in both forest, semi-forest and home garden coffee systems (Woldemariam, 2003; Hylander and Nemomissa, 2008).

3.3 A framework for managing trade-offs between
regulating and provisioning services

Here we propose a general framework for handling undesired trade-offs between
provisioning and regulating services. The framework is based on a typology of
landscapes: (1) intensive agricultural landscape; (2) conservation landscape; and
(3) degraded landscape. Each has a distinct configuration of levels of provisioning and regulating services (Figure 3.4). We define landscape at a spatial scale
that is sufficiently large to incorporate important ecological processes (e.g. large-
scale disturbances) and thus on a scale of hundreds of square kilometres.
Although most landscapes would represent a mix of the three types in Figure 3.4,
it is useful to discuss them as distinct points of departure, since transitions to a
more desirable state involve different types of management and governance strategies. None of the landscape typologies in Figure 3.4 are likely to be stationary,
but subject to changing biophysical, social and economic drivers. We need to
analyse the conditions under which these systems tend to move along the more
undesirable trajectories indicated by hatched arrows in Figure 3.4. Moving along
the more desirable alternative trajectories, indicated by solid arrows in Figure 3.4,

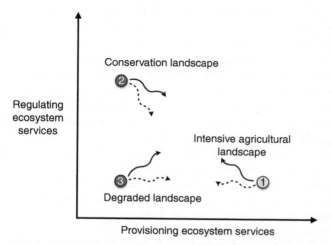

Figure 3.4 Different trajectories of change for (1) intensively used agricultural landscapes; (2) conservation landscapes; and (3) degraded landscapes (modified after Brussard *et al.*, 2010).

is only partly dependent on technology and new innovations. Even more important are incentive schemes, institutions and governance structures that may either
encourage or provide barriers to such a development (cf. Folke *et al.*, 2005).

Intensively used agricultural landscapes are located at the far right, where high
generation of provisioning services is maintained at least temporarily at the expense
of regulating services. In the future, increasing fossil fuel prices, climate change and
water shortage may drive many such areas to the left. For example, the IPCC pre-
dicts that even slight global warming will substantially decrease agricultural productivity in many tropical and subtropical countries, mainly due to water shortage for
irrigation (IPCC, 2007). Further, as stated earlier, nitrogen fertilizer is increasingly
expensive and supplies are therefore not sustainable. We may already have passed a
critical threshold (Rockström *et al.*, 2009). Sustainable agricultural systems will
therefore increasingly have to rely on nitrogen fixation by organisms in the future.

The transformation of intensive agriculture under this scenario may occur
along at least two trajectories, one representing a monotonic decrease in productivity (response type A), another representing a simultaneous increase in regulating services (type B or C) such as biological control, nitrogen fixing and climate
regulation. We still lack financial incentives and institutions for encouraging
type B or C responses, although in some cases these may be triggered by new
financial mechanisms where, for example, conversion of cropland to forests has
a very large effect on carbon sequestration (Righelato and Spracklen, 2007).

Conservation landscapes are characterized by conservation and protected-
area policies, where high levels of regulating services also means low generation
of provisioning services. Demographic and market pressures will, in most parts

of the world, lead to intensification of land use and drive such areas down and right (i.e. losing regulating and cultural services while gaining provisioning services). For example, natural areas will continue to be converted to agricultural land and land currently under extensive (low impact) forms of agriculture will be increasingly converted to intensive agricultural use with 7.5 million square kilometres expected to be converted by 2050 (Braat *et al.*, 2008). Also, two trajectories are possible, one leading to increases in provisioning services but a sharp decline in regulating services (type A), the other to maintaining higher levels of regulating services (type B or C). What institutions and incentives should be put in place for the type B or C trajectories? One important and yet unresolved question in this context is to what extent the net production of regulating and provisioning services is greater when a portion of the landscape is converted to very intensive agriculture and the rest turned to conservation, or when most of the landscape is under land uses that aim to balance agricultural production with biodiversity conservation (Bengtsson *et al.*, 2003; Fischer *et al.*, 2008).

Degraded landscapes may generate few services as a result of extremely low productivity and often absence of institutions to regulate boom and bust economic drivers. However, there are currently incentives building up to transform such areas towards production of biomass energy. Global terrestrial annual plant growth is more than five times the eight billion tons of carbon released into the atmosphere in fossil fuel combustion. In principle, diverting a small fraction of total plant growth into biomass energy could satisfy the majority of global energy needs. The large potential for producing biomass energy without negative effects on climate and food production lies in using degraded and abandoned agricultural lands (Field *et al.*, 2007). Houghton *et al.* (1991) estimated the area of degraded abandoned land to be around 500 Mha globally, with 100 Mha in Asia, 100 Mha in Latin America and 300 Mha in Africa, while Field *et al.* (2007) estimated the global area at 386 Mha. Metzger and Hüttermann (2009) argue that the world energy needs could be provided sustainably and economically primarily from lignocellulosic biomass grown on areas that have been degraded by human activities in historical times. With the right incentives, additional advantages such as CO_2-sequestration, soil formation, water conservation and desertification control are easily achieved. Increased market demand for energy offers an opportunity for conversion of these degraded landscapes. If the conversion is profitable and novel in character, there is a window of opportunity for influencing this shift so that many regulating services are enhanced, corresponding to a B or C type response rather than an A type response (Figure 3.4)

3.5 Conclusion

The simplified example with one manager, here a farmer, and one agricultural system in a landscape, as shown in Figure 3.3, highlights that though many options are available in the trade-off of space, most do not currently provide an improved economy for the farmer and, hence, does not present an economic incentive. However, when a farmer reduces yield to make room for biodiversity and promote regulating services, compensating this with higher prices thanks to a certification scheme, the situation could be a zero-sum game for the farmer but a real improvement for the landscape as a whole. In this context, two important and urgent questions that need to be addressed are:

1   What institutions are required to obtain more sustainable landscape manage-
    ment by "mainstreaming" ecosystem services and, for example, promoting
    choices that might be zero-sum for the individual manager, but are of great
    value for the larger landscape?
2   What are the impediments to ecosystem services being incorporated into the
    everyday land-use decision-making of individuals, companies and govern-
    ments (cf. Polasky *et al.*, 2008)?

One solution suggested by Goldman *et al.* (2007) is the development of incentives within "ecosystem services districts", where the full range of services generated within a landscape is monitored, valued and forms a part of respons-ible decision-making processes. The district could be a combination of regula-tion and incentive, as well as voluntary and non-voluntary approaches. A potential advantages is that such districts facilitate cooperation among landown-ers who are then more likely to manage common-pool resources sustainably (Ostrom, 1990), with cooperation reducing individual direct costs and transac-tion costs (Wagner and Kreuter, 2004). An ecosystem service district would allow landowners to bundle services and offer the provision of multiple services within one defined boundary, enabling them to address type B and C responses in land-management decisions. Novel solutions like this need to be developed and practically tested and evaluated in real landscapes (Cowling *et al.*, 2008).

Acknowledgements

We thank the NRM-group at the Department of Systems Ecology for a stimulat-ing discussion around the theme of this chapter. This work has been supported by a grant from Formas to Thomas Elmqvist. We also thank SIDA for providing support for J. Krishnaswamy and exchange between SRC and ATREE and support of research and fieldwork in Ethiopia for K. Hylander.

Note

1   www.accessmylibrary.com/coms2/summary_0286-7587403_ITM (accessed 28 Sep-
    tember 2009).

References

Anand, M.O., Krishnaswamy, J. and Das, A. 2008. Proximity to forests drives bird con-
    servation value of shade-coffee plantations: Implications for certification. *Ecological
    Applications* 18 (7), 1754–1763.

Bali, A., Kumar, A. and Krishnaswamy, J. 2007. The mammalian communities in coffee plantations around a protected area in the Western Ghats, India. *Biological Conservation* 139, 93–102.

Bengtsson, J., Angelstam, P., Elmqvist, T., Emanuelsson, U., Folke, C., Ihse, M., Moberg, F. and Nystrom, M. 2003. Reserves, resilience and dynamic landscapes. *Ambio* 32 (6), 389–396.

Bohensky, E.L., Reyers B. and Van Jaarsveld, A.S. 2006 Future ecosystem services in a Southern African river basin: A scenario planning approach to uncertainty. *Conservation Biology* 20: 1051–1061.

Borkhataria, R.R., Collazo, J.A. and Groom, M.J. 2006. Additive effects of vertebrate predators on insects in a Puerto Rican coffee plantation. *Ecological Applications* 16, 696–703.

Braat, L., ten Brink, P., Bakkes, J., Bolt, K., Braeuer, I., ten Brink, B., Chiabai, A., Ding, H., Gerdes, H., Jeuken, M., Kettunen, M., Kirchholtes, U., Klok, C., Markandya, A., Nunes, P., van Oorschot, M., Peralta-Bezerra, N., Rayment, M., Travisi, C. and Walpole, M. 2008. *The Cost of Policy Inaction (COPI): The Case of not Meeting the 2010 Biodiversity Target.* Brussels: European Commission.

Brussaard, L., Caron, P., Campbell, B., Lipper, L., Mainka, S., Rabbinge, R., Babin, D. and Pulleman, M. 2010. Reconciling biodiversity conservation and food security: Scientific challenges for a new agriculture. *Current Opinion in Environmental Sustainability* (in press).

Brussaard, L., de Ruiter, P.C. and Brown, G.G. 2007. Soil biodiversity for agricultural sustainability. *Agriculture, Ecosystems and Environment* 121 (3), 233–244.

Carpenter, S.R., DeFries, R., Dietz, T., Mooney, H.A., Polasky, S., Reid, W.V. and Scholes, R.J. 2006. Millennium Ecosystem Assessment: Research needs. *Science* 314, 257–258.

Carpenter, S.R., Mooney, H.A., Agard, J., Capistrano, D., DeFries, R.S., Diaz, S., Dietz, T., Duraiappah, A.K., Oteng-Yeboah, A., Pereira, H.M., Perrings, C., Reid, W.V., Sarukhan, J., Scholes, R.J. and Whyte, A. 2009. Science for managing ecosystem services: Beyond the Millennium Ecosystem Assessment. *Proceedings of the National Academy of Sciences of the United States of America* 106 (5): 1305–1312.

Carr, D., Barbieri, A., Pan, W. and Iranavi, H. 2006. Agricultural change and limits to deforestation in Central America. In: Brouwer, F. and McCarl, B.A. (eds), *Agriculture and Climate Beyond 2015.* Dordrecht: Springer, pp. 91–107.

Cowling, R.M., Egoh, B., Knight, A.T., O'Farrell, P.J., Reyers, B., Rouget'll, M., Roux, D.J., Welz, A. and Wilhelm-Rechman, A. 2008. An operational model for mainstreaming ecosystem services for implementation. *Proceedings of the National Academy of Sciences* 105 (28), 9483–9488.

Daily, G.C., Polasky, S., Goldstein, J., Kareiva, P.M., Mooney, H.A., Pejchar, L., Ricketts, T.H., Salzman, J. and Shallenberger, R. 2009. Ecosystem services in decision making: Time to deliver. *Frontiers in Ecology and the Environment* 7 (1): 21–28.

Das, A., Krishnaswamy, J., Bawa, K.S., Kiran, M.C., Srinivas, V., Samba Kumar, N. and Karanth, K.U. 2006. Prioritization of conservation areas in the Western Ghats, India. *Biological Conservation* 133, 16–31.

Díaz, S., Fargione, J., Chapin III, F.S. and Tilman, D. 2006. Biodiversity loss threatens human well-being. *PLoS Biology* 4 (8), e277.

Dolia, J., Devy, M.S., Aravind, N.A. and Kumar, A. 2008. Adult butterfly communities in coffee plantations around a protected area in the Western Ghats, India. *Animal Conservation* 11, 26–34.

FAO. 2006. Livestock's long shadow. Available at: http://virtualcentre.org/en/library (accessed 20 September 2009).

FAO. 2009. State of food insecurity in the world 2009: Economic crises – impacts and lessons learned. Available at: ftp://ftp.fao.org/docrep/fao/012/i0876e/i0876e.pdf.

Field, C.B., Lobell, D.B. and Peters, H.A. 2007. Feedbacks of terrestrial ecosystems to climate change. *Annual review of Environment and Resources* 32, 1–29.

Fischer, J., Brosi, B., Daily, G.C., Ehrlich, P.R., Goldman, R., Goldstein, J., Lindenmayer, D.B., Manning, A.D., Mooney, H.A., Pejchar, L., Ranganathan, J. and Tallis, H. 2008. Should agricultural policies encourage land sparing or wildlife-friendly farming? *Frontiers in Ecology and the Environment* 6 (7), 380.

Folke, C., Hahn, T., Olsson, P. and Norberg, J. 2005. Adaptive governance of social-ecological systems. *Annual Review of Environment and Resources* 30, 441–473.

Goldman, R.L., Thompson, B.H. and Daily, G.C. 2007. Institutional incentives for managing the landscape: Inducing cooperation for the production of ecosystem services. *Ecological Economics* 64, 333–343.

Gordon, C., Manson, R., Sundberg, J. and Cruz-Angón, A. 2007. Biodiversity, profitability, and vegetation structure in a Mexican coffee agroecosystem. *Agriculture Ecosystems and Environment* 118, 256–266.

Gordon, L.J., Peterson, G.D. and Bennett, E. 2008. Agricultural modifications of hydrological flows create ecological surprises. *Trends in Ecology and Evolution* 23, 211–219.

Gove, A.D., Hylander, K., Nemomissa, S. and Shimelis, A. 2008. Ethiopian coffee cultivation: Implications for bird conservation and environmental certification. *Conservation Letters* 1, 208–216.

Houghton, R.A. 1991. Tropical deforestation and atmospheric carbon-dioxide. *Climatic Change* 19 (1–2), 99–118.

Hylander, K. and Nemomissa, S. 2008. Home garden coffee as a repository of epiphyte biodiversity in Ethiopia. *Frontiers in Ecology and the Environment* 6, 524–528.

IPCC. 2007. *Climate Change 2007: The Physical Science Basis.* Geneva: IPCC Secretariat.

Klein, A., Cunningham, S.A., Bos, M. and Steffan-Dewenter, I. 2008. Advances in pollination ecology from tropical plantation crops. *Ecology* 89, 935–943.

Klein, A., Vaissière, B.E., Cane, J.H., Steffan-Dewenter, I., Cunningham, S.A., Kremen, C. and Tscharntke, T. 2007. Importance of pollinators in changing landscapes for world crops. *Proceedings of the Royal Society of London B* 274, 303–313.

Krishnaswamy, J., Bawa, K.S., Ganeshaiah, K.N. and Kiran, M.C. 2009. Quantifying and mapping biodiversity and ecosystem services: Utility of a multi-season NDVI based Mahalanobis distance surrogate. *Remote Sensing of Environment* 113, 857–867.

Kumar, B.M. and Nair, P.K.R. 2006. *Carbon Sequestration Potential of Tropical Homegardens in Tropical Homegardens: A Time-Tested Example of Sustainable Agroforestry.* Dordrecht: Springer.

Larsen, T.H., Williams, N.M. and Kremen, C. 2005. Extinction order and altered community structure rapidly disrupt ecosystem functioning. *Ecology Letters* 8, 538–547.

Lavelle, P. and Spain, A.V. 2001. *Soil Ecology.* Netherlands: Kluwer Academic Publishers.

Losey, J.E. and Vaughan, M. 2006. The economic value of ecological services provided by insects. *Bioscience* 56, 331–323.

Luck, G.W., Daily, G.C. and Ehrlich, P.R. 2003. Population diversity and ecosystem services. *Trends in Ecology and Evolution* 18 (7), 331–336.

Luck, G.W., Harrington, R., Harrison, P.A., Kremen, C. and Berry, P.M. *et al.* 2009. Quantifying the contribution of organisms to the provision of ecosystem services. *Bioscience* 59, 223–235.

MA (Millennium Ecosystem Assessment) (2005) *General Synthesis Report.* Washington, DC: Island Press.

Metzger, J.O. and Hüttermann, A. 2009. Sustainable global energy supply based on ligno-cellulosic biomass from afforestation of degraded areas. *Naturwissenschaften* 96, 279–288.

Meyer, F.G. 1965. Notes on wild *Coffea arabica* from Southwestern Ethiopia, with some historical considerations. *Economic Botany* 19, 136–151.

Meyerson, L.A., Baron, J., Melillo, J.M., Naiman, R.J., O'Malley, R.I., Orians, G., Palmer, M.A., Pfaff, A.S.P., Running, S.W. and Sala, O.E. 2005. Aggregate measures of ecosystem services: Can we take the pulse of nature? *Frontiers of Ecology and Environment* 3 (1): 56–59.

Moguel, P. and Toledo, V.M. 1999. Biodiversity conservation in traditional coffee systems of Mexico. *Conservation Biology* 13, 11–21.

Naidoo, R., Balmford, A., Costanza, R., Fisher, B., Green, R.E., Lehner, B., Malcolm, T.R. and Ricketts, T.H. 2008. Global mapping of ecosystem services and conservation priorities. *Proceedings of the National Academy of Sciences* 105 (28), 9495–9500.

Olchev, A., Ibrom, A., Priess, J., Erasmi, S., Leemhuis, C., Twele, A., Radler, K., Kreilein, H., Panferov, O. and Gravenhorst, G. 2008. Effects of land-use changes on evapotranspiration of tropical rain forest margin area in Central Sulawesi (Indonesia): Modelling study with a regional SVAT model. *Ecological Modelling* 212 (1–2), 131–137.

Ostrom, E. 1990. *Governing the Commons: The Evolution of Institutions for Collective Action.* New York: Cambridge University Press.

Perfecto, I., Mas, A., Dietsch, T. and Vandermeer, J. 2003. Conservation of biodiversity in coffee agroecosystems: A tri-taxa comparison in southern Mexico. *Biodiversity and Conservation* 12, 1239–1252.

Perfecto, I., Vandermeer, J., Mas, A. and Pinto, L.S. 2005. Biodiversity, yield, and shade coffee certification. *Ecological Economics* 54, 435–446.

Philpott, S.M. and Armbrecht, I. 2006 Biodiversity in tropical agroforests and the ecological role of ants and ant diversity in predatory function. *Ecological Entomology* 31, 369–377.

Philpott, S.M., Bichier, P., Rice, R. and Greenberg, R. 2007. Field-testing ecological and economic benefits of coffee certification programs. *Conservation Biology* 21, 975–985.

Philpott, S.M., Perfecto, I. and Vandermeer, J. 2008 Effects of predatory ants on lower trophic levels across a gradient of coffee management complexity. *Journal of Animal Ecology* 77, 505–511.

Polasky, S., Nelson E., Camm, J., Csuti, B., Fackler, P., Lonsdorf, E., Montgomery, C., White, D., Arthur, J., Garber-Yonts, B., Haight, R., Kagan, J., Starfield, A. and Tobalske, C. 2008. Where to put things? Spatial land management to sustain biodiversity and economic returns. *Biological Conservation* 141 (6), 1505–1524.

Pretty, J.N., Noble, A.D., Bossio, D., Dixon, J., Hine, R.E., de Vries, F.W.T.P. and Morison, J.I.L. 2006. Resource-conserving agriculture increases yields in developing countries. *Environmental Science and Technology* 40 (4), 1114–1119.

Ricketts, T.H. 2004. Tropical forest fragments enhance pollinator activity in nearby coffee crops. *Conservation Biology* 18, 1262–1271.

Righelato, R. and Spracklen, D.V. 2007. The carbon benefits of fuels and forests: Response. *Science* 318 (5853), 1066–1068.

Rockström, J., Steffen, W., Noone, K., Persson, A., Chapin, F.S., Lambin, E.F., Lenton, T.M., Scheffer, M., Folke, C., Schellnhuber, H.J., Nykvist, B., de Wit, C.A., Hughes, T., van der Leeuw, S., Rodhe, H., Sorlin, S., Snyder, P.K., Costanza, R., Svedin, U., Falkenmark, M., Karlberg, L., Corell, R.W., Fabry, V.J., Hansen, J., Walker, B., Liverman, D., Richardson, K., Crutzen, P. and Foley, J.A. 2009. A safe operating space for humanity. *Nature* 461 (24), 472–475.

Scheffer, M., Carpenter, S.R., Foley, J.A., Folke, C. and Walker, B. 2001. Catastrophic shifts in ecosystems. *Nature* 413, 591–596.

Schmitt, C.B. 2006. Montane rainforest with wild *Coffea arabica* in the Bonga region (SW Ethiopia): Plant diversity, wild coffee management and implications for conservation. PhD thesis. University of Bonn.

Schroter, D., Cramer, W., Leemans, R., Prentice, I.C., Araujo, M.B., Arnell, N.W., Bondeau, A., Bugmann, H., Carter, T.R., Gracia, C.A., de la Vega-Leinert, A.C., Erhard, M., Ewert, F., Glendining, M., House, J.I., Kankaanpaa, S., Klein, R.J.T., Lavorel, S., Lindner, M., Metzger, M.J., Meyer, J., Mitchell, T.D., Reginster, I., Rounsevell, M., Sabate, S., Sitch, S., Smith, B., Smith, J., Smith, P., Sykes, M.T., Thonicke, K., Thuiller, W., Tuck, G., Zaehle, S. and Zierl, B. 2005. Ecosystem service supply and vulnerability to global change in Europe. *Science* 310, 1333–1337.

Senbeta, F. and Denich, M. 2006. Effects of wild coffee management on species diversity in the Afromontane rainforests of Ethiopia. *Forest Ecology and Management* 232, 68–74.

Shennan, C. 2008. Biotic interactions, ecological knowledge and agriculture. *Philosophical Transactions of the Royal Society B* 363 (1492), 717–739.

Sidle, R.C., Ziegler, A.D., Negishi, J.N., Nik, A.R., Siew, R. and Turkelboom, F. 2006. Erosion processes in steep terrain: Truths, myths, and uncertainties related to forest management in Southeast Asia. *Forest Ecology and Management* 224 (1–2), 199–225.

Soto-Pinto, L., Perfecto, I. and Caballero-Nieto, J. 2002. Shade over coffee: Its effects on berry borer, leaf rust and spontaneous herbs in Chiapas, Mexico. *Agroforestry Systems* 55, 37–45.

Steffan-Dewenter, I., Kessler, M., Barkmann, J., Bos, M.M., Buchori, D., Erasmi, S., Faust, H., Gerold, G., Glenk, K., Gradstein, S.R., Guhardja, E., Harteveld, M., Hertel, D., Hohn, P., Kappas, M., Kohler, S., Leuschner, C., Maertens, M., Marggraf, R., Migge-Kleian, S., Mogea, J., Pitopang, R., Schaefer, M., Schwarze, S., Sporn, S.G., Steingrebe, A., Tjitrosoedirdjo, S.S., Tjitrosoemito, S., Twele, A., Weber, R., Woltmann, L., Zeller, M. and Tscharntke, T. 2007. Tradeoffs between income, biodiversity, and ecosystem functioning during tropical rainforest conversion and agroforestry intensification. *Proceedings of the National Academy of Sciences of the United States of America* 104, 4973–4978.

Sylvain, P.G. 1955. Some observations on Coffea arabica L. in Ethiopia. *Turrialba* 5, 37–53.

Tallis, H., Kareiva, P., Marvier, M. and Chang, A. 2008. An ecosystem services framework to support both practical conservation and economic development. *Proceedings of the National Academy of Sciences of the United States of America* 105 (28), 9457–9464.

TEEB. 2008. *The Economics of Ecosystems and Biodiversity: An Interim Report*. Brussels: European Commission. Available at: www.teebweb.org (accessed 1 September 2009).

TEEB. 2009. *The Economics of Ecosystems and Biodiversity*. Available at: www. teebweb.org (accessed 29 September 2009).

Wagner, M.W. and Kreuter, U.P. 2004. Groundwater supply in Texas: Private land considerations in a rule-of-capture state. *Society and Natural Resources* 17, 359–367.

Woldemariam, T. 2003. Vegetation of the Yayu Forest in SW Ethiopia: Impacts of human use and implications for in situ conservation of wild Coffea arabica L. populations. PhD thesis. University of Bonn.

4 The "ecosystem service framework"

A critical assessment

R. David Simpson[1]

4.1 Introduction

In recent years considerable enthusiasm has grown for an "ecosystem service framework" (Daily and Turner, 2008) to conservation policy. Gretchen Daily and Pamela Matson write that such an approach has sparked

> a growing feeling of Renaissance in the conservation community. This flows from the promise in reaching, together with a much more diverse and powerful set of leaders than in the past, for new approaches that align economic forces with conservation, and that explicitly link human and environmental well-being. And this promise is flowering thanks to substantial recent advances in key areas of inquiry, such as ecology, economics, and institutions, and their integration.
>
> (Daily and Matson, 2008; references omitted)

Many hope that the ecosystem services framework will provide a new and generous source of conservation funding. Heather Tallis and Peter Kareiva (2005) write that "realization of the market worth of ecosystem services has the potential to increase conservation funding by orders of magnitude".

This enthusiasm has sparked an impressive volume of work within the ecosystem service framework (Turner and Daily, 2008). Fisher and co-authors (2009) document an exponential increase in the number of published papers employing the terms "ecosystem services" or "ecological services", beginning from essentially none in the early 1980s to more than 250 in 2007, the last year for which they have data. Some rough idea of the currency of the term can be gleaned from the fact that entering "ecosystem services" in the Google search engine returns about 4.7 million entries.[2] The Millennium Ecosystem Assessment (MA), a multi-year, multi-million dollar international undertaking involving over 1,300 scientists from around the world was conducted to assess the consequences of ecosystem change, and consequent alterations in the flow of ecosystem services, for human well-being (MA, 2005). This work may continue under a recently proposed "intergovernmental platform on biodiversity and ecosystem services" (IPBES), modeled on the Nobel-prize-winning Intergovernmental Panel on Climate Change (IPCC). In November 2008 representatives of 78 nations and 25 international NGOs met to consider establishment of an IPBES (UNEP, 2008a). At the meeting a "program of work and budget" of approximately $18.4 million was presented (although not yet adopted) (UNEP, 2008b).

Organizations around the world are adopting an ecosystem services approach to ecological decision-making. Yet the elements of that approach are not as settled as its widespread adoption might make it appear. One often encounters passages such as the following: "Although the societal benefits of native ecosystems are *clearly immense*, they remain *largely unquantified* for all but a few services" (Ricketts *et al.*, 2004, emphasis added; see also Kareiva and Ruffo, 2009; Daily *et al.*, 2009). But if benefits are "largely unquantified", what is the basis for concluding that they are "clearly immense"? Is there really much evidence supporting the contention that the services supplied by natural ecosystems are of great value and that they are being squandered by unwise land-use decisions?

In this chapter I suggest that evidence to that effect remains sparse. This is so for several reasons, and I will consider them in turn. The first is that many contributions to the literature on ecosystem service values would appear to be intended to motivate research on ecosystem services rather than to document the findings of such research. There are certainly numerous, and in many instances eloquent, statements of the *hypothesis* that natural ecosystems provide valuable services, but fewer careful tests of that hypothesis.

In some studies the interpretation of evidence concerning ecosystem service values is problematic. It is worth underscoring that evidence of ecosystem service values will only motivate different conservation decisions if such values outweigh costs. It is not sufficient simply to note that there is *some* value to conserving what is already in place without comparing that value to other possibilities.

Closely related to the above observation is the economic truism that "value is determined on the margin". The relevant concern is typically not that biodiversity or ecosystem services will perish in their entirety. Any monetary estimate of such a calamity would necessarily be, to borrow Michael Toman's (1998) characterization, a "serious underestimate of infinity". The relevant policy question, then, is whether preserving *specific components* of ecosystems provides benefits in excess of those that would arise from their forgone uses.

If ecosystem services are not assigned their true value in land-use decision-making, it is because such services are *public goods*; that is, they are benefits which, when supplied by one person are necessarily accessible to many. Yet the more compact the scale on which such public goods are provided – the fewer members of the "public" who benefit from their provision – the less likely it is that ecosystem services will be underprovided. Consequently, we should be most concerned about the provision of ecosystem services whose benefits are very widely dispersed.

This observation, in turn, leads to a couple of other issues. First, there is what I call below a "paradox of valuation". The things we would most like to be able to place an economic value on are those public goods whose benefits are the most widely dispersed. But these are precisely the goods whose value is most difficult to estimate. Second, the most compelling argument for conserving relatively pristine ecosystems may prove to be that they provide the global public goods of carbon sequestration and biodiversity protection. If this is, in fact, the most important argument for conservation, however, the ecosystem service framework does not appear to be adding much new to the debate on conservation policy.

This last observation poses the main question motivating this chapter. How *does* adopting the ecosystem service framework alter the ways in which we think about conservation policy? If the point is simply that we ought to regard natural ecosystems as assets that provide value to society and should, therefore, compete with alternative land uses as we make choices about how to allocate the earth's surface among our wants and needs, the argument is unexceptionable. It is also not novel, however. Underscoring such a fundamental principle is useful, but it alone cannot account for current enthusiasm for the ecosystem service framework.

That enthusiasm derives, rather, from the sense that the ecosystem service framework has already demonstrated, or can soon be expected to demonstrate, the general economic superiority of conservation to alternative land uses. Most of the remainder of this chapter is devoted to considering and, generally, rebutting these assertions. As these are controversial points, I should hasten to point out a handful of caveats. I most certainly do not dispute that the services of natural ecosystems are valuable to humanity. Nor do I dispute that the services of some such ecosystems are *more* valuable than are any alternative uses that might be made of the areas they occupy. Consequently, there are surely instances in which land use could be made more rational and, generally, socially beneficial by undertaking public policy to preserve natural habitats.

What has not been satisfactorily established is the generality of such propositions. In the body of this chapter I pursue two major themes. The first is that many well-known tracts on ecosystem services do not, in fact, make a general and compelling case for their economic value. The second is that there is a good reason for the first observation: valuing ecosystem services is an extraordinarily difficult undertaking. In the final section of the chapter I return to my main question in light of these observations. What *does* an ecosystem service framework imply for conservation policy, and does adopting it move the debate forward?

4.2 The value of ecosystem services: some prominent examples

In this section I review some prominent examples of empirical work on the economic valuation of ecosystem services. The point I wish to make with this review is that some of the works in which the perception that ecosystem service values are important and significant are controversial. They do not establish a *prima facie* presumption that the benefits of ecosystem preservation exceed those of alternative use. Nor, it should be pointed out, does the selection of a handful of studies whose methods can be faulted or the generality of whose conclusions can be disputed establish that ecosystem services are *not* valuable or important. It does, however, suggest that we should consider more carefully the empirical evidence for that assertion. This is the inquiry to which I turn after discussing a handful of prominent examples.

4.2.1 The Millennium Ecosystem Assessment

Publications discussing ecosystem services and their value often reference the recently concluded Millennium Ecosystem Assessment (MA) (MA, 2005). Despite the characterizations one sometimes reads of the MA, the reader should appreciate a few things about its purposes and results. First, the Millennium Eco-system *Assessment* did not conduct and report new research. Rather, as my emphasis suggests, it *assessed* work already in the literature. Second, the MA was, in the final analysis, restrained in its assessment. It did not make as bold claims for ecosystem service values as have appeared elsewhere in the literat-ure.[3] Finally, some commentators appear to have confused the MA's suggested *definitions* and *classification schemes* for *estimates* of value. The MA proposed a division of ecosystem service values among provisioning, regulating, cultural and supporting services. While this taxonomy may be useful,[4] definition and estimation remain very different undertakings. The reader must, then, look else-where for empirical estimates of ecosystem values.

4.2.2 "The value of the world's ecosystem services and natural capital"

Perhaps the best-known example of ecosystem service valuation remains a paper published in *Nature* in 1997 by Robert Costanza and 12 co-authors. In "The value of the world's ecosystem services and natural capital", Costanza *et al.* sug-gested that a "minimum estimate" of such values was $33 trillion.[5] I will con-sider below, in somewhat more detail, the "benefit transfer" approach taken by Costanza *et al.* For now, however, I will just note that the study set off a fire storm of criticism, particularly, albeit not exclusively, from economists (Ayres, 1997; Smith, 1997; Toman, 1998; Freeman, 1998; Pearce, 1998). If the point of Costanza *et al.* were to demonstrate the value of natural ecosystems in sustaining life, it delivered, as Michael Toman (1998) noted, "a serious underestimate of infinity". If, on the other hand, it was intended to provide an economically mean-ingful measure, it reported a logical impossibility: a *willingness* to pay that exceeded world income which would, in turn, limit the *ability* to pay (Smith, 1997). While it might reasonably be argued that this logical oversight was more semantic than substantive,[6] a more fundamental criticism of the Costanza *et al.* (1997) work is that it confused marginal and total values. In economic theory the value of a good is determined by how much benefit we receive from a little more of that good, phrased in terms of the other goods we might give up to obtain it. Costanza *et al.* (ibid.) have often been criticized (see, recently, for example, Plummer, 2009) for applying values obtained for ecosystems at one place and supposing that such values could be applied to superficially similar but very differently situated systems at other places. Since Costanza *et al.* (1997) continues to be widely cited – and some subsequent work could be subjected to the same criticisms (Mates, 2007) – readers of work on ecosystem services may be surprised to discover that most economists who have reviewed this work have found it seriously defective.

4.2.3   *"Economic reasons for conserving wild nature"*

Motivated in part by the criticisms offered of the work by Costanza *et al.* (1997), some of the same authors joined with Andrew Balmford and others to produce another piece that was published in *Science* in 2002. Balmford *et al.* (2002) attempted carefully to identify studies that reported the marginal value of land retained in natural habitat and compared it to the projected value of the same land if it were converted to more intensive use. This study has also been widely cited, but is also problematic in several respects.

The first concerns coverage and representativeness. Balmford *et al.* reported that they had surveyed over 300 case studies, but ultimately identified only five that compared the benefits of ecological preservation with its opportunity costs and used broad and generally accepted measures of opportunity costs. Of the five studies identified, two were not published in peer-reviewed journals (despite having been written, respectively, eight and four years before Balmford *et al.* (ibid.)). It is open to question whether such a limited sample is in any way representative of broader circumstances in conservation policy.

Moreover, two of the five studies cited relied in part on the ecosystem service of carbon sequestration to generate values in excess of the opportunity cost of habitat preservation. The inclusion of such values is entirely appropriate if the objective is to demonstrate that the *global* benefits of conservation exceed the *local* costs. However, the international community has, by and large, still not developed a consistent set of rules for crediting developing countries for carbon sequestered in forests and other ecosystems.[7] This observation begs the question of what an emphasis on ecosystem services is intended to accomplish for international conservation. If the objective is to convince local communities to preserve natural habitats because of the benefits they will confer on themselves directly, work such as that by Balmford *et al.* (ibid.) does not necessarily make the case (see also Kremen *et al.*, 2000; Naidoo and Ricketts, 2006). If the objective is to convince global donors that "purchasing" ecosystem services from developing countries would be wise, work such as that by Balmford *et al.* may be more compelling, but this argument has been made in the conservation literature for many years (see, e.g. Pearce and Moran, 1994).

4.2.4   *"The Catskills parable"*[8]

The next example for consideration is one of the most often cited pieces of "evidence" for the importance of ecosystem services. In the late 1990s New

York City sought to secure the safety of water provided from its reservoir in the Catskills outside the city. In a widely praised (Levin, 1999) and cited, albeit brief, piece in *Nature*, economists Geoffrey Heal and Graciela Chichilnisky (1998) argued that the city had avoided the substantial capital and operating costs of a new water treatment plant by devoting a fraction of their expense to the preservation of natural habitat in the vicinity of the reservoir. While this example has often been cited as evidence of the value ecosystem services provide, it is problematic on several counts. First, the city faced the requirement to construct a treatment plant based on a *regulatory* rather than an actual demand. The United States Environmental Protection Agency (EPA) required that municipalities drawing from surface sources either treat their water or obtain a waiver from the regulatory requirement. There was no evidence that New York City's drinking water was unsafe or required treatment (NRC, 1999; Sagoff, 2002). While one positive aspect of maintaining more "natural" habitat for wildlife around the reservoir was that it could then support more wildlife and biodiversity that some constituents valued, there was no evidence that citizens were willing to pay extra for water in order to support wildlife conservation, an observation made at the time by some advocates of biodiversity protection (Salzman *et al.*, 2001).

Moreover, the assertion that what happened in the Catskills approximated a situation in which payments were made for ecosystem services is not well supported by the evidence. Mark Sagoff (2002) reports that while the 1997 Memorandum of Agreement between the EPA and New York City called on the latter to solicit purchase of 355,000 acres of land in the watershed, by February of 2002 only a little over 19,000 acres had been acquired, most of them in the form of conservation easements restricting use, rather than of simple purchase. Environmental organizations expressed dissatisfaction with the pace of acquisitions (ibid.). On the other hand, however, some efforts to restrict land use without what were regarded by owners and developers as adequate compensation were decried as "thievery" (Daily and Ellison, 2002). However one characterizes what happens in the Catskills, it seems reasonable to conclude that it was not what it has often been described as: a set of large-scale transactions entered into voluntarily to realize the preservation of important ecosystem services.

Perhaps the most troubling aspect of "The Catskills parable" is the lack of scrutiny to which it has been exposed by those who cite it as evidence of the importance and value of ecosystem services. While the episode is widely cited in the literature on ecosystem services, tracing such citations back to their origin leads one to the two-page 1998 Chichilnisky and Heal *Nature* article, a piece that lists no references, but would appear to contain significant and material factual mis-statements (Sagoff, 2002). It is troubling that so slight a piece has been so influential in the discourse about ecosystem services. This provides a useful cautionary tale. One should be careful in the "evidence" one cites to support the importance of ecosystem services.

4.2.5 Vittel

The next two examples are, I believe, more substantively valid, but each begs an important question. The first is of the Vittel water bottling facility near the Vosges Mountains in northeastern France.[9] The company bottles water from a spring in the region, which it then markets worldwide.[10] In recent decades the quality of water from the underground aquifer in the area has been threatened by more intense cattle operations in the region. The presence of the cattle could lead to increased nitrate in the groundwater and, eventually, a decline in the quality of water from the spring. As the process by which the nitrate would enter groundwater is well understood, as is the relationship between nitrate and cattle ranching operations, Vittel readily perceived how it could maintain the value of its franchise by compensating local ranchers for modifying their practices. Consequently, it entered into an arrangement to do so.

The Vittel example has often been cited as an example of the importance of ecosystem services (Ranganathan *et al.*, 2008; US Forest Service, 2007; Perrot-Maître, 2006). Indeed, it does seem to be a very apposite case. While it does not speak to the difficulties or methods of valuation per se, it is clearly an instance in which improved environmental performance would create large enough gains for the beneficiary to induce it to compensate the party that restricts its options in order to supply such benefits. The only question is whether this is an exception that proves a rule. *Reducing* the intensity of agricultural use is perhaps a step back toward a more "natural" ecosystem, but is a far cry from adopting measures to preserve relatively pristine landscapes. The Vittel example is a good one for showing the benefits of less intensive use of the landscape. In as much as even this relatively straightforward effort to conclude a transaction in relatively minimal "ecosystem services" was difficult to consummate, it begs the question of what realistically are the prospects for concluding deals for still more difficult, diffuse and diverse ecosystem services.

4.2.6 Pollination on the Finca Santa Fe

Another case study that briefly (we will see momentarily why interest was transitory) attracted interest among practitioners and advocates occurred on a coffee plantation in Costa Rica. One ecosystem service that has attracted considerable attention has been pollination. Areas of retained natural habitat in the vicinity of agricultural fields provide refuge for insects and birds that may pollinate agricultural crops. In a carefully conducted study, Taylor Ricketts and his colleagues (2004) demonstrated that coffee yields were about 20 percent greater on plants within 1 km of retained forest areas, presumably because they are better served by native pollinators.

This observation begs a question. All 480 hectares of habitat located within 1 km of preserved forest habitat in the study by Ricketts *et al.* were owned by a single owner. If it were, in fact, the case, that the value of coffee production on the plantation would be higher if 157 hectares of adjoining forest were preserved, what would prevent the owner of the coffee plantation from acquiring the forest and preserving it for his own benefit? In fact, however, careful consideration of the numbers reported in the Ricketts *et al.* (ibid.) study suggest that the coffee plantation owner might have been better off if, rather than acquiring the 157 hectares to assure that it remained in forest, he had instead acquired the land, cut down the trees and planted more coffee on it. While yields might have declined elsewhere on his land, the increase in production on the newly cleared land would have more than compensated for it. As it turned out, events have revealed a related phenomenon. Douglas McCauley (2006) reports that the coffee plantation was subsequently uprooted and replaced by a pineapple farm. Pineapple does not require insect pollination at all.

The point of this and the above examples is not to suggest that ecosystem services are not important. They surely are in aggregate, and they may well be "on the margin" in a number of situations of policy interest. The point, rather, is that cases in which such values are most easily demonstrated often lead to unsurprising and not very illuminating policy implications. The value of ecosystem services can be most easily estimated when simple, often private transactions can be structured to assure that they are maximized. Conversely, the cases of greatest policy interest arise precisely when the benefits of ecosystem services are diffuse and most difficult to measure.

4.3 Impediments to estimating ecosystem service values

In this section I discuss why the value of ecosystem services is so difficult to measure, as well as why some of the published estimates of such values might be taken with a grain of salt.

4.3.1 The production function approach

A number of recent papers and studies have suggested that researchers take a "production function" approach to the estimation of ecosystem service values (Boyd and Banzhaf, 2007; Daily *et al.*, 2009; SAB, 2009). Under this approach natural ecosystems would be regarded as an element of "machinery" that can, in combination with manufactured capital, labor and other such inputs, produce outputs of value to humanity. Such processes might generate products for sale, such as agricultural commodities, lumber or fish, or through the process of "household production" they might create goods and services such as pleasant household settings or family health that are valuable even though they are not generally traded in markets.

The economic logic behind the "production function" approach is impeccable. The value of an input to production is, from elementary economic theory, the price[11] of the output in whose production it is employed multiplied by the marginal product of the input in the production of the output. The problem arises, however, when we have to impute such a price in the absence of market data. Empirical economists typically cannot observe the marginal product of an input in the production of an output. The thought experiment implied – "What would happen to the production of good Y if we varied the quantity of good X_1 by a small amount *while holding the quantities of goods X_2, X_3, ..., X_N constant?*" – can rarely be conducted in practice.

The alternative is to specify a production function – positing a functional relationship between the quantities of inputs employed and the quantity of output[12] produced – and estimate it employing statistical techniques. This approach has indeed been used, both in the general empirical economic literature and in work on ecosystem services (Acharya and Barbier, 2000). Several comments and caveats are in order, however. I begin with some of the more basic.

The first is that estimating production functions has long been regarded as problematic by empirical economists. The reasons for their caution are instructive in the context of ecosystem services. When an economist estimates a production function she must make certain assumptions about the variables that she assumes affect production. Naturally enough, if she wants accurately to estimate the effects of particular inputs on production, she must suppose that she has accounted for all relevant factors. If she has not, it is likely that some of the factors she presumes to account for higher levels of production in one area relative to another are not actually contributing to production but, rather, capturing the effect of one or more variables that have not been considered explicitly.

The canonical example of this phenomenon is the application of fertilizer in agriculture.[13] If an econometrician were to estimate the effects of capital, labor and fertilizer applications on agricultural outputs, he might well find that the effects of fertilizer appear to be negative: farmers who are observed to apply more fertilizer harvest less output than those that use less. Why would this be? Are the farmers making foolish choices, paying to buy more of an expensive input that is actually hurting, rather than helping, them?

Not necessarily. A more plausible explanation is that farmers who apply more fertilizer are attempting to make up for the absence of another factor that has not been measured, and are not fully able to do so. Perhaps farmers who have inherently less fertile soil apply more fertilizer.

I suggest that this example is instructive in the context of ecosystem service value estimation. The simplest solution to this problem of "unobserved" variables would be to make the effort to observe them. Yet this is not the solution typically prescribed by econometricians. Rather, it is more common to employ a bit of theoretical sleight-of-hand to obviate the problem. The problem of unobserved variables arises because some of the explanatory factors that *are* observed are correlated with some that are not, and consequently "pick up" the effect of the unobservable variables. If it were possible to express the production relationship as a function of variables that are uncorrelated with any unobserved factors, the problem would be solved. This is exactly what econometricians try to do. They typically prefer to estimate "cost functions" or, better yet, "profit functions". A cost function relates a producer's cost of production to the *prices* of the inputs he purchases and the *quantity* of output he produces. A profit function relates profit to the prices of inputs *and* output. As such, prices are typically not correlated with local production conditions, and estimation can proceed.[14]

The point I want to emphasize here is that if including variables such as the effects of ecosystem services on production were easy, empirical economists would have done so a long time ago, as the need to develop more sophisticated methods of estimation would have been obviated. Of course, virtually any worthwhile empirical undertaking will be difficult. So, the relevant question is whether these difficulties have been, or will be, overcome in empirical work.

4.3.2 A paradox of valuation

Even indifferent students of economics are likely to remember the "paradox of value": why is water, which is so essential to life, so cheap, while diamonds, which have such limited, and largely ornamental, uses so expensive? The answer is that water is (generally) abundant with respect to the uses to which it is put, while diamonds are (generally) scarce relative to the demand for them. The exceptions prove the rule: someone dying of thirst – experiencing an extreme scarcity of water – would surely trade all the diamonds he had for a drink.

One might propose a corollary, a "paradox of valu*ation*". If something is more or less valuable depending on whether it is more or less scarce, then the only way to place a value on a good that does not have an evident market price is to identify some circumstances under which it is more scarce and others under which it is less so. Now this will be relatively easy to do if the public good whose value we are trying to establish is relatively local; that is, it has a discernable effect on those who are close enough to its source as to enjoy its benefits, but others who are more distant receive only negligible benefits.

If the benefits afforded by such a public good are localized, however, it begs the question as to whether the good in question ought to be considered "public" at all. If the radius of dispersal is compact enough, why would it not make sense for affected parties to merge their interests and "internalize the externality" by placing the source and the beneficiary of the good under common ownership? This is essentially what Vittel did in the example cited above; it "internalized the externality" of cattle ranching in its watershed by purchasing a portion of local ranchers' land-use rights. For ecosystem services dispersed over somewhat broader areas, a number of authors have documented instances in which local communities evolve rules for their management (Ostrom, 1991; Baland and Platteau, 1996; more generally, Coase (1960) discusses ways in which affected parties might reach agreement for the provision of public goods or private goods with extensive externalities).

There are also instances in the literature in which it would appear that private parties may be behaving optimally already with respect to the provision of – at least local – ecosystem services. This would appear to have been the case in the pollination services example developed by Ricketts *et al.* (2004). In a similar study, Thorsnes (2002) finds that construction lots abutting retained natural areas command modestly higher prices than those at a greater distance. It would appear, however, that, absent legal restrictions against doing so, residential developers would make more money by clearing more land for construction than they would lose by reduced sales prices on lots now rendered less attractive by the reduction in adjoining natural areas.

When there is enough spatial variability to facilitate easy measurement of values, then, it seems reasonable to suppose that local people would develop an appreciation for such values and evolve institutions to preserve them. The opposite situation is more problematic from a policy perspective. What if the services provided by natural ecosystems are provided to very large publics? This would be the case if the intensity of service provision does not vary greatly over the landscape. There would, then, be little variation, and little prospect for inferring value from observing differences in the volume of service flows received from different areas. In extreme instances, such as the sequestration of atmospheric carbon dioxide and the preservation of endangered species valued for moral and aesthetic reasons, the public goods are truly global and it would be impossible to value them by observation of cross-sectional variation.

Moreover, even if it were possible to identify *some* variation in the intensity with which ecosystem services are provided across the landscape by different sources, it becomes increasingly difficult to disentangle the effect of any particular wetland, forest, meadow, etc., from that of the multitude of others that would influence production if the benefits of each do not dissipate relatively quickly in the distance from source to receptor areas.

Thus, there is a "paradox of valuation". We would like to know the value of services whose benefits accrue over such large areas of the landscape that efficient arrangements for their private or communal provision are unlikely to evolve. Yet these are exactly the circumstances under which the exercise of valuation will prove most difficult.

4.3.3 *Spatial correlation and endogeneity*

The estimation of production, cost or profit functions is often forgone for a related technique: hedonic estimation. A hedonic model is one in which the value of some good or asset – such as a hectare of land – is determined by its attributes.[15] Two other fundamental results from economic theory are, first, that the rental value of an asset, such as a hectare of land, is determined by the profits that can be earned from using that land in its "highest and best use", and second, that the purchase price of such land is determined by the net present value of the stream of rental earnings that could be realized from its ownership. So, the value of ecosystem services should be reflected in the rental and purchase prices of land receiving them.

There is a long history of hedonic studies of land value based on the uses made of nearby lands. Some of the statistical issues discussed above reappear with a vengeance in this context, however. Since it is often extremely difficult to measure the actual services provided to one parcel of land relative to those provided to another, a more common empirical procedure is to estimate the value of land as a function of (among other factors) proximity to features of the landscape such as wetlands or forests. This raises a difficult issue. Reliable estimation of the empirical relationships between land values and the factors that explain them requires that *all* of the latter be included in the analysis. If they are not, some of the other "explanatory" factors included may not themselves explain variations in value so much as proxy for other factors that are not included. This becomes particularly problematic when land values are determined by similar factors in adjoining or nearby places in the landscape.

The essential points to appreciate here are that: (1) the goal of a hedonic pricing exercise is to understand how land *value* at one point in a landscape is determined by land *use* at another; (2) it is more likely that more intensive *use* will be made of land when the features of its location imply that greater value will arise from more intensive use; and (3) the value-determining features of the landscape are likely to be highly correlated for properties that are relatively close to one another. This combination of considerations will likely imply that the benefits of ecosystem services will be *under*estimated in hedonic studies. The reasoning encapsulates the points above. Consider a farm located adjacent to an area of retained natural forest. The value of that farm may well be lower than that of a similar farm situated amidst other farms and far from remaining forest areas. Both the isolated farm and the forest adjoining it are likely situated in areas identified as having been less advantageous for farming.

In recent years econometricians have derived techniques for dealing with the combined effects of correlation in values across space and omitted variables. Such techniques presume the existence of adequate "instrumental variables" – factors that may explain the decision not to devote nearby land to more intensive use while not affecting the value of land that has been placed into more intensive use. Such variables are difficult to identify, however. While work such as that of Irwin and Bockstael (2001) illustrates the approach, results cannot yet be considered definitive.

4.3.4 Taking the "con" out of econometrics[16]

Despite the conclusion of the last paragraph, most hedonic studies relating land value to the retention of relatively pristine ecosystems show that proximity to ecosystem services affords positive benefits. In as much as the factors explicated above would seem to suggest that estimates of value would be biased *downwards* by the factors considered, one might suppose that existing studies make the case that ecosystem services are valuable a fortiori.

There are, however, other concerns. It is difficult to do controlled experiments in economics on a temporal, spatial, social and financial scale relevant to the resolution of important policy questions. Thus, rather than having the researcher control the circumstances under which experiments are conducted, as would be the case in laboratory sciences, economists must typically look for "natural experiments" in which circumstances have fortuitously crafted situations in which variables of policy interest – in our case, areas preserved for the provision of ecosystem services – differ while other relevant circumstances remain relatively constant. Perfect natural experiments are vanishingly rare, however, and researchers must instead attempt to correct for the influence of variables they cannot control directly.

This is typically done in practice by supposing that there exists a functional relationship between all of the explanatory variables of interest and the dependent variable (in the case of a hedonic model, the price of a property). The empirical procedure works, then, by seeing how well the function "fits" the data.

This procedure is problematic, however, as it does not comport well with the statistical theory on which empirical procedure is supposedly based. That theory presumes "hypothesis testing". The researcher forms a hypothesis – for example, that property values increase with the proximity of a property to a wetland – and can test this conjecture by seeing whether or not the estimated effects of proximity are greater than those that might arise simply from random variation in the data.

In testing such a hypothesis, however, researchers inevitably must posit certain "maintained hypotheses": that the set of other explanatory variables they have included is appropriate and complete, that the functional form they have chosen is correct, and that the spatial and, in some instances, temporal coverage of the data is adequate and representative. It is, however, very unusual for a researcher to collect a set of data, perform a single statistical procedure on it (in the parlance of the discipline, a single "regression"), and report the results of that procedure. Rather, it is common for researchers to experiment with a number of different "specifications" – typically, different functional forms, combinations or variables, and/or special techniques – and report only a subset of the results obtained from doing so. To give an example, Robert Costanza *et al.* (2008), in their study of the value of coastal wetlands in protecting inland areas against hurricane damage, report that they experimented with nine different models, but report results for the one that, in their judgment, best fit the data.[17]

There is widespread agreement that this type of "pre-test bias" is prevalent and problematic (Leamer, 1983; Kennedy, 2002; Glaeser, 2006), although there is probably less agreement as to the severity of the problem and the appropriate solution. There are certainly examples from other areas of economics in which researchers have exposed the sensitivity of results to specific assumptions (Easterly *et al.*, 2004).

4.3.5 The battle of the Bayesians

Even if researchers do violate the principles of statistics in conducting "specification searches", is there a reason to suppose their results will be biased in predictable ways? There may be. Edward Glaeser writes:

> Economists are quick to assume opportunistic behavior in almost every walk of life other than our own. Our empirical methods are based on assumptions of human behavior that would not pass muster in any of our models.... While economists assiduously apply incentive theory to the outside world,

we use research methods that rely on the assumption that social scientists are saintly automatons.

(Glaeser, 2006)

What are the incentives that might motivate economic researchers? One that has often been suggested (Pearce, 2007) is *publication bias*.[18] Academic economists obtain recognition and advancement in their field by publishing in scholarly journals. It is seen as almost a de facto requirement for publication that one find a "significant" – in the statistical sense of that term[19] – result. It may, then, be that journals disproportionately accept papers that report statistically significant results (suggesting that they may then reject large numbers of papers that do not report such results). Of course, if we *do* apply economic theory to economists, it seems unlikely that large numbers of economists would spend the time and effort required to write up results they knew would likely be rejected when submitted for journal publication. They might instead pre-screen research projects, bringing to fruition only those that yield significant results. They might also be tempted to engage in specification searches until they derive results that are (ostensibly, ignoring the pre-testing that may have occurred) statistically significant.

It is too cynical to suppose that researchers slant their results simply to get them published. Another reason researchers might find and report strong positive results is that the researchers firmly believe that such results are correct. The process of specification search can be given a Bayesian[20] interpretation. Suppose I believe that the services performed by a particular forest ecosystem are of considerable value. Suppose also that I amass a set of data, choose what seems to be a plausible functional form, and perform a statistical analysis to test the hypothesis: "The value of ecosystem services provided by this area of forest are no greater than the opportunity cost of its preservation." Finally, suppose that I cannot reject the hypothesis. I can react to this information in one or a combination of two ways. First, I can say "That's surprising! I must have been wrong", and change my mind. Or, I can say "I'm pretty sure I'm right about the value of ecosystem services. Since I didn't get the 'right' result, some other aspect of my analysis must be wrong. I'm going to try a different specification and see if I get the 'right' result with it".[21]

The reader of such work is then faced with her own problem of inference, informed by her own beliefs. If confronted with a claim that ecosystem services are of significantly greater value than the opportunity cost of their preservation, but dogged by the suspicion that such a claim is based on extensive specification searching, does she believe the claim or discount it? It seems that the general answer will be that she will follow her own prior beliefs on the matter.

Such a scenario could lead to what I suggest might be "a battle of Bayesians". A researcher believing that ecosystem services are important and valuable would credit those formulations of the empirical model that led to the confirmation of his prior beliefs. A skeptical reader could dismiss the researcher's findings on the presumption that the researcher had continued to test specifications until he found the one that comported best with his prior beliefs.

Which is right? In a sense – and despite the contradiction between their positions – both are. Each is equally entitled to her prior beliefs concerning ecosystem services, and there is nothing necessarily irrational or inconsistent in each updating her beliefs as she has. Such divergent positions cannot be reconciled absent agreement on an "experiment" – a set of data on which a hypothesis can be tested – that each agrees will resolve the matter.[22]

4.3.6 An extreme example of a Bayesian standoff: stated-preference studies

Nowhere is the problem of defining agreed-upon procedures for the estimation of value more vexing than with stated-preference studies. Economists often distinguish their discipline from other social science approaches by noting that they base their analyses on what people actually *do* rather than on the subjective thought processes that people *say* motivate their actions. It is, then, not surprising that sharp disputes have broken out between economists citing the above distinction and those who abandon it by *asking* people what they *would* do rather than *observing* what people *have* done.[23]

Adherents of the latter procedure conduct "stated-preference" studies (as contrasted to "revealed-preference" studies). Examples include "contingent valuation studies", in which survey respondents are asked how much they would pay for a particular good or service,[24] and "conjoint analysis" and "choice experiments", in which respondents are asked to choose among different combinations of public and private goods to determine their preference for the former and the consistency of their preferences between them.

Stated-preference methods have often been used in the valuation of ecosystem services. Richardson and Loomis (2009; see also Loomis and White, 1996) survey a number of stated-preference studies that have been conducted on the value of threatened and endangered species. Naidoo and Adamowitz (2005) consider the value of birds to protected areas in Uganda. Many such studies exhibit a troubling feature, however. As Brown and Shogren (1998) commented in reviewing 18 earlier stated-preference studies, "the average person was willing to pay about $1000 to protect 18 different species.... Many will find these figures suspiciously high." They are "suspiciously high" because there are so many public goods to whose maintenance a survey respondent might be asked to contribute. More generally, critics have long alleged that respondents to stated-preference surveys regard them as opportunities to "purchase moral satisfaction" (Kahneman and Knestch, 1992) – albeit without having to actually pay for it – rather than as considered statements of budget-constrained choices. Peter Diamond (1996) has suggested that relatively simple "adding-up" tests can be conducted to determine the consistency of stated-preference studies, although other authors suggest that Diamond's conditions are more stringent than need be implied by received theory (Smith and Osborne, 1996).

This is precisely the problem, however: commentators disagree as to what received theory requires, and hence, as to whether stated-preference studies provide valid estimates of the social values of things like imperiled ecosystem services. While V. Kerry Smith was writing over a decade ago, it is likely that his assessment remains accurate:

> Indeed, there is a curious dichotomy in the research using CV for nonmarket valuation. Environmental economists actively engaged in nonmarket valuation continue to pursue very technical implementation or estimation issues, while the economics profession as a whole seems to regard the method as seriously flawed when compared with indirect methods. They would no doubt regard this further technical research as foolish in light of what they judge to be serious problems with the method.
>
> (Smith, 1997: 42)

The profession has, essentially, agreed to disagree as to the validity of the approach.[25] Obviously, this state of affairs makes any estimates of ecosystem values based on stated-preference approaches problematic.

4.3.7 Benefit transfer

Another approach has been employed in a number of ecosystem service valuation studies. Probably the most prominent of these was the study published in *Nature* in 1997 by Robert Costanza and his colleagues. In that piece the authors combined data from scores of earlier studies reporting the value of services generated by particular ecosystems. They then extrapolated these service values on a per-hectare basis to other ecosystems of similar types around the world. As has already been noted, this procedure is problematic. If, as may often be the case, ecosystems that are unusually valuable because of their proximity to centers of population or sources of pollution are the subjects of study, extrapolation of estimated values to more remote areas will be inaccurate.

The general technique of applying estimates derived in one setting to the valuation of services generated in another is known as "benefit transfer", and has been the subject of considerable research (see, e.g. the survey in Navrud and Ready, 2007). Best practice now gravitates to "function" rather than "estimate" transfer, wherein researchers transfer a set of parameters describing monetary benefits as a function of underlying site attributes rather than simply a numerical measure of monetary benefits themselves. Other approaches attempt to "calibrate preferences" by imposing consistency across different methods of estimation and categories of value (Smith *et al.*, 2006).

One troubling aspect of existing benefit transfer studies – and related "meta-analyses"[26] – however, is that they often find that the *methods* employed in individual studies may explain the *results* they derive (Richardson and Loomis, 2009). At the very least this suggests that some approaches may be more reliable than others. More generally, any approach that aggregates other studies can be no more reliable than the studies on which it is based.

One might counter the above observation by saying that aggregation of individual studies should, by the law of large numbers, smooth the errors found in each. This would be true if the underlying studies themselves were unbiased. If, however, the potential sources of bias discussed above are matters of concern, the biases of the individual studies would be transferred to the study that aggregates them.

4.4 How does the ecosystem services framework change conservation policy?

Its more enthusiastic advocates have hailed the adoption of an ecosystem services framework as a watershed event in the evolution of conservation policy. Is it likely to prove to be one?

The underlying logic of the ecosystem services framework is impeccable. Natural ecosystems do, of course, provide a host of valuable services to society. There is no denying that the water purification, pollinator habitat, recreational opportunities, erosion protection, soil regeneration, etc. provided to humanity are valuable. Of course, there are also questions as to how such values compare to alternative uses, how valuable they are on the margin, and what disamenities natural ecosystems also generate. Some contributors to the literature on ecosystem services note, for example, that there may be rapidly diminishing returns in certain services with respect to the size of the ecosystem providing them (Tallis, 2006),[27] and that completely *un*natural systems might provide equal or superior services in some respects (Turpie *et al.*, 2003).[28] With respect to disamenities, it is instructive to note that many of Europe's wetlands were drained in eighteenth- and nineteenth-century efforts to control malaria (Bate, 2001; McCauley, 2006).

It should also be remembered that many of the values ascribed to ecosystem services arise precisely because of the benefits they provide to decidedly *un*natural systems: large areas of monoculture crops benefit from pollination, vulnerable urban structures benefit from flood control, etc. If the benefits of maintaining areas in natural ecosystems depend on the size and location of unnatural areas, there is obviously a balance to be struck between preservation and development. This observation would not come as any revelation to advocates of an ecosystem services approach, but it does underscore the importance of evaluating marginal trade-offs.

It may be problematic if the general conclusion drawn from an analysis of conservation versus development trade-offs is that they are currently drawn with too much emphasis on development. There is an important result in economics known as the "general theory of the second best" (Lipsey and Lancaster, 1956). Put in very colloquial terms, it says that "two wrongs may make a right" in some circumstances, or, perhaps put more accurately, "correcting" one problem may not improve welfare when other problems are not addressed. While the situation is certainly very complicated, it is not clear, for example, that taking steps to provide greater ecosystem services for one community would always and necessarily be the best measures to combat other environmental problems, such as global warming. Kareiva and Ruffo (2009), for example, note that "[M]assive infrastructure projects, monocultures of plantation trees, seawalls and levees,

[and] biofuels that ultimately accelerate land conversion" are among the strategies suggested for combating climate change. While noting again that the science is complicated and appears to remain in some dispute, one cannot simply assume that the maintenance of natural ecosystems is necessarily consonant with other ecological or social objectives.

These observations may be particularly trenchant as it would appear that concern for ecosystem services arises largely from conservation advocates' concern for the preservation of biodiversity. There is some discussion in the ecosystem service literature concerning the degree to which biodiversity preservation and ecosystem service provision are, in fact, consistent objectives (Balvanera *et al.*, 2001; Tallis and Kareiva, 2005; Turner *et al.*, 2007; Nelson *et al.*, 2009).

These concerns are likely to be particularly acute when considering particular strategies for realizing the purported value of ecosystem services. In the absence of clear evidence of the demand for ecosystem services, conservation (and, in some instances, development) donors have often underwritten "integrated conservation and development projects" (ICDPs) in which local communities are subsidized to undertake projects such as the collection of non-timber forest products, "ecotourism" and pharmaceutical research and development based on natural products. Such ICDPs have proved to be very controversial, with both their ecological (Terborgh, 1999; Terborgh *et al.*, 2002) and economic (Wells and Brandon, 1991; Ferraro, 2001; Ferraro and Simpson, 2002) benefits in considerable dispute. Many commentators are likely to be extremely disappointed if the current interest in ecosystem services turns out to be only a recycled argument for a conservation strategy that has already been tried and, in the opinion of many, failed dismally, in developing countries.

Yet some authors who have extolled the promise of the ecosystem service framework write hopefully of the possibility of "ecosystems services ... aligning conservation values and poverty alleviation" (Tallis and Kareiva, 2005), largely in hopes of tapping into international development funding.[29] To those who have followed the evolution of conservation strategy over the past two decades, such suggestions elicit a disheartening sense of *déjà vu*. While the new emphasis on ecosystem services – and the operational mechanisms of payments for their provision – differ in some important ways from the ICDP strategies that have often prevailed in recent decades, they are also similar in one fundamental way. To the extent that the ecosystem services emphasized in recent conservation literature call for the preservation of natural ecosystems in order to provide *local* public goods – services such as water purification, erosion control, pollinator habitat, etc. – they presume that local communities have proved incapable of recognizing and safeguarding these services on their own.

It is almost tautological that poor communities are poor because they fail in some respects to take the actions that would be required to improve their collective welfare. Having stipulated this fact, however, it seems disingenuous to suppose that poor communities will be better off if they conserve ecosystems whose preservation would also benefit an international conservation community whose underlying interest is in the preservation of biological diversity, not the welfare of local communities per se.

How, then, should the ecosystem service framework affect conservation policy? It seems reasonable to suppose that research should continue into the valuation of ecosystem services. If clear and compelling evidence can be assembled to suggest that the local value of preserved ecosystems will compensate the opportunity costs of their preservation, perhaps local development and international biodiversity interests can be aligned.

For the reasons cited above, however, research has not yet established that case. Given the circumstances, we might consider two paradigms in deciding on policy. The first is that provided by the theory of options. When faced with uncertainty and irreversible consequences, it is prudent to exercise an abundance of caution. The second, competing, view is provided by Ockham's razor. While there may be other possibilities, the most parsimonious explanation for why local people do not preserve their ecosystems is that they do not believe it is in their interest to do so.

While some poor communities may be sufficiently forward-looking as to wait for the resolution of uncertainty before making irrevocable choices concerning their ecological assets, it would be surprising if this were the norm. So, whether or not one thinks local communities are making wise choices in liquidating their natural capital,[30] they are likely to continue to do so in the absence of international payments for conservation. In the final analysis, then, it seems that the consideration of ecosystem services does not leave conservation planners in a much different position than they were before with respect to practical conservation strategy. Payments will likely be required from the wealthier to the poorer nations of the world on the basis of carbon sequestration in standing forests or intangible values of biodiversity if natural ecosystems are to be preserved. We may choose to call the goods for which such payments are made "ecosystem services", but the designation makes little difference with regard to the practical need to structure international payments for conservation.

Notes

1 The opinions expressed in this chapter are the author's, and do not necessarily reflect those of the United States EPA. I thank Emma Roach for research assistance and my colleagues at the National Center for Environmental Economics for many helpful comments.
2 Search conducted 17 April 2009. To get some idea of societal priorities and the *zeitgeist*, this is about half the number returned when one searches for "Julia Roberts", and slightly more than are returned for "Matthew McConaughey".
3 A summary of the MA's findings is often reported as that 15 of 24 of the ecosystem services studied in the MA are in decline or are being degraded. While perhaps cause for considerable alarm, this is not a statement concerning the value of ecosystem services.
4 Taxonomic and definitional matters are not yet settled, however. No fewer than five definitions of "ecosystem services" have been proposed in the literature (Costanza *et al.*, 1997; Daily, 1997; MA, 2005; Boyd and Banzhaf, 2007; Fisher *et al.*, 2009).

Moreover, it is not clear to me what the last decade's consideration of "ecosystem services" has added over and above earlier suggestions for the classification of "total economic value" of natural systems as proposed by the late David Pearce and R. Kerry Turner (1990).

5 Costanza *et al.* (1997) derived a range of value estimates from $18 trillion to $54 trillion, but, because of exclusions, suggested that the "average" estimate of $33 trillion was a lower bound on actual values.

6 Willingness to pay is, in economic theory, the amount someone would *and can* pay for a good or collection of goods. It is necessarily limited by the resources at one's disposal, i.e. wealth. There is not anything necessarily logically inconsistent about saying that the benefits we receive "for free" from nature are of equal or greater subjective value to us than those we purchase in markets.

7 Developing such guidance is the mission of the REDD (Reduced Emissions from Deforestation and Degradation) program.

8 I have borrowed this designation from the title of Mark Sagoff's (2002) paper, on which I have drawn heavily.

9 I rely heavily on Perrot-Maître (2006) for this paragraph.

10 One might also pause in passing to speculate as to the aggregate ecological consequences of maintaining the purity of a spring so that its water can continue to be shipped to customers as far as 10,000 km away.

11 More generally, we might say that the value of an input in utility terms is the *marginal utility* afforded by the output times the marginal product of the input in its production, but a still more fundamental result of economic theory holds that the price of any product is determined by the ratio of the marginal utility it affords to that of some other good denoted as *numeraire*.

12 More generally, we might say positing a relationship between the quantities of inputs employed and the quant*ies* of output*s* produced, but I'll keep the example simple for now.

13 I base this statement on the fact that this was the example my instructor employed when I took my introductory econometrics course some 30 years ago.

14 Explaining the reasons for this gets complicated. Basically, principles of "duality" assure that production processes may be expressed equivalently by relating the *quantity* of output to the *quantities* of inputs or by expressing the *cost* (or *profit*) associated with production to the *prices* of inputs and the quantity of output, in the case of the cost function, or prices of inputs and output in the case of the profit function. There is also a general preference for estimating profit rather than cost functions, as the quantity of production may also be affected by unobserved factors. For this reason, much of the early empirical work on estimating cost functions was conducted on regulated public utilities, on the argument that output was determined by regulatory authorities rather than by factors that might also affect costs.

15 "Hedonic" is derived from the same Greek root as "hedonism", and, like the latter term, relates to "pleasures". A "hedonic" valuation exercise attempts to estimate the price of a good by the "pleasures" or, more generally, "attributes" its ownership offers.

16 The title of this subsection is borrowed from Edward Leamer's 1983 paper (and plea) "Let's take the 'con' out of econometrics".

17 My point in citing this work is not to criticize the authors so much as to credit them for having been more forthright than are many of their peers in describing their procedures.

18 Publication bias is also perceived as a problem in the pharmaceutical research industry, where some allege that results favorable to a research funder's interests tend to be published, while those that are not are "stuck in the file drawer".

19 A result is said to be "statistically significant at the x per cent level" if the probability that it would have been found to be as large as it is if it did not, in fact, have any consistent effect, is less than x per cent.

20 The Reverend Thomas Bayes (*c.*1702–1761) was a British mathematician best known for formulating Bayes' Law, a theorem describing how probabilities are updated in the presence of new information. Bayesian analysis concerns the ways in which "prior distributions" are updated on the basis of new information so as to form "posterior distributions".

21 I do not believe that this is unusual. I have certainly proceeded in this fashion myself at times. It is not unusual to overhear one colleague ask another "Did that new specification you tried work?" where I presume "work" means "produce statistically significant results of the sign and magnitude expected".

22 This standard echoes Karl Popper's (1959) notion distinguishing science as a realm of inquiry whose propositions must be falsifiable if they are to be meaningful. If we are to credit statements such as "the services provided by a natural ecosystem are more valuable than the opportunity cost of its maintenance", or the opposite, we must have some agreed-upon set of techniques for measuring values and opportunity costs. My concern in much of the empirical literature on ecosystem services is that one side or the other in the debate can too easily say "You have reported the wrong 'experiment'."

23 See, for example, Nordhaus and Kokkelenberg (1999), who write:

> Some techniques such as hedonic-price or travel-cost studies rely *on behavioral or market-based estimates*; while these estimates are subject to significant measurement problems, *they are conceptually appropriate* in economic accounts. Other techniques, such as contingent valuation, *are not based on actual behavior*, are highly controversial, and are subject to potential measurement errors. (Emphasis added.)

24 I simplify greatly in the interests of brevity. Open-ended questions of the form "How much would you pay for x?" are no longer asked by most state-of-the-art practitioners of stated-preference studies. A more likely question would be a variant of "Would you pay y for x?", possibly followed by "If you would pay y, would you also pay $y + z$ for x?" The difference between the answers given to "willingness to pay" and "willingness to accept" questions has also generated great controversy in the literature.

25 "We agree to disagree" is the phrase employed by a presenter at a recent workshop at which I discussed his and other papers using stated-preference methods. Much the same message was conveyed by a prominent representative of the other side of the stated-preference debate, Peter Diamond, in a personal communication in 2005.

26 A meta-analysis is a "study of studies". It typically takes the estimates of earlier studies as a set of "dependent variables", which it then seeks to explain as functions of the location, methods or other attributes of the studies.

27 The author notes that increases in forest cover above 70 percent of a land area have no demonstrable effect on water purification. See also Kareiva and Ruffo (2009).

28 The authors note that South African mountains might provide better water supply to the cities and farmers below them "if the mountains were covered in concrete" than if the native vegetation were restored.

29 The passage quoted here follows immediately after that quoted in Section 4.1, in which Tallis and Kareiva suggest that the "realization of the market worth of ecosystem services has the potential to increase conservation funding by orders of magnitude".

30 It is worth remembering in this context that some authors who are sympathetic to the ecosystem services perspective believe such choices *are*, in fact, wise, in the absence of international payments; see Kremen *et al.* (2000); Naidoo and Ricketts (2006).

References

Acharya, G. and Edward Barbier. 2000. Valuing groundwater recharge through agricultural production in the Hadejia-Nguru wetlands in northern Nigeria. *Agricultural Economics* 23 (3), 299–310.

Ayres, R.U. 1997. *On the Economic Valuation of Ecosystem Services.* Fontainebleu: INSEAD.

Baland, Jean-Marie and Jean-Philippe Platteau. 1996. *Halting Resource Degradation: Is There a Role for Communities?* Rome: FAO.

Balmford, Andrew, Aaron Bruner, Philip Cooper, Robert Costanza, Stephen Farber, Rhys E. Green, Martin Jenkins, Paul Jefferiss, Valma Jessamy, Joah Madden, Kat Munro, Norman Myers, Shahid Naeem, Jouni Paavola, Matthew Rayment, Sergio Rosendo, Joan Roughgarden, Kate Trumper and R. Kerry Turner. 2002. Economic reasons for conserving wild nature. *Science* 297 (5583), 950–953.

Balvanera, Patricia, Gretchen C. Daily, Paul R. Ehrlich, Taylor H. Ricketts, Sallie-Anne Bailey, Salit Kark, Claire Kremen and Henrique Pereira. 2001. Conserving biodiversity and ecosystem services. *Science* 291 (5511), 2047.

Bate, R. 2001. *Malaria and the DDT Story.* London: Institute of Economic Affairs.

Boyd, James and Spencer Banzhaf. 2007. What are ecosystem services? The need for standardized accounting units. *Ecological Economics* 63 (2–3), 616–626.

Brown, Jr., Gardner and Jason Shogren. 1998. Economics of the Endangered Species Act. *Journal of Economic Perspectives* 12, 3–20.

Chichilnisky, G. and G. Heal. 1998. Economic returns from the biosphere: Commentary. *Nature* 391 (6668), 629–630.

Coase, Ronald. 1960. The problem of social cost. *Journal of Law and Economics* 1, 1–44.

Costanza, R., R. d'Arge, R. de Groot, S. Farber, M. Grasso, B. Hannon, K. Limburg, S. Naeem, R. O'Neill, J. Paruelo, J. Raskin, P. Sutton and M. van den Belt. 1997. The value of the world's ecosystem services and natural capital. *Nature* 387: 253–260.

Costanza, R., Octavio Pérez-Maqueo, M. Luisa Martinez, P. Sutton, S.J. Anderson and K. Mulder. 2008. The value of coastal wetlands for hurricane protection. *Ambio* 47 (4), 241–248.

Daily, Gretchen C. and Katherine Ellison. 2002. *The New Economy of Nature: The Quest to Make Conservation Profitable.* Washington, DC: Island Press.

Daily, Gretchen C. and P. Matson. 2008. Ecosystem services: From theory to implementation. *Proceedings of the National Academy of Sciences* 105 (28), 9455–9456.

Daily, Gretchen C., Stephen Polasky, Joshua Goldstein, Peter M. Kareiva, Harold A. Mooney, Liba Pejchar, Taylor H. Ricketts, James Salzman and Robert Shallenberger. 2009. Ecosystem services in decision-making: Time to deliver. *Frontiers in Ecology* 7 (1), 21–28.

Diamond, P.A. 1996. Testing the internal consistency of contingent valuation surveys. *Journal of Environmental Economics and Management* 30 (3), 337–347.

Easterly, William, Ross Levine and David Roodman. 2004. New data, new doubts: A comment on Burnside and Dollar's "Aid, Policies, and Growth". *American Economic Review* 94 (3), 774–780.

Ferraro, Paul J. 2001. Global habitat protection: Limitations of development interventions and a role for conservation performance payments. *Conservation Biology* 15 (4), 990–1000.

Ferraro, Paul J. and R. David Simpson. 2002. The cost-effectiveness of conservation performance payments. *Land Economics* 78 (3), 339–353.

Fisher, Brendan, R. Kerry Turner and Paul Morling. 2009. Defining and classifying eco-system services for decision making. *Ecological Economics* 68 (3), 643–653.

Freeman III, A. Myrick. 1998. Notes for valuing nature workshop: Commentary on methods and data used by Costanza *et al.* Paper prepared for the Bowdoin College Environmental Studies Program Workshop on Valuing Nature, August.

Glaeser, Edward. 2006. Researcher incentives and empirical methods. National Bureau for Economic Research, Working Paper T0329.

Irwin, E.G. and Bockstael, N.E. 2001. The problem of identifying land use spillovers: Measuring the effects of open space on residential property values. *American Journal of Agricultural Economics* 83 (3), 698–704.

Kahneman, Daniel and Jack Knetsch. 1992. Valuing public goods: The Purchase of moral satisfaction. *Journal of Environmental Economics and Management* 22 (1), 57–70.

Kareiva, Peter and Susan Ruffo. 2009. Using science to assign values to nature. *Frontiers in Ecology* 7 (1), 3.

Kennedy, Peter. 2002. Sinning in the basement: What are the rules? The ten commandments of applied economics. *Journal of Economic Surveys* 16 (4), 569–589.

Kremen, C., J. Niles, M. Dalton, G. Daily, P. Ehrlich, P. Fay, D. Grewal and R.P. Guillery. 2000. Economic incentives for rain forest conservation across scales. *Science* 288, 1828–1832.

Leamer, Edward. 1983. Let's take the "con" out of econometrics. *American Economic Review* 73 (1), 31–43.

Levin, Simon. 1999. *Fragile Dominion: Complexity and the Commons*. Cambridge, MA: Perseus.

Lipsey, R.G. and K. Lancaster. 1956. The general theory of second best. *Review of Economic Studies* 24, 11–32.

Loomis, J.B. and D.S. White. 1996. Economic benefits of rare and endangered species: Summary and meta-analysis. *Ecological Economics* 18, 197–206.

MA (Millennium Ecosystem Assessment). 2005. Overview of the Milliennium Ecosystem Assessment. Available at: www.millenniumassessment.org/en/About.aspx# (accessed 17 April 2009).

McCauley, Douglas. 2006. Selling out nature. *Nature* 443, 27–28.

Mates, William. 2007. Valuing New Jersey's natural capital: An assessment of the economic value of the state's natural resources. State of New Jersey Department of Environmental Protection. Available at: www.state.nj.us/dep/dsr/naturalcap/nat-cap-3.pdf (accessed 23 May 2009).

Naidoo, Robin and Wiktor L. Adamowicz. 2005. Economic benefits of biodiversity exceed costs of conservation at an African rainforest reserve. *Proceedings of the National Academies of Science* 102 (46), 16712–16716.

Naidoo, R. and T.H. Ricketts. 2006. Mapping the economic costs and benefits of conservation. *PLoS Biology* 4 (11), e360.

Navrud, Ståle and Richard Ready (eds). 2007. *Environmental Value Transfer: Issues and Methods*. Dordrecht: Springer.

Nelson, K.C., M.A. Palmer, J.E. Pizzuto, G.E. Moglen, P.L. Angermeier, R.H. Hilderbrand, M. Dettinger and K. Hayhoe. 2009. Future long-term changes in global water resources driven by socio-economic and climatic changes. *Journal of Applied Ecology*, 46(1).

Nordhaus, William and Edward Kokkelenberg. 1999. *Nature's Numbers: Expanding the National Economic Accounts to Include the Environment*. Washington, DC: National Academies Press.

NRC (National Research Council) of the US National Academies of Science. 1999. *Watershed Management for Potable Water Supply: Assessing the New York City Strategy.* Washington, DC: National Academies Press.

Ostrom, E. 1991. Managing our common resources: Introduction. *Nature and Resources* 27 (4), 2–3.

Pearce, David. 1998. Auditing the Earth. *Environment* 40 (2), 23–28.

Pearce, David. 2007. Do we really care about biodiversity? *Environmental and Resource Economics* 37 (1), 313–333.

Pearce, David and R. Kerry Turner. 1990. *Economics of Natural Resources and the Environment.* Baltimore, MD: Johns Hopkins University Press.

Pearce, David and Dominic Moran. 1994. *The Economic Value of Biodiversity.* London: Earthscan.

Perrot-Maître, Danielle. 2006. *The Vittel Payments for Ecosystem Services: A "Perfect" PES Case?* London: International Institute for Environment and Development.

Plummer, Mark. 2009. Assessing benefit transfer for the valuation of ecosystem services. *Frontiers in Ecology* 7 (1), 38–45.

Popper, Karl. 1959. *The Logic of Scientific Discovery.* New York: Basic Books.

Ranganathan, Janet, Ciara Raudseppe-Hearne, Nicolas Lucas, Frances Irwin, Monika Zurek, Karen Bennett, Neville Ash and Paul West. 2008. *Ecosystem Services: A Guide for Decision-Makers.* Washington, DC: World Resources Institute.

Richardson, Leslie and John Loomis. 2009. The total economic value of threatened, endangered and rare species: An updated meta-analysis. *Ecological Economics* 68, 1535–1548.

Ricketts, Taylor H., Gretchen C. Daily, Paul R. Ehrlich and Charles D. Michener. 2004. Economic value of tropical forest to coffee production. *Proceedings of the National Academy of Sciences of the United States of America* 101 (34), 12579–12582.

SAB (Science Advisory Board) to the US Environmental Protection Agency. 2009. *Valuing the Protection of Ecological Systems and Services.* Washington, DC: US EPA.

Sagoff, Mark. 2002. On the value of natural ecosystems: The Catskills parable. *Politics and the Life Sciences* 21 (1), 19–25.

Salzman, James, Barton H. Thompson, Jr. and Gretchen C. Daily. 2001. Protecting ecosystem services: Science, economics, and law. *Stanford Environmental Law Journal* 20, (2), 309–332.

Smith, V. Kerry. 1997. Mispriced planet. *Regulation* 20 (3), 16–17.

Smith, V. Kerry and Laura L. Osborne. 1996. Do contingent valuation estimates pass a "scope" test? A meta-analysis. *Journal of Environmental Economics and Management* 31 (3), 287–301.

Smith, V. Kerry, Subhrendu K. Pattanayak and George L. van Houten. 2006. Structural benefits transfer: An example using VSL estimates. *Ecological Economics* 60, 361–371.

Tallis, Heather. 2006. Introduction to ecosystem services. *Science Chronicles* 4 (3). Online at www.naturalcapitalproject.org/pubs/tallis_science_chronicles_2006 (accessed 14 May 2009).

Tallis, Heather, and Peter Kareiva. 2005. Ecosystem services. *Current Biology* 15 (18), 746–748.

Terborgh, John. 1999. *Requiem for Nature.* Washington, DC: Island Press.

Terborgh, John, Carel van Schaik, Lisa Davenport and Madhu Rao. 2002. *Making Parks Work: Strategies for Conserving Tropical Nature.* Washington, DC: Island Press.

Thorsnes, Paul. 2002. The value of a suburban forest preserve: Estimates from sales of vacant residential lots. *Land Economics* 78, 426–441.

Toman, Michael. 1998. Why not to calculate the value of the world's ecosystem services and natural capital. *Ecological Economics* 35, 57–60.

Turner, R.K. and G.C. Daily. 2008. The ecosystem services framework and natural capital conservation. *Environmental and Resource Economics* 39 (1), 25–35.

Turner, Will R., Katrina Brandon, Thomas M. Brooks, Robert Costanza, Gustavo A.B. da Fonseca and Rosimeiry Portela. 2007. Global conservation of biodiversity and ecosystem services. *BioScience*. Available at: www.bioone.org/doi/abs/10.1641/B571009 (accessed 28 April 2009).

Turpie J.K., B.J. Heydenrych and S.J. Lamberth. 2003. Economic value of terrestrial and marine biodiversity in the Cape Floristic Region: Implications for defining effective and socially optimal conservation strategies. *Biological Conservation* 112, 233–251.

UNEP (United Nations Environment Program). 2008a. Report of the ad hoc intergovernmental and multi stakeholder meeting on an intergovernmental science policy platform on biodiversity and ecosystem services. Available at: http://ipbes.net/en/adHoc_intgvmntlMulti_stakeholderMeeting.aspx (accessed 17 April 2009).

UNEP (United Nations Environment Program). 2008b. Programme of work and budget of an intergovernmental science-policy platform on biodiversity and ecosystem services. Available at: http://ipbes.net/Documents/IPBES_meeting_Report_UNEP_IPBES_1_6%20_en.pdf (accessed 17 April 2009).

US Forest Service. 2007. Valuing ecosystem services: Capturing the true value of nature's capital. Available at: www.fs.fed.us/ecosystemservices/pdf/ecosystem-services.pdf (accessed 3 May 2009).

Wells, Michael and Katrina Brandon. 1991. *People and Parks: Linking Protected Areas with Local Communities*. Washington, DC: World Bank.

Part II

Methodological applications

5 Evaluating the economic impacts of water harvesting in Burkina Faso

Rodney B.W. Smith, Laura A. Hildreth and Kimsey Savadago

5.1 Introduction

Food security, or lack thereof, is an increasing concern throughout sub-Saharan Africa. Increases in agricultural output during the past decade have primarily been driven by the expansion of agricultural land. However, this increase in agricultural output has not kept pace with population growth (Fox *et al.*, 2005), and has typically been driven by the cultivation of marginal lands. In order to close the increasing gap between agricultural output and demand, the search is on for yield-improving seeds or technologies.

In sub-Saharan Africa, the primary limiting factor to improved crop yields is water availability (ibid.). While low rainfall levels are detrimental to crop growth, the irregular occurrence of rainfall during critical growing stages is the major constraint in crop production, leading to a gap between actual output and potential output (Fox and Röckstrom, 2003; Barron and Okwach, 2005; Röckstrom and Falkenmark, 2000). Water shortages have profound consequences on small-holder farmer welfare, and are a major obstacle to reducing poverty levels (Hatibu *et al.*, 2006). Previous research indicates soil nutrient deficiency is also a limiting factor for crop growth (Fox and Röckstrom, 2003). Thus, both water availability and soil quality interact to limit productivity growth.

To mitigate the effects of water shortage and soil nutrient deficiency, subsistence farmers are turning to yield-improving measures like water harvesting. Several water harvesting techniques exist, each being a small-scale technology employed in regions where irrigation is not available. They are broadly defined as the collection of runoff for productive use. The primary objective of this analysis is to evaluate the impact of water harvesting on crop yields. We consider the potential impact of two water harvesting techniques: mulching and zai.

With mulching, a farmer simply spreads mulch over soil with the hope the mulch will help retain moisture for subsequent crop uptake. Mulch is typically derived from a basic ecosystem resource – local grasses and plant cuttings. Mulching is a relatively simple technique to implement and requires very little in terms of education or skill to implement.

A "zai" is a hole dug in the ground, typically 10–15 cm deep and 20–30 cm in diameter. Depending on the distance between them, a farmer can dig

12,000–15,000 zai per hectare. In each zai, the farmer places a mixture of soil and organic matter like manure, and then adds either the seed to be planted or an entire plant. Farmers add manure to attract termites. The termites dig tunnels in the soil, which in turn improves the water retention properties of the soil. They also bring nutrients from deep soil layers closer to the surface for uptake by the plant (Drechsel *et al.*, 2005). Drechsel *et al.* suggest zai are effective because they concentrate water and manure at the same point. This concentration is facilitated by the soil restructuring and nutrient cycling services of termites.

Previous studies suggest water harvesting has a positive impact on crop yields in sub-Saharan Africa. The present study uses data from semi-subsistence households in Burkina Faso to estimate two different production technologies: millet monocropping and white sorghum monocropping. The millet and white sorghum technologies are approximated by a quadratic production function. Results suggest for both millet monocropping and white sorghum monocropping, water harvesting typically increases the marginal product of inputs.

The chapter is arranged as follows: Section 5.2 discusses previous studies and Section 5.3 describes the dataset used in this analysis and the empirical models employed. Section 5.4 reports the results of these empirical models and Section 5.5 concludes.

5.2 Previous research

Sub-Saharan Africa faces different types of water limitations, including meteorological droughts and dry spells. Due to a general absence of irrigation, many small-holder farmers mitigate the impact of dry spells through the use of *in situ* water harvesting techniques, which in practice has proved beneficial in decreasing runoff and evapotranspiration, and boosting agricultural output (Fox *et al.*, 2005; Walker *et al.*, 2005; Hatibu *et al.*, 2006). Water harvesting is broadly defined as the collection of runoff for productive use and is divided into two major classifications – runoff farming water harvesting (RFWH) and supplemental irrigation (SI) (Oweis *et al.*, 1999). Several differences exist between RFWH and SI. SI is a temporal intervention that supplies crops with water from either surface storage or the exploitation of groundwater when rainfall is insufficient for plant growth. RFWH directly applies runoff to crops and does not include surface storage, as the soil profile serves as the water reservoir (ibid.). See Oweis *et al.* (ibid.), and Hatibu *et al.* (2006) for detailed discussions of water harvesting.

Analysts have used several techniques to evaluate the economics of water harvesting. The simplest approach is to compare the yields of a particular crop obtained using water harvesting and traditional cultivation practices under the same set of experimental conditions – typically applying the same type and quantity of fertilizer to similar soil conditions. Tabor (1995) conducted one such study for millet and sorghum. In this study, yields for both millet and sorghum under water harvesting increased as compared to traditional cultivation, but the increase in yield depended on whether it was a dry or wet year.

Several studies improved upon this analysis and compared the yields of a given crop under four different scenarios: traditional practices, water harvesting only, fertilizer use only, and a combination of water harvesting and fertilizer use. These studies examined maize (Barron and Okwach, 2005) and sorghum (Fox and Röckstrom, 2000, 2003; Carsky *et al.*, 1995; Carter and Miller, 1991) production under the above scenarios. The general finding was that water harvesting alone can boost yields, but the greatest increase in yields occurs when water harvesting is combined with fertilizer use. As with Tabor (1995), these increases depend on the total rainfall realized during the growing season. The exception to these results is Carsky *et al.* (1995), who find that water harvesting alone boosts yields more than when combined with fertilizer use. Finally, Zougmoré *et al.* (2004) compared sorghum yields from two separate water harvesting techniques under three scenarios: water harvesting without fertilizer use, fertilizer use without water harvesting, and the combination of water harvesting and fertilizer use. They concluded that the combination of water harvesting and fertilizer use increases water-use efficiency and increases yields.

The above studies were primarily field experiments that examined the relation between inputs and an output, with or without water harvesting. Another set of studies used more sophisticated models designed to capture the economic benefits of water harvesting. One common technique is gross margins analysis, which is conducted using the following deterministic relationship:

$$ GM_{jk} = \frac{1}{n} \left(\sum_{i}^{n} P_{ij} V_{ijk} - VC_{ijk} \right). $$

Here, GM_{jk} is the gross margin (or farmer rent) for the *j*th crop, under the *k*th water harvesting system. The parameter n is the number of farmers producing crop *j* under the *k*th water harvesting system, while P_{ij} is the unit output price the *i*th farmer receives for the *j*th crop. V_{ijk} is the volume of crop *j* marketed by the *i*th farmer under the *j*th water harvesting system, and VC_{ijk} is the total variable cost for the *i*th farmer producing crop *j* under the *k*th water harvesting system (Hatibu *et al.*, 2006). The advantages of this approach are that market prices can vary, farmers can produce multiple crops, and a farmer may use several water harvesting techniques. Gross margin analysis is appropriate when fixed costs are insignificant or non-existent. This approach assumes labor is the major investment in water harvesting and labor opportunity costs are very low or zero.

Hatibu *et al.* (ibid.) found that in Tanzania water harvesting increased the economic returns to both land and labor, as water harvesting allowed farmers to grow rice and vegetables – commodities with greater economic value than the traditional crops of maize and sorghum. They found increased rice and vegetable production helped in poverty alleviation. Jensen *et al.* (2003) found similar results for maize and maize–cowpea intercropping in that water harvesting provided more income for both market-oriented and subsistence-oriented households, though the market-oriented households receive larger gross margins. The

Jensen *et al.* study also suggests water harvesting is highly beneficial under intercropping as gross margins under these systems were higher as compared to monocropping. Senkondo *et al.* (2004) found water harvesting allowed Tanzanian farmers to produce rice and onion, which was not feasible without water harvesting, allowing for a higher gross margin and return to labor. This study also found that returns to maize were considerably higher with water harvesting.

Due to the high cost of field studies regarding water harvesting, several researchers use simulations to assess the impact of water harvesting. The study by Röckstrom and Falkenmark (2000) employed a green water crop model to assess the effect of dry spells on crop yields in the Sahel. Their results suggest that poor rainwater partitioning and low plant water uptake reduce yields to 10 percent of potential yields. According to the study, with small changes to rainwater portioning – possible via water harvesting – it is agro-hydrologically possible to double crop yields in sub-Saharan Africa. Stephens and Hess (1999) directly assessed the effect of water harvesting on maize crop yields in the Machakos district, Kenya. Using a predicting arable resource capture in hostile environments (PARCH) model, Stephens and Hess simulate the effect of runoff water harvesting on crop yields, assuming either dry, average or wet rainfall seasons. Results suggest that during average years runoff control and runoff water harvesting significantly increase crop yields, while in dry years, crop yields increase only slightly. Yield increases were negligible during wet years as compared to yields during typical runoff conditions. Walker *et al.*, 2005) assessed the risk to crop yields of maize using a crop growth model combined with a deterministic runoff model and a stochastic rainfall model in South Africa. This study simulated crop yields with water harvesting (mini-catchment) and conventional total soil tillage under varying agronomic practices. Under a wide range of conditions, water harvesting increased the probability of higher crop yields.

While these previous studies provide useful insight to the economic viability of water harvesting, they are burdened with several disadvantages. The largest drawback is that none of the studies capture practices actually used by farmers. Many of the studies were designed experiments, with fixed levels of fertilizer use and soil conditions. In practice, however, farmers use varying levels and types of fertilizer under varying soil conditions. These studies also tend to ignore labor's contribution to agricultural production. While the opportunity costs of labor may be low in subsistence agriculture in sub-Saharan Africa, it is unlikely that the cost is zero. Labor is arguably the most significant investment in subsistence agriculture, and failing to include labor as an input may not allow for an accurate representation of agricultural production.

5.3 Data and the empirical model

5.3.1 Data

Data for this analysis consist of a two-year panel of 46 semi-subsistence households from Kolbila and Ouonon villages, Passore province in Burkina Faso. The observations are for the years 2001 and 2002. The collected data include crop production information, including the type and volume of crops produced, and the inputs used to produce these crops. The variables relevant to this analysis are discussed in greater detail as needed.

Each household has several family members, with each typically cultivating one or more plots. This analysis focuses on the plots of heads of households – a total sample size of 622 observations. The major crops produced were millet, white sorghum, red sorghum, cowpea, rice, ground nut, maize, sesame and several other smaller crops. In terms of volume for 2001 and 2002, the most important crops in this region were white sorghum, millet, cowpea and red sorghum. Among the households surveyed, two of the most common production choices were monocropping millet ($n=77$) and monocropping white sorghum ($n=78$). Data inconsistencies forced us to drop four millet and five white sorghum observations. As noted in the introduction, this study focuses on these two cropping scenarios.

Each crop has its own production technology, and hence, a different mix of fixed and variables factors.[1] In this analysis, the allocatable fixed factors are the hectares planted with each crop, the number of cartloads of manure applied to each plot and household labor in person-days. The variable factors in this analysis are the amount of fertilizer used in kilograms, the quantity of hired labor measured in person-days, and the use of water harvesting. The mean, standard deviation, minimum and maximum values of each input, for each crop are presented in Table 5.1. In the tables below, the following variables are assigned to each input: x_1=fertilizer (kg); x_2=manure (cartloads); x_3=hired labor (person-days); x_4=family labor (person-days); x_5=land (hectares); x_6=mulching (dummy, 1=yes); and x_7=zai (dummy, 1=yes).

As noted earlier, some farmers in this region use water harvesting to increase yields. The type of water harvesting used on a plot depends on the type of crop grown. For millet production, 14 percent of plots used mulching, while for white sorghum production, 22 percent of the plots used either zai or mulching.

Table 5.1 Descriptive statistics of inputs

Variable	Mean	Standard deviation	Minimum	Maximum
Millet				
Manure	0.2	0.5	0	2
Hired labor	2.1	4.7	0	17
Family labor	40.9	34.7	3.25	197
Land	0.5	0.5	0.012	1.633
White sorghum				
Fertilizer	7.4	14.3	0	50
Manure	1.9	3.2	0	10
Hired labor	2.4	5.8	0	20
Family labor	54.2	60.9	1.3	400
Land	0.7	0.8	0.008	3.018

A typical finding of previous studies is that water harvesting (e.g. mulching) increases crop yields. Table 5.2 presents output levels for plots/crops with and without water harvesting, and reveals that on average fields that use at least one type of water harvesting have higher yields than those that do not. The table reveals the effect of water harvesting is more pronounced in the case of white sorghum production.

5.3.2 The production technology

We approximate the millet and white sorghum production technology with the quadratic function

$$y = f\left(x_1, \ldots, x_N\right) = \beta_0 + \sum_{i=1}^{N}\beta_i x_i + \sum_{i=1}^{N}0.5\beta_{ii}x_i^2 + 0.5\sum_{i=1}^{N}\sum_{j=i+1}^{N}\beta_{ij}x_i x_j + \varepsilon.$$

In the case of millet production we have $n=4$ inputs (manure, hired labor, family labor, land),[2] the mulching dummy variable, and a dummy variable for time:

$year = 1$ if year is 2001, 0 if year is 2002.

The estimated equation for millet production is:

$$y_{millet} = \beta_0 + \sum_{i=2}^{6}\beta_i x_i + \sum_{i=2}^{5}0.5\beta_{ii}x_i^2 + 0.5\sum_{i=2}^{6}\sum_{j=i+1}^{6}\beta_{ij}x_i x_j + \beta_t year + \varepsilon.$$

where β_t is the coefficient on the dummy variable for year.

On white sorghum plots we have $n=5$ inputs (fertilizer, manure, hired labor, family labor, land), the mulching and zai dummy variables and the dummy variable for year. Our estimated equation for white sorghum production is:

$$y_{whitesorghum} = \beta_0 + \sum_{i=1}^{7}\beta_i x_i + \sum_{i=1}^{5}0.5\beta_{ii}x_i^2 + 0.5\sum_{i=1}^{7}\sum_{j=i+1}^{7}\beta_{ij}x_i x_j + \beta_t year + \varepsilon.$$

Table 5.2 Average output with and without water harvesting

Crop	Average output	Average output with water harvesting	Average output without water harvesting	Percentage difference
Millet	154.42	192.01	141.08	36
White sorghum	166.11	243.71	132.66	84

5.4 Results

We use ordinary least squares to estimate each production technology. Due to the large ratio between maximum and minimum values and the panel nature of the dataset, heteroskedasticity was a concern. Consequently the standard errors reported are White's heteroskedasticity-corrected standard errors.

5.4.1 Millet

The estimated coefficients for millet production are presented in Table 5.3. The inputs used to produce millet were manure (on a few plots), hired labor (also on a few plots), family labor and land. Zai was introduced only on one plot, and hence dropped as an explanatory variable. The coefficient estimates for the direct effects on family labor and land were significant and had the expected signs.

The coefficient estimates for the direct effects of family labor, land and mulching were positive and statistically significant. The coefficient on manure was positive and hired labor was negative, but both insignificant. These results

Table 5.3 Coefficient estimates for millet production

Coefficient	Estimate	Std error[§]	t value	$Pr > |t|$
α_0 **	−55.889	25.831	−2.16	0.04
β_2	82.739	80.350	1.03	0.31
β_3	−6.089	10.263	−0.59	0.56
β_4 ***	4.055	1.116	3.63	0.00
β_5 ***	286.645	81.543	3.52	0.00
β_6 **	127.327	63.269	2.01	0.05
β_{22}	−177.213	141.916	−1.25	0.22
β_{23}	21.864	53.515	0.41	0.68
β_{24}	−0.078	2.611	−0.03	0.98
β_{25}	51.940	40.753	1.27	0.21
β_{26}	78.862	85.215	0.93	0.36
β_{33}	0.872	1.241	0.70	0.49
β_{34}	−0.025	0.073	−0.34	0.74
β_{35}	0.354	5.547	0.06	0.95
β_{36}	−1.510	11.553	−0.13	0.90
β_{44}	−0.007	0.022	−0.31	0.76
β_{45} *	−2.653	1.513	−1.75	0.09
β_{46}	−0.543	1.662	−0.33	0.75
β_{55}	−150.766	152.954	−0.99	0.33
β_{56}	−75.334	84.070	−0.90	0.37
D_1 **	60.280	26.774	2.25	0.03

Notes
$R^2 = 0.5368$, adjusted $R^2 = 0.3771$.
[§] Stata, robust standard errors.
* significant at the 10 percent level.
** significant at the 5 percent level.
*** significant at the 1 percent level.

are reasonable, especially given that so few plots used manure or hired labor, and those that used either input used a small amount. Of greater interest in this analysis, however, is the sign on the mulch dummy variable. The results suggest mulching has a positive and statistically significant impact on millet production. These results, however, are possibly problematic, as the squared terms for each input typically had the desired negative sign, but none were significantly different from zero. Hence, the estimated millet production technology might not be strictly concave in inputs.

Evaluating the estimated quadratic millet technology at the mean values for manure, hired labor, household labor and land suggest mulching can lead to a 41 percent increase in yields in 2000: from a predicted average of 188 bushels with no mulching to 268 bushels of millet with mulching. Mulching led to a 32 percent increase in yields in 2001: from a predicted average of 248 bushels with no mulching to 328 bushels of millet with mulching. Note that rainfall was 758 cm in 2000 and 500 cm in 2001, suggesting mulching has higher value in higher rainfall seasons.

The results on yield improvements from mulching are consistent with the calculated values reported in Table 5.2, and lend support to the hypothesis that water harvesting increases crop yield. Of course, one could argue the econometric exercise above is a complex method to use to arrive at the same conclusion presented in Table 5.2. With this observation in mind, we next examine two other measures of economic interest: the direct elasticity of substitution among inputs and the marginal value product of inputs – with and without mulching. The direct elasticity of substitution is defined as:

$$\sigma_{ij} = \frac{\dfrac{1}{x_i f_i} + \dfrac{1}{x_j f_j}}{-\dfrac{f_{ii}}{f_i f_i} + 2\dfrac{f_{ij}}{f_i f_j} - \dfrac{f_{jj}}{f_j f_j}}$$

and "is the elasticity of the input ratio of factors i and j with respect to the marginal rate of substitution of these factors, taken along a fixed isoproduct curve, with all remaining factor quantities fixed" (McFadden, 1963). A value of $\sigma_{ij} > 0$ indicates inputs i and j are substitutes, while a negative value suggests the pair are complements. Table 5.4 presents the direct elasticity of substitution for each of the input pairs. The results suggest that with no water harvesting, all input pairs except family labor/land are substitutes. With mulching, all inputs are substitutes with one another, typically with stronger degrees of substitution than the case without mulching.

Although not reported here, the marginal products of hired labor, family labor and land each fall with mulching, while the marginal product of manure increases with mulching. One possible reason for this outcome is that millet is a low-value crop, typically produced for household consumption only and not intensively cultivated.

Table 5.4 Direct elasticity of substitution in millet production

	Manure		Hired labor		Family labor	
	No mulch	*Mulching*	*No mulch*	*Mulching*	*No mulch*	*Mulching*
Manure	–	–	–	–	–	–
Hired labor	0.28	0.69	–	–	–	–
Family labor	3.86	6.17	0.40	1.25	–	–
Land	1.86	0.65	0.39	2.00	−4.12	2.30

5.4.2 *White sorghum*

The estimated coefficients for the white sorghum technology are presented in Table 5.5. The inputs used to produce white sorghum were fertilizer, manure, hired labor, family labor and land. Zai was present in ten of the 78 plots, and mulching was used on ten of the 78 plots. In 2001 zai and mulching were both used on three plots. The coefficient estimates for the direct effects of fertilizer, manure, hired labor, family labor and land each had the expected sign, with family labor and land being statistically significant. The coefficients for both mulching and zai were positive and statistically significant.

Evaluated at the average input levels given in Table 5.1, the estimated technology consistent with the coefficients in Table 5.5 yield the following results. In 2000, average white sorghum output is 259 bushels per hectare with no water harvesting, 574 bushels per hectare with mulch and 243 bushels per hectare with zai. In 2001, average white sorghum output is 330 bushels per hectare with no water harvesting, 645 bushels per hectare with mulch, and 314 bushels per hectare with zai. Hence, the results suggest mulching can more than double yield, while zai leads to a small decrease in average yields. The unfavorable prediction result for zai stems from the cross terms interacting zai with manure, fertilizer, hired and family labor and land. Each of these terms is negative, but statistically insignificant. Another word of caution, however, is in order. Our zai data only tells us whether or not a plot has zai. It does not tell us if the entire plot has been dug, or one-half of the plot, or some other percentage.[3] Likewise, the mulching data is also only a dummy variable. A measure of the average biomass per plot would likely convey better information.

Table 5.6 presents the direct elasticity of substitution for the five inputs with no water harvesting. The results suggest that manure and hired labor are complements, but all other input pairs are substitutes. These results are similar to those found with millet production.

Table 5.7 presents the direct elasticity of substitution for the five inputs with mulching. As contrasted with the case for millet, in white sorghum production fertilizer is a complement with each other productive factor; manure is a complement with hired and family labor; and family labor is a complement with land.

Table 5.5 Coefficients for white sorghum production

Coefficient	Estimate	Std error	t value	Pr > |t|
α_{0**}	−33.646	18.689	−1.80	0.08
β_1	4.639	5.527	0.84	0.41
β_2	8.263	23.389	0.35	0.73
β_3	35.539	27.138	1.31	0.20
β_4*	1.309	0.746	1.76	0.09
β_5**	147.730	69.845	2.12	0.04
β_6***	308.770	115.057	2.68	0.01
β_7**	259.488	118.834	2.18	0.03
β_{11}	−0.414	0.413	−1.00	0.32
β_{12}	0.000	1.794	0.00	1.00
β_{13}	1.208	0.931	1.30	0.20
β_{14}	0.057	0.088	0.65	0.52
β_{15}	−6.462	8.655	−0.75	0.46
β_{16}**	−11.200	4.784	−2.34	0.02
β_{17}	−3.635	5.899	−0.62	0.54
β_{22}	−1.683	4.473	−0.38	0.71
β_{23}	−5.323	6.555	−0.81	0.42
β_{24}	−0.113	0.115	−0.98	0.33
β_{25}	50.953	33.381	1.53	0.13
β_{26}***	−62.127	18.939	−3.28	0.00
β_{27}	−34.964	25.785	−1.36	0.18
β_{33}	−2.179	2.403	−0.91	0.37
β_{34}	−0.137	0.202	−0.68	0.50
β_{35}	−4.945	11.759	−0.42	0.68
β_{36}*	56.263	30.056	1.87	0.07
β_{37}	−3.140	23.977	−0.13	0.90
β_{44}***	−0.030	0.011	−2.77	0.01
β_{45}**	2.095	0.930	2.25	0.03
β_{46}	−7.082	5.384	−1.32	0.20
β_{47}	−1.848	2.964	−0.62	0.54
β_{55}*	−198.127	110.497	−1.79	0.08
β_{56}*	652.189	364.605	1.79	0.08
β_{57}	−107.176	235.405	−0.46	0.65
D_1**	71.636	28.521	2.51	0.02

Notes
$R^2 = 0.7718$, adjusted $R^2 = 0.6001$.
* significant at the 10 percent level.
** significant at the 5 percent level.
*** significant at the 1 percent level.

Hired and family labor are substitutes, and land is a substitute input with manure and hired labor. The results suggest that when a white sorghum plot is mulched, the plot is cultivated more intensively. Similar results obtain for the substitution elasticities when a plot has zai, and when a plot has both mulch and zai.

The marginal products of hired labor and land increase significantly with mulching. The marginal product of hired labor more than triples and the mar-

Table 5.6 Direct elasticity of substitution in white sorghum production with no water harvesting

	Fertilizer	Manure	Hired labor	Family labor
Manure	1.42	–		
Hired labor	0.71	−2.82	–	
Family labor	0.57	1.92	2.01	–
Land	2.06	0.82	2.91	0.44

Table 5.7 Direct elasticity of substitution in white sorghum production with mulching

	Fertilizer	Manure	Hired labor	Family labor
Manure	−4.08	–		
Hired labor	−4.16	−1.50	–	
Family labor	−2.10	−17.35	1.40	–
Land	−1.75	6.36	13.88	−4.83

ginal product of land increases four-fold. Under zai, the marginal product of each input falls.

5.6 Discussion and conclusion

The above results provide further evidence that water harvesting generally has a positive effect on crop yields, and hence on household income. These results also provide insight on the substitutability of inputs. While previous studies have alluded to the fact that certain input combinations are complementary or that certain inputs can be substituted for one another, by not using a flexible production technology it is difficult to ascertain whether such relationships exist or not. The data reported here suggest substitution patterns depend on the crop produced. For instance, virtually all inputs are substitutes in millet production, while complementarities among inputs are prevalent in white sorghum production. Previous studies indicate that while fertilizer alone increases output, the greatest increases in output occur when fertilizer is used with other yield-enhancing inputs. This study provides evidence for such conjecture.

Despite the encouraging results found in this analysis, we acknowledge several shortcomings. First, the range of data is only over two years, and consequently the estimates could be markedly different for different years due to stochastic events such as rainfall and pest infestations. Second, two factors that are not controlled for in the regressions are soil quality (many plots have similar soil conditions) and rainfall (levels are the same for each plot in a given year and consequently this variable would lead to similar results as year dummies). Lastly, and most importantly, in this study the proxy used for mulching and zai is a dummy variable – a likely better measure of mulching is biomass per hectare, and a better measure of zai is percentage of plot converted to zai.

Despite these shortcomings, the analysis does provide potentially useful insights on the effect of water harvesting that have not been found in prior studies. Since this study uses actual data from households as opposed to previous data from designed experiments, the measured effect of water harvesting is consistent with the actual agricultural practices adopted by farmers in this region. At the moment, one can conclude that water harvesting could be a viable poverty reduction strategy in sub-Saharan Africa.

Notes

1 Strictly speaking these fixed factors are more properly defined as "fixed but variable inputs" in that the head of the household allocated his endowment of fixed factors over several productive activities.
2 Because millet is such a low-value crop, less than 5 percent of households in this region use fertilizer.
3 Digging zai is quite a labor-intensive endeavor, requiring over 300 person-hours to fill a hectare of land with zai. Typically, farmers convert 0.2 hectares each year (Kaboré and Reij, 2004).

References

Barron, J. and Okwach, G. (2005) Runoff water harvesting for dry spell mitigation in maize (*Zea mays* L.): Results from on-farm research in semi-arid Kenya. *Agricultural Water Management* 74, 1–21.

Carsky, R.J., Ndikawa, R., Singh, L. and Rao, M.R. (1995) Response of dry season sorghum to supplemental irrigation and fertilizer N and P on Vertisols in northern Cameroon. *Agricultural Water Management* 28, 1–8.

Carter, D.C. and Miller, S. (1991) Three years' experience with an on-farm macro catchment water harvesting system in Botswana. *Agricultural Water Management* 19, 191–203.

Chambers, R., Chung, Y. and Fare, R. (1996) Benefit and distance functions. *Journal of Economic Theory* 70, 407–419.

Drechsel, P., Olaleye, A., Adeoti, A., Thiombiano, L., Barry, B. and Vohland, K. (2005) Adoption drivers and constraints of resource conservation technologies in sub-Saharan Africa. Available at: www.iwmi.cgiar.org/africa/west_africa/projects/Adoption Technology/AdoptionConstraints-Overview.pdf.

Fox, P. and Rockstrom, J. (2000) Water-harvesting for supplementary irrigation of cereal crops to overcome intra-seasonal dry-spells in the Sahel. *Physics and Chemistry of the Earth* 25 (3), 289–296.

Fox, P. and Röckstrom, J. (2003) Supplemental irrigation for the dry-spell mitigation of rainfed agriculture in the Sahel. *Agricultural Water Management* 61, 29–50.

Fox, P., Röckstrom, J. and Barron, J. (2005) Risk analysis and economic viability of water harvesting for supplemental irrigation in semi-arid Burkina Faso and Kenya. *Agricultural Systems* 83, 231–250.

Hatibu, N., Mutabazi, K., Senkondo, E.M. and Msangi, A.S.K. (2006) Economics of rainwater harvesting for crop enterprises in semi-arid areas of East Africa. *Agricultural Water Management* 80, 74–86.

Jensen, J.R., Bernhard, R.H., Hansen, S., McDonagh, J., Moberg, J.P., Nielsen, N.E. and Nordbo, E. (2003) Productivity in maize based cropping systems under various soil–

water–nutrient management strategies in a semi-arid, alfisol environment in East Africa. *Agricultural Water Management* 59, 217–237.

Kaboré, D. and Reij, C. (2004) The emergence and spreading of an improved traditional soil and water conservation practice in Burkina Faso. IFPRI, EPTD Discussion Paper 114. Available at: www.ifpri.org/divs/eptd/dp/papers/eptdp114.pdf.

McFadden, D. (1963) Constant elasticity of substitution production functions. *The Review of Economic Studies* 30 (2), 73–83.

Oweis, T., Hachum, A. and Kijne, J. (1999) Water harvesting and supplemental irrigation for improved water use efficiency in dry areas. SWIM Paper 7, IWMI. Available at: www.iwmi.cgiar.org/pubs/SWIM/Swim07.pdf.

Röckstrom, J. and Falkenmark, M. (2000) Semi-arid crop production from a hydrological perspective: Gap between potential and actual yields. *Critical Reviews in Plant Sciences* 19 (4), 319–346.

Senkondo, E.M.M., Msangi, A.S.K., Xavery, P., Lazaro, E.A. and Hatibu, N. (2004) Profitability of rainwater harvesting for agricultural production in selected semi-arid areas of Tanzania. *Journal of Applied Irrigation Science* 39 (1), 65–81.

Stephens, W. and Hess, T.M. (1999) Modeling the benefits of soil water conservation using the PARCH model: A case study from a semi-arid region of Kenya. *Journal of Arid Environments* 41, 335–344.

Tabor, J.A. (1995) Improving crop yields in the Sahel by means of water-harvesting. *Journal of Arid Environments* 30: 83–106.

Walker, S., Tsubo, M. and Hensley, M. (2005) Quantifying risk for water harvesting under semi-arid conditions. Part II: Crop yield simulation. *Agricultural Water Management* 76, 94–107.

Zougmoré, R., Mando, A. and Stroosnijder, L. (2004) Effect of soil and water conservation and nutrient management on the soil–plant water balance in semi-arid Burkina Faso. *Agricultural Water Management* 65, 102–120.

6 Accounting for regulating services

Karl-Göran Mäler, Sara Aniyar and Åsa Jansson

6.1 Why valuation?

Almost all decisions made by agents (individuals, households, companies, associations, governments, etc.) are preceded by some comparisons of the expected gains from making the decision compared with the cost of making the same decision. These comparisons may be completely informal, involving only some rough thoughts on the consequences of the decision, or they may involve the use of an elaborate decision theoretic model.[1] Most decisions made by a household do not need any elaborate theoretical analysis. The decisions are mainly made on the basis of experience. But when a household is going to make a major investment such as buying a house, they will try to make a rational choice, given the information they have available. Based on this information, they will make a valuation of the consequences, in order to see which side will dominate – buying the house now or waiting for another opportunity. In this example, the household will probably consult experts that can translate the consequences of buying the house for the household into something concrete, such as the net income of the household. Then the household is performing a valuation. Similarly, when a society is going to make a decision on, say, the construction of a new highway, the society should know how this new highway affects the citizens: higher taxes, shorter transport time, more air pollution, deforestation where the highway is going to be built, etc. before making a decision. In the end, all these factors – and many, many more – have to be compared in some way or another so that a decision can be made. Valuation is a technique for doing just that. In theory, it tries to identify the consequences of the construction of the highway for each affected household, and then aggregate this over all households. The former part – identifying the consequences for households – can in principle be done without imposing any moral or ethical values. We are simply interested in whether a household is better or worse off. However, the second part, aggregation, needs values on how we should think of the interpersonal consequences of the construction. Some households may be better off, while others will be worse off.

The first part is valuation, and economists have developed a rich toolbox for assessing household-specific values. We will later give a brief presentation of some of the tools in this toolbox.

Thus, valuation was developed as a tool for decision making. However, it is also used to find out whether the welfare of a society has increased over a specified time period. It is very common in newspapers to find references to the gross national product as an index of whether welfare has increased or not. In this review we will introduce a different and more relevant index, namely wealth per capita. In constructing such an index, it is necessary to value ecosystem services and, more important, the capital stocks embodied in an ecosystem. In doing so, essentially the same valuation techniques as used in decision making will be used.

6.2 Ecosystems and ecosystem services

6.2.1 Key definitions

Ecosystems. An ecosystem is a dynamic complex of plant, animal, and microorganism communities and the nonliving environment interacting as a functional unit. Humans are an integral part of ecosystems. Ecosystems vary enormously in size, a temporary point in a tree hollow and an ocean basin can both be ecosystems.

Ecosystem services. Ecosystem services are the benefits people obtain from ecosystems. These include provisioning services such as food and water; regulating services such as regulation of floods, drought, land degradation, and disease; supporting services such as soil formation and nutrient cycling; and cultural services such as recreational, spiritual, religious and other nonmaterial benefits.

Well-being. Human well-being has multiple constituents, including basic material for a good life, freedom of choice and action, health, good social relations and security. Well-being is at the opposite end of a continuum from poverty, which has been defined as a "pronounced deprivation in well-being." The constituents of well-being, as experienced and perceived by people, are situation-dependent, reflecting local geography, culture, and ecological circumstances.

(Millennium Ecosystem Assessment, 2005: Box 1.1, 1.2, p. 3)

The definition of an ecosystem given above does not give a precise guide on how to delimit an ecosystem. In principle, organisms in one area can (and will) interact with organisms elsewhere on the planet. Given enough time, we would end up with one global ecosystem. That is obviously very impractical, so we should try to adopt a more practical rule for differentiating between one ecosystem and another, and the only way of doing that is to use common sense. When does it seem acceptable to exclude some connections and when is it necessary to include others? These questions may seem academic for an ecologist, but an economist needs to delimit a system very precisely in order to develop the tools for valuing the services and managing the system in a rational way. The same problem is familiar to regional economists who, more or less arbitrarily, define the spatial extent of the regions to be studied. In the end, only experience, theoretical insights and common sense can resolve this problem.

We will in the next section treat ecosystems as capital assets. How do we measure the "size" of these assets? We will discuss this question shortly.

6.2.2 Classification of ecosystem services

The Millennium Ecosystem Assessment suggested a classification system of ecosystem services, briefly illustrated in Figure 6.1. This classification is more or less obvious. Provisional services are services that are directly used by man. Examples are many: fish from the seas, timber from the forests, agricultural output from cultivated land, etc. Cultural services are services that are not material, but still affect man directly. To see large mammals – whales, elephants, lions, moose, wolves – is something many people would be willing to pay substantial amounts for, which is a clear indication that the existence of these animals is welfare-enhancing. Similarly, giant Sequoias, rare orchids, a cloud forest in Costa Rica or a boreal forest in northern Scandinavia, may, by their existence, provide well-being to many citizens. Thus, these sorts of assets often generate *intrinsic* values. An intrinsic value is roughly defined as the value of a change in a resource, even if this change in the resource does not change the behaviour of individuals. We will come back later to a discussion of intrinsic values.

Regulating services do not directly provide welfare to humans. Their importance derives from the fact that they are essential in providing intermediary

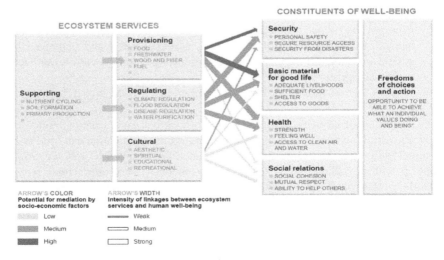

Figure 6.1 Linkages between ecosystem services and human wellbeing (source: Millenium Ecosystem Assessment, 2005).

goods and services. Thus their value derives from the values of the provisional services they are inputs to. Similarly, supporting services are another kind of intermediary service that derive their values from the value of provisioning services. We will call the regulating and supporting services simply intermediary services. Of course, it may happen that an intermediary service is, besides providing a necessary input to provisional services, also providing a provisional service. An example is given by a forest that regulates the local hydrology (the regulating service) but also provides fuel-wood or recreational opportunities. From a valuation point of view there is, therefore, not much difference between regulating and supporting services, and we will treat them under one heading.

As provisional services are generating either direct inputs to human production agencies (households, private and public organizations, etc.) we often call the provisional services final demand (or final consumption) in order to keep the text in line with established economic definitions.

Thus, we have for our analysis two different kind of services:

• final consumption
• intermediary services.

However, it is important to remember the remark made above that an intermediary service may also be generating final consumption, and we will give many examples of this later. It may be desirable also to repeat that the values of intermediary services are derived from their role in providing final consumption, and we will see many examples of this later.

For our discussion on valuation techniques later, it may be worthwhile to recall that both final consumption and intermediary services may either be characterized as public goods or as private goods. This distinction has nothing to do with whether the producer is a private or public agency. It has to do with whether the output from a service shares the characteristic of a private or a public good. A private good is a service such that an increase of the use of this service by one household will diminish the potential use by other households. A public good is just the opposite – a service such that an increase of the use of which by one household will not diminish the potential use by other households. We will see several examples on the analytical use of this distinction soon. However, two examples may illustrate the distinction.

A forest provides many provisional services, but for now let us only consider the supply of fuel-wood. If one household increases its collection of fuel-wood, there will be less available for other households to collect (if fuel-wood is scarce). Thus, there is a competition between households for fuel-wood. This is true irrespective of the institutional arrangements – more fuel-wood to one household will necessarily reduce the use of fuel-wood in other households. Thus, the consumption of fuel-wood is a private good. The forest also controls the hydrology of the surrounding area. A clearing of parts of the forest will change the pattern of water flows. That change will be the same for all inhabitants of the forest area and/of the downstream area. The change in hydrology is a public (dis)service. The only way for a household to avoid experiencing this change in hydrology is by moving away from the catchment area. But all those who remain in this area will face the same change in the water flows!

The reasons these concepts are important are:

- · valuation depends on whether an ecosystem service is a private or a public good; and
- management of the ecosystem will very much be influenced by the distinction between private and public goods.

We will mainly deal with valuation in this chapter.

6.3 Sustainable development and accounting prices

Before beginning a discussion of valuation techniques, it is necessary to discuss the purposes of valuation. Here, we will argue that valuation is primarily a tool for first assessing whether the economic development is sustainable or not, and second for allowing decision making in a way that supports sustainable development. The discussion will take place within the framework developed by Dasgupta and Mäler (2000) and Arrow *et al.* (2003). A more comprehensive presentation is given in the forthcoming book, *Accounting for Ecosystem Services* by Sara Aniyar and Karl-Göran Mäler.

6.3.1 Wealth as an indicator of sustainable development

Let $Cs = (C_{1;s}, C_{2;s}, \ldots, C_{m;s})$ be a list (or vector) of consumer goods and services in period s. The list must contain not only what we traditionally regard as consumer goods, but also environmental amenities, public goods, etc. These are also included because all of them contribute to human well-being in one way or another.

We add the critical assumption that we have a forecast of the future consumption vectors. Such a forecast obviously must depend on at least three factors: the present stocks of capital $K_{i;t}$ (where the current period is t and i denotes the ith capital stock); a forecast of future knowledge (including technological knowledge); and a forecast of the future institutions of the economy. Given such a forecast, the forecasted consumption will depend on these three factors. We will focus on the role of the present stocks of capital (but we will touch upon the remaining two a few times later).

Let $K_s = K_{1;s}, K_{2;s}, \ldots, K_{n;s}$ be a list (or a vector) of capital stocks in the beginning of period s. Given a dynamic system that determines the future capital stocks, we can write

$$K_{t+1} - K_t = \theta(C_t, K_t, t) \tag{1}$$

We assume, as is standard in economics, that there is a utility function $U(C_1, C_2 \ldots, C_m)$ that describes the production of well-being in any given period. Note that the list of consumption "goods" is not equivalent to what we ordinarily measure as consumption. The list $(C_1, C_2 \ldots, C_m)$ of consumption goods includes all goods and services that affect the feeling of well-being: food, recreation, health, natural amenities and even the improvement of other people's well-being; and also those goods and services that reduce the feeling of well-being (bads), such as pollution, labour time, etc. Given the assumption in the previous paragraph, the future consumption C_τ will be a function of the present stocks:

$$C_\tau = \alpha(\tau, t, K_{1,t}, K_{2,t}, K_{2,t}, K, K_{m,t})$$ (2)

The α-function will be called a resource allocation mechanism and the characteristics of this function are determined by our forecasts of the future knowledge and the future institutions.

We will define social welfare as the present value of the stream of future utilities.

$$W_t = \sum_{a=t}^{\infty} \frac{U(C_s)}{(1+\delta)^{s-t}}$$ (3)

We will return to the interpretation of the discount rate and the utility function later.

Mathematically, the accounting price on asset i at time t is defined as

$$\tilde{p}_{i,t} = \sum_{s=t}^{\infty} \frac{\frac{\partial U(Cs)}{\partial K_{i,t}}}{(1+\delta)^{s-t}}$$ (4)

It is worth remembering that forecasted future consumption is a function of the current capital stocks.

The intuition behind this definition should be clear: the accounting price of capital stock i at time t, with utility as the numéraire, is the present value of the future marginal return (measured in utility units) of a small perturbation of the stock at time t. Very often in the rest of this chapter, we will replace the list with a single variable, C, but it would be quite easy intellectually to carry with us the whole list, although it might be typographically boring.

We will make the rather strong assumption that there is only one individual in society in order to avoid difficulties associated with interpersonal comparisons. For a complete analysis see Aniyar and Mäler (forthcoming).

One can now show that

$$W_{t=1} - W_t = \sum_{i=1}^{n} \tilde{p}_i (K_{i,t+1} - K_{i,t}) + \upsilon_t$$ (5)

Neglecting the last term, Equation 4 says that the change in social welfare between two time periods is equal to the sum over all capital stocks of the value of changes in these stocks, when the value is calculated with the accounting prices. Thus, the economy is on a sustainable path if the change in welfare from one period to the next is always non-negative.

6.3.2 Choice of numéraire

The analysis above is with utility as the numéraire. The accounting price of one stock is a price in utility – that is, how much utility we would be willing to abstain from in the current period in order to have the stock in the end of the period increased by one unit of utility. In empirical studies it would not be very convenient to use utility as the numéraire. Instead we would like to use consumption in the current period as the numéraire – that is, using the cost of a basket of consumption goods in the current period as the numéraire. In order to simplify, we assume that the basket contains only one good, Good 1. With this as the numéraire, the accounting prices $p_i(s)$ are defined as

$$p_i(s) = \frac{\tilde{p}_i(s)}{\dfrac{\partial U}{\partial c_1(1)}}$$

However, in order to use these prices with consumption as the numéraire, we need to use the discount rate with consumption as the numéraire r instead of the utility discount rate δ. This is discussed in the next section.

6.3.2.1 Discounting

The way of looking at δ is a moral parameter indicating how we want to compare well-being of future generations with well-being of the present generations. The utility discount rate is related to the consumption rate of discount rate. This latter concept – r – is basically measuring the marginal rate of future consumption for present consumption. The relation follows from the Ramsay equation:

$$r = \delta + \eta g \tag{6}$$

That is, the consumption rate equals the utility rate δ plus the elasticity of marginal utility $\eta = -\frac{u'}{u''}$ of consumption times the predicted future growth rate ηg.

η can be interpreted as our value for equity between different generations, regardless of when these generations live,[2] g as how much better a future generation will find life compared to the present generation, and δ as our preference for individuals living in the future relative to current individuals.

The Ramsay equation can be interpreted as a rule that provides us with an "exchange rate" between measuring well-being in utility terms and in consumption terms.

One can show that these accounting prices for stocks and flows are the correct prices for marginal cost–benefit analysis of "small" projects (see Arrow *et al.*, 2003).

Let us now go back to Equation 5. In this equation, the first term gives the "endogenous" change in social welfare – that is, the change which is due to changes in resources inside the system. The last term, v_t, reflects changes in social welfare due to causes outside the studied system. For example, change in a country's terms of trade is, for a small country, independent of changes inside the country. The term will also reflect autonomous changes in technology (that is, technical changes that are independent of capital accumulation in the country).

Although both terms of trade and technical change can be quite important for social well-being, we will neglect these effects in this article – that is, we will neglect the "drift term". For the motivation for this, see Dasgupta and Mäler (2000), Arrow *et al.* (2003) and Xepapadeas (2001). However, the main reason for us not including these terms is that we want to focus on how to include eco-system services in this framework.

6.4 Ecosystems as capital assets

We will regard ecosystems as collections of organisms that are interacting with each other. These interactions can be described as a dynamic system and the biomass of the various organisms can be interpreted as capital assets. Thus, the assumption implies that we can interpret an ecosystem as a dynamic system with the interactions described by dynamical equations. However, the number of different organisms in an ecosystem may be extremely large, and in order to perform empirical analysis of an ecosystem, we need to aggregate them to a small number of measurable variables. We assume, from now, that the systems we are studying have been simplified in this way. We will illustrate with specific models.

6.4.1 The Schaefer model of a fishery

Although the Schaefer model (see Clark (2005) for a thorough introduction to this and other fishery models) is not an ecosystem model – only one species – we start our discussion on valuation with an analysis of this surplus model, as it will set the tone for more general models.

Let x_t be the stock of fish in the beginning of period t. The dynamics of this stock is given by

$$x_{t+1} - x_t = gx_t(1 - \frac{x_t}{\bar{x}}) - h_t \tag{7}$$

where h_t is the harvest in period t, g is the intrinsic growth rate and $\bar{x}$ is the carrying capacity of the system. The harvest is, of course, a provisional service and there are no regulating services generated in the system. We can now try to derive the accounting price for the fish stock at the beginning of period *t*. However, we must first make a forecast of the future of this fishery. Such a forecast will be influenced by the institutions controlling the use of the fishery. Let us start by assuming the system to be optimally managed. The optimum is defined as the harvest strategy that maximizes the present value of future harvests:

$$\sum_{s=t}^{\infty} \frac{ph_t - C(e_t)}{(1+r)^{s-t}} \tag{8}$$

where e_t is the fishing effort in period *t* (measured, say, by the number of boats in the fishery), $C(e_t)$ the cost of this effort and *p* is the net price of fishing costs for the harvest.

Conditions for an optimal management defines the existence of an accounting price, q_s, on the fish stock

$$q_s = p - \frac{C(e_s)}{x_s}. \tag{9}$$

In a steady state, the accounting price is thus equal to output price minus the marginal cost of effort per unit of fish stock.

Note that the service of the fish stock is a provisional service (final service in our terminology) that is a private good with a market price, and if our assumption of the dynamics is correct, the estimation of the accounting price is very simple.

Let us now assume that the fishery is an open-access fishery – that is, anyone can enter and leave the fishery without cost.[3] This implies that as soon as expected profit is positive, fishermen will enter the fishery, and when it is negative, they will leave. In equilibrium, net revenues must be zero.[4] The rent from the fishery has been completely dissipated. But that implies that the accounting price must be zero! On the margin, an increase in the fish stock is worth nothing.

This example shows that valuation of ecosystem services must be seen in an institutional context. Accounting for ecosystem services is, thus, very closely connected with the institutions that determine the management of the ecosystems.

6.5 Estimation of accounting price for a regulating service

6.5.1 Mangrove forests and fisheries

The carrying capacity of the fish stock in the previous example is, in general, determined by the physical and biological environment in which the fish reproduce. One example of this is the importance of mangrove forests for fisheries. Thus, let us assume that the carrying capacity $\bar{x}$ is a function of the size of the mangrove forest. Once again, we have to face the problem of how we should define size. Possibly, the best way is to simply define it as the area covered by the forest. For our purpose, the exact definition is of no importance. Of course, the mangrove forest offers many more services (wood for charcoal production, wood for construction, recreational area, protection of coastal land, etc.), but we will neglect them here and concentrate on the regulating service. Thus we postulate that

$$\bar{x}_s = \bar{x}(M_s),\tag{10}$$

where M_s is the size of the forest.[5] While keeping the Schaefer model, we could also have assumed that the intrinsic growth rate is affected by the size of the mangrove forest. However, the case we are going to study is enough to show the general principles.

The dynamics of the fish stock can, as in the previous section, be written

$$x_{s+1} - x_s = rx_s\left(1 - \frac{x_s}{x(M_s)}\right) - h_s\tag{11}$$

We also need to know the dynamics of the mangrove forest. The simplest (but perhaps erroneous) assumption is that the logistic model describes the forest growth sufficiently well.

$$M_{s+1} - M_s = r_M M_s\left(1 - \frac{M_s}{\bar{M}}\right) - h_{M,s}\tag{12}$$

where $h_{M,s}$ is the harvest of forest products in period s.

We now have two different equations and it is not possible to derive closed-form solutions to them. However, it very simple to use simulation software, Stella[6] for example, to calculate the accounting price on both mangrove forest and the fish stock, given the predicted future prices on fish catches.

Note that the accounting price for the regulating service of the mangrove forest is derived from the price of fish catches.

6.5.2 Plaice fishery and an environmental disservice

Plaice (a fish belonging to the flounders) is an important fish in the North Atlantic. Its reproduction requires bare sea bottoms (hard or sandy bottoms). Reproduction areas are threatened by eutrophication (for example, due to runoff of nitrogen from agricultural land or discharge of sewage). When the sea bottom has been covered by algae, it can no longer be used for reproduction. Thus, the growth of algae can be seen as a regulatory disservice and the accounting price for suitable reproduction areas is an asset that has an accounting price. This accounting price can be estimated as follows.

The biology of plaice is such that the Schaefer model is not a good choice. Instead, the Beverton-Holt model is most appropriate for describing the dynamics of plaice populations (in fact, it was developed for plaice fisheries in the North Sea). In this model the focus is on the growth of individuals over time. This growth is described by the so-called van Bertanlanffy growth equation. Thus, the total biomass of one cohort in one year is determined by multiplying the weight of the average individual (given by the van Bertanlanffy equation) with the number of individuals in the surviving generation, and finally summed over all cohorts. The model is complicated and it is impossible to derive mathematical solutions except in some extremely simple cases (see Clark, 2005). Instead, one can use GAMS (general algebraic modelling system) to simulate the fishery and thereby estimate the accounting price of suitable reproduction areas. This was done by Sandra Silva Paulsen in her PhD thesis (see the appendix for the GAMS code for the model). She used ecological knowledge to relate the spawning of plaice in an area of suitable habitats on the Swedish west coast, as well as the growth of the number of species during the first two years when the young fish were recruited. She then obtained the information on the age structure for each year since 1950. Based on this, she then developed the Beverton-Holt model and studied how the fisheries performed under different conditions (only one scenario is described in her thesis). By then changing the initial area of suitable habitat a little, she could develop an analogous scenario. By comparing the present value of these two runs of the model, she generated the accounting price per square metre of the habitat.

The Beverton-Holt model is non-convex, which is behind the difficulties in deriving mathematical results, but also causes empirical algorithms to go astray. Dr Paulsen had to work quite hard for a long time to make the algorithms in the GAMS program converge. Anyone trying something similar should be well trained in GAMS.

6.5.3 *Pollination services from wild bumble-bees*

This is based on a study that we carried out on the sustainable development of Stockholm County. We will report on the way we studied land-use changes.

Many types of rapeseed (canola), a major cash crop in North America, are pollinator dependant. For certain canola lines, the seed weight per plant can increase over 80 per cent with bumble-bee pollination (Steffan-Dewenter *et al.*, 2002). The growing demand for urban development has significant impacts on terrestrial ecosystems (McIntyre *et al.*, 2000) and on habitat fragmentation (Sala *et al.*, 2000), which represents a major threat to wild pollinators (Allen-Wardell *et al.*, 1998). In this context, it is relevant to assess the pollination ecosystem services. In our Stockholm County Project we attempted to estimate the accounting price for the pollination regulating service by calculating how the pollination potential of canola can vary due to land-use change in an urban development.

It has been shown that the availability of mass flowering crops (such as canola) has strong positive effects on bumble-bee densities; and that the strongest correlation between the proportion of mass flowering crops and bumble-bee (*B. terrestris*, *B. lucorum*, *B. lapidarius*, *B. pascuorum*) densities was found for landscape sectors with a 3,000 m radius (Westphal *et al.*, 2003). The bumble-bees also require a 2 per cent area of semi-natural habitat within the circles sur-rounding the canola fields in order to obtain adequate nesting sites.

By using a geographical information system (Arc View) and information on the area and geographical location of canola fields, we could then place circles (3,000 m radius) around the canola fields of the study area (Stockholm County, Sweden) and calculate the pollination potential in each circle. By changing the land use according to the regional development plan (Stockholm Regional Planning Office, 2001) of the study area, we could then estimate the change in the pollination potential of the canola. The parameters upon which our esti-mates of pollination potential changes were based were the proportion of mass flowering crops within the circle and the minimum requirement of semi-natural habitat.

As there is also a correlation between bumble-bee density and harvest index (30), the change in pollination potential can be linked to crop output. The change in crop output can then, in turn, be translated into monetary units through a market price method. Using a similar approach, it has been shown (Ricketts, 2004; Ricketts *et al.*, 2004) that forest-based pollinators increased coffee yield in plantations in Costa Rica by 20 per cent, and estimated that during 2000–2003 pollination services from two forest fragments translated into about $60,000.

Furthermore, the scales of operation of ecosystem services are of essential consideration when valuing ecosystem services (Hein *et al.*, 2006). The scale of operation of solitary wild bees, as well as some long-tongued bumble-bees (Walther-Hellwig *et al.*, 2000), is in the realm of hundreds of metres, as opposed to several thousand metres, as is the case for the included generalist bumble-bees. In our example, there are potentially several scales of operation to consider.

The distribution of resources at the landscape scale is an important issue to consider in the context of mobile organisms contributing to ecosystem services (Kremen, 2007). Landscape connectivity is needed for different pollinators and potentially also for relevant pest control species; the freedom of choice to switch between different crops in the face of, for example, climate change, is enhanced. This freedom allows adaptation to future environmental issues and other changes, and should also be considered an option value, at least partly ascribed to the pollination service.

The dynamics of the interactions between the wild pollinators needs, there-fore, at least two capital stocks, the size of the canola plantation and the size of the natural and semi-natural habitat. The bee population seems to adjust very quickly to changes in the canola cultivation. Thus there is a very fast positive feedback from increases in the canola area to the increase in the stock of bees and the following increase in canola production. On the other hand, the impact of increases in the size of the natural or semi-natural habitat seems to reach a saturation point with regard to impacts on the size of the bee populations. If the habitat is smaller than saturation size, a decrease of habitat will result in lower bee population and therefore lower harvest of canola.

We will try to summarize the above description by the following model structure:

Let

x_t be the stock of bumblebees in the beginning of period t
y_t be the production of canola
N_t be the size of the natural habitat for the bumble-bees
L_t be the land used for canola cultivation.

Then we could represent the dynamics of the bumble-bees by

$$x_{t+1} - x_t = rx_t \left(1 - \frac{x_t}{\bar{x}_t}\right). \tag{13}$$

Here we have assumed that there is no predation of bumble-bees. However, it is possible to change that assumption without difficulty. This is a logistic growth model with carrying capacity given by

$$\bar{x}_t = \bar{x}(N_t, L_t). \tag{14}$$

The canola production y_t is described by

$$y_t = \psi(L_t). \tag{15}$$

Here we have assumed that the canola production is determined by the size of land allocated to its growth. Of course, labour, fertilizers, etc. will affect the production, but we will disregard such factors in this presentation.

The production of canola seeds (S_t) is given by

$$S_t = \phi(y_t, x_t). \tag{16}$$

Finally, the value of the seed production in year t is

$$v_t = q_t S_t - C(L_t) \tag{17}$$

where $C(Lt)$ is the cost of cultivating the land Lt.

Finally, the accounting prices for the stocks of natural land N, cultivation land L, and bumble-bees are defined as the partial derivatives with respect to these variables of

$$\sum_{s=t}^{\infty} \frac{v_t}{(1+r)^{s-t}}. \tag{18}$$

Assuming rapid bumble-bee population dynamics, Equation 13 can be simplified to

$$x_t = \bar{x}(N_t, L_t), \tag{19}$$

which would simplify the estimation of the accounting prices substantially.

In flow accounting (standard SNA procedure), the only quantity of interest (at least in the production account) is vt, which can easily be found from agricultural statistics. The contributions from the bumble-bees do not need to be accounted for, as these are already in v_t.

6.5.4 Forests and water

In all previous examples, the value of a regulating service has been calculated from an assumed knowledge of the value of a provisional service. We will in this example study a case in which we first have to estimate the marginal value of the provisional service before we can estimate the value of the regulating service and the accounting prices for the relevant stocks.

It seems to be accepted that a forest will retain water in greater quantities and for longer periods than a corresponding area in which all trees have been removed. In particular, the transport of water in the soil will be much slower in the forested area, which indicates a higher quality, both of groundwater as well as surface water. This can be studied by using detailed hydrological models. We will thus assume that we have access to such a model that relates changes in the forested area to changes in water flow, the variance of this flow and the quality of the flow. Thus, associated with a change, ΔF, of forested area, there are corresponding changes in the average water flow, ΔZ, the variance in the flow, $\Delta\sigma$, and the quality (measured, for example, by its turbidity), ΔQ. If we can value these changes, we will be able to estimate the accounting price, p, for the forested area.

Assume now that the water is used for irrigation. Then the turbidity does not matter. The variance of the flow does matter, however, as large flows may not correspond to times when much water is used for irrigation. Furthermore, the runoff may create degradation of land through erosion. Thus, an increase in the variance will damage agricultural production. Of course, the farmer downstream can always build a tank to moderate the water flows to reduce erosion and even out the flow. In order to keep things simple, we assume that those options are too costly to be considered (anyone interested can easily generalize what follows to include that option).

Thus, we have a situation in which there is a water flow that is characterized by the average amount of water flowing and by its variance. We could (or better should) regard the variance as a quality measure of the water flow. The strategy now is to find ways of estimating the marginal value of the average flow and of the variance (which of course will be negative). We proceed as follows.

If there is a market price on water, p_w, used by the farmers for irrigation, this is the correct estimate of the marginal value of the flow (provided there are no taxes or subsidies on water use or quantity rationing of water consumption). We then have to make a forecast for the future development of this market price. Suppose now that we have a hydrological model able to predict future changes in the water flow, ΔZ_τ, from a hypothetical marginal change today in the forested

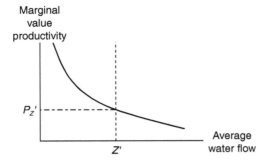

Figure 6.2 Ecosystem services and their links to human well-being (Millennium Ecosystem Assessment, 2005).

area. The accounting price for the forest (in period *t*, neglecting the variance of the water flow as well as direct provisional services the forest may generate) is then

$$p_{f,t} = \sum_{\tau=t}^{\infty} \frac{p_{w,\tau} \Delta Z_{\tau}}{(1+r)^{\tau-t}} \tag{20}$$

6.5.4.1 Agronomic knowledge

However, the assumption of the existence of a water market may not cover most cases in real life, and so we have to consider the case where such a market does not exist. In that case we have to estimate $p_{w,t}$ indirectly. There are many ways of doing so. The most obvious one is to consult an agronomist to find out the marginal value productivity of water in the farms using the water. Basically, how much does agriculture output increase if the average water flow increases by one unit per unit of time? If this information is available, the product of the forecasted prices of agriculture output with the marginal product of the water flow, for each possible size of the stream flow, would provide us with the marginal value productivity of water, and by using this information we can then, for each size of the stream flow, read off the shadow or accounting price of the water flow. The situation is described in Figure 6.3.

Suppose that we have been able to estimate the marginal value productivity of average water flow curve as depicted in the Figure 6.3, and assume that the current water flow is Z'. The appropriate shadow price of water is P'_Z. If we then make a forecast of the water flows in the future, we can for each point in time read the corresponding accounting price for water flow. This means that we can use Equation 20 for calculating the accounting price for forest land! What is needed for all this is a model that connects the size of forestland to the average water flow – now and in the future.[7]

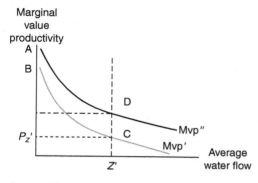

Figure 6.3 Determining the shadow price for water (P'Z).

Now let us focus on the variance of the stream flow. What is the value of a reduction of this variance? Now it is immediately seen that this is a case of weak complementarity.[8] Weak complementarity is by definition a situation when consumption of one commodity is zero and the marginal value of another commodity is also zero. When the average flow of water is zero, we don't care about the variance (which of course is zero). The weak complementarity principle can be illustrated as follows.

MVP' is, as before, the original marginal value productivity curve. Assume that the variance increases, forces the curve to shift to MV". It can now be shown that the value of the change in the variance (or any other quality indicator that satisfies the weak complementarity principle) is equal to the area ABCD. Thus the weak complementarity principle gives us the option to estimate the accounting price of the variance in the stream flow, assuming that our expert agronomist can provide us not only with the marginal productivity curve of the average water flow, but also tell us how this curve will shift due to a change in the variance of the flow.

6.5.4.2 Econometric techniques

Instead of using agronomic knowledge, there may sometimes by the possibility of using econometric estimation techniques. There are two possibilities: using cross-sectional data or time-series data. In both cases, we would like to estimate the production function with water, labour, capital, etc. as inputs and agricultural products as the output. If we can do that, we would end up with an estimated production function

$$Y_\tau = f(K_\tau, L_\tau, Z_\tau, M_\tau, \sigma)) \tag{21}$$

where Y_τ, is farm output, K_τ stock of man-made capital, L_τ, input of labour, Z_τ input of water, M_τ the size of the cultivated area, and σ, as before, the variance of the flow (or any other quality variable). With forecasts for output and input prices (with water as the exception), we can immediately derive the marginal value product for water

$$p_{w,\tau} = \frac{p_{o,\tau}\partial f}{\partial Z_\tau}$$

where $p_{w,\tau}$ is the accounting price of the average water flow and $p_{o,\tau}$ is the price of the output from agriculture, and

$$p_{\sigma,\tau} = \frac{p_{o,\tau}\partial f}{\partial \sigma_\tau}$$

where $p_{\sigma,\tau}$ is the accounting price in period τ for the variance of the water flow. The analysis continues as in the previous subsection.

6.5.5 Resilience

Whenever there are positive feedbacks in the ecosystem, one may expect multiple equilibriums and the possibility of fast flips from one set of equilibriums to another when the system is perturbed. The maximum perturbation that the system can be exposed to without flipping to a different basin of stability is known as the resilience of the system.[9] Resilience is thus a measure of what resistance the system can create to a change to a different equilibrium with different functions (that is, different provision of services).

Sometimes, the value of resilience is negative – the present state is rather bad compared with a different state. But we will assume from now on that resilience is something we value positively. In this case resilience can be regarded as capital stock that will protect us from undesirable changes in the system. But then, this stock might have a positive accounting price indicating its value as insurance capital. The theory for this is developed in Mäler *et al.* (2008) and applied in Walker *et al.* (2009). The case Walker *et al.* studied was the Goulburn Broken watershed in south-eastern Australia. The Goulburn Broken flows through a forest downhill into an area heavily cultivated by vegetables. Because of the high use of fertilizers in this area, the groundwater has been highly salinized. Added to this, deforestation upstream has increased the water flow in the stream, which in turn brings the water table closer to the surface. If the water table comes within 2 m of the surface, capillary forces will suck up the water to the surface, and as a result the soil will no longer be usable for the cultivation of vegetables. Thus, if the current water table is at 8 m depth, there is still 6 m it can rise without killing off the cultivation, but if it rises further, the whole industry will be destroyed. Thus, we have two possible equilibriums, one in which the water table is more than 2 m from the surface, in which cultivation can go on, and one in which the water table rises so the soil becomes salinized and the industry will go out of business for at least 30–50 years (probably forever as it takes a very long time for rain to wash out the salinity from the soil).

If we were able to predict the water table perfectly, we could always manage the level of the water table in order to avoid a catastrophe. However, the stream flow is a stochastic variable and we are therefore not in a position to predict the water table perfectly. We will only know the historic mean and variance of the water flow (some exceptions to this will be briefly discussed below). This means that we are able to predict the probability that the water table will reach the critical 2 m level – at which all resilience has been exhausted – within one year, five years, 20 years, etc. This, together with the predicted future net gains from the cultivation in the valley (and, of course, the zero value of cultivation if resilience is exhausted), means we are able to answer the question: What is the increase in the expected net gains from an increase in resilience today of 1 m? The answer to this question is the accounting price of the resilience of the groundwater! The actual calculations were based on historical estimates of the stochastic process that generated the recorded variations in the water table. However, it seems that we should have taken one further critical step in including the most recent forecasts of climate change. During the last few years, Australia has suffered from repeated droughts, which have been predicted as consequences of climate change. We should therefore have based our analysis partly on the historic variations and partly on the forecasted change in precipitation in the area.

However, the main point of the analysis was to show that it is possible to estimate an accounting price on resilience. The techniques used can easily be applied to almost all situations in which it is desirable to estimate an accounting price for resilience.

6.6 Conclusions

We have seen above how to estimate accounting prices for ecological assets. As long as we can rely on market prices, these estimations are rather straightforward but, unfortunately, ecosystems are rarely transacted on markets and we, the researchers, have to estimate these prices ourselves. In order to do so, we must know the dynamics of the systems and we must be able to make satisfactory predictions of the future development of the social–economic–ecological system. As long as this is roughly true, we are able to estimate the accounting prices approximately. With these prices, we can then quantify the contributions from ecosystem services to sustainable development and also use them for social cost–benefit analysis. We can also extend the analysis to "non-convex" ecosystems, i.e. systems that have multiple equilibriums and therefore may flip from one equilibrium to another (see Dasgupta and Mäler, 2004). In particular, we showed the way of estimating an accounting price of resilience in an ecosystem.

In summary, we should remember the following important points:

- It matters for which purpose we are doing the valuation.

- The value of regulating (and supporting) services is derived from the value of one or more provisional services (which includes cultural services).
- Ecosystems are capital assets and we are therefore forced to do an intertemporal analysis.
- In order to do a correct intertemporal analysis, we need predictions of the future values of all important variables.
- Predictions depend on the current stocks of assets, on the expected future "technology" and on the present and expected future institutions that determine resource use.
- Capital assets evolve over time according to their dynamics, and it is necessary to take those dynamics into account.
- Given the conditions above, we need accounting prices of assets that reflect the impact on social well-being from a small perturbation of an asset.
- These accounting prices are the correct prices for doing a cost–benefit analysis of a "small" project.
- The value of the change in assets, evaluated with these accounting prices, is the correct measure of sustainability.
- In order to apply these methods, it is necessary that the researcher has a very good understanding of the idea of an accounting price and that she is not following prescriptions slavishly.

6.7 Appendix: GAMS code for the plaice model

Set as text – see original PDF if unclear

GAMS code for the plaice model, written by Sandra Paulsen, Swedish Environment Protection Agency
Optimal Fish Harvesting subject to the van Bertalanffy function
$onupper
SETS k Time in which the Kth cohort enters the fishery /1970*2054/
t(k) Time period of the model /2000*2054/,
tf(t) First period of the model,
tl(t) Last period of the model,
a(k,t) Tuple indicating which cohorts are alive at time t;
*Set up logic for the first and last period:
tf(t) = yes$(ord(t) = 1):
tl(t) = yes$(ord(t) = card(t));
SCALARS p Price of plaice /13/
r Discount rate /0.01/
Rk Recruitment at times k (millions) /62/
m Natural fish mortality /0.1/;
PARAMETER yr(k) Year corresponding to cohort k,
w(k,t)Weight of a cohort k fish in year t,
pv(t) Present value price;

```
yr(k) = ord(k)-1;
pv(t) = 1/1+r)**ord(t);
w(k,t)$(yr(t) ge yr(k)) = 2.867 * (1 – EXP(-0.095*(yr(t)-yr(k)+1)))**3;
VARIABLES
OBJ Objective function;
POSITIVE VARIABLES
N(k,t) Number of fish belonging to the kth cohort at time t,
B(k,t) Fish biomass of the kth cohort,
C(t) Cost of fishing,
Q(k,t) Harvest in numbers,
H(k,t) Harvest biomass of fish from cohort k;
EQUATIONS
EQNB Defines the objective function
EQN(k,t) Equation for number of fish belonging to the kth cohort at time t,
EQB(k,t) Equation for the fish biomass of the kth cohort,
EQH(k,t) Harvest biomass for a given cohort,
EQC(t) Equation for the cost function,
QLAST(k,t) Limit on harvest in final period;
EQNB .. OBJ =E= SUM(t, pv(t) * (p * sum(a(k,t),H(k,t)) – C(t)));
EQN(k,t+1)$a(k,t).. N(k,t+1) =E= N(k,t) – Q(k,t) – m * N(k,t);
QLAST(k,tl)$a(k,tl).. N(k,tl) =g= Q(k,tl);
EQB(k,t)$a(k,t) .. B(k,t) =E= N(k,t) * w(k,t);
EQH(k,t)$a(k,t) .. H(k,t) =E= Q(k,t) * w(k,t);
* Cost function
EQC(t).. C(t) =E= SUM(a(k,t), exp(2.494)* H(k,t))**(0.9898) *
SUM(a(k,t), B(k,t))**(-0.146);
*Introduce fish into the active population only when their biomass is non-
negligible:
a(k,t) = yes$(yr(k) le yr(t));
N.L(k.t)$a(k,t) = RK;
* Assuming that fish cannot live more than 30 years:
B.L.(k,t) = 0$(yr(t) –yr(k) ge 30);
* Assume that no harvesting has occurred prior to the first year:
N.FX(k,tf)$a(k,tf) = RK;
N.FX(t,t) = RK;
B.L.(k,t)$a(k,t) = N.L(k.t) * w(k,t);
H.L.(k,t)$a(k,t) = RK/10;
* Avoid divide by zero errors:
H.LO(k,t) = 0.0001;
B.LO(k,t) = 0.0001;
MODEL PLAICE/ALL/;
SOLVE PLAICE USING minos MAXIMIZING OBJ;
DISPLAY OBJ.L;
$if not exist "%gams.sysdir%wgnup132.exe" $exit
* Produce some graphical output using GNUPLOT:
```

PARAMETER wvalue(t,k) Weight of Selected Cohorts Through the Model Horizon; set kplot(k) Cohorts to be plotted /1970,1980,1990,2000,2010,2020,2030,2040,2050/;
wvalue(t,kplot) = w(kplot,t);
set tlbl(t) Time periods to label in plots /2000,2010,2020,2030,2040,2050/;
$setglobal gp_opt0 'set key outside width 3'
$Setglobal domain t
$setglobal labels tlbl
$libinclude plot wvalue
PARAMETER QH(t,k) Fish Harvest Quantity,
NF(t,k) Numbers of Fish
BF(t,k) Biomass of Fish
HF(t,k) Harvest biomass,
SUMMARY(t,*) Summary statistics;
SUMMARY(t,"Q") = sum(k, Q.l(k,t));
SUMMARY(t,"N") = sum(k, N.I(k,t));
SUMMARY(t,"B") = sum(k,B.I(k,t)):
SUMMARY(t,"H") = sum(k,H.I(k,t));
$libinclude plot summary
Set ksol(k) Cohort solutions to plot
/1970,1975,1980,1985,1990,1995,2000,2005,2010,2015,2020,2025,2030,2040,2050/;
QH(t,ksol) = na;
QH(t,ksol)$a(ksol,t) = Q.L(ksol),t);
$libinclude plot qh
NF(t,ksol) = na;
NF(t,ksol)$a(ksol,t) = N.L.(ksol,t);
$libinclude plot nf
BF(t,ksol) = na;
BF(t,ksol)$a(ksol,t) = B.L.(ksol,t);
$libinclude plot BF
HF(t,ksol) = na;
HF(t,ksol) $a(ksol,t) = H.L.(ksol,t);
$libinclude plot HF

Notes

1 For a good introduction to decision theory, see Raiffa and Schleifer (1961).
2 It can also be interpreted as the relative risk aversion.
3 See Mäler *et al.* (1996) for the case when access is defined in terms of a dynamic process.
4 For a complete analysis, including the case of fixed costs, see Mäler *et al.* (1996).
5 See Mäler *et al.* (1996) for a detailed analysis of this approach.
6 See Mäler *et al.* (1996) for details.
7 One should remember that the forecasts of productivity and average stream flow will depend on many factors, economic as well as environmental. For example, climate

change will certainly change the water flows in the future and economic development will change the demand for the agriculture output and therefore the farm prices!

8 This was first explored in Mäler (1971) and developed further in Mäler (1974) and in Mäler (1985).

9 This is rather imprecise. We always have to ask the question: Resilience of what to which disturbance? For simplicity, we will assume that the answers to this question are known – that is we know what "what" is and also that the perturbation is one dimensional so we also know what "which" is.

References

Aniyar, S. and K.-G. Mäler (forthcoming) *Accounting for Ecosystems.* Preliminary manuscript.

Arrow, Kenneth, Partha Dasgupta and Karl-Göran Mäler (2003) "Evaluating projects and assessing sustainable development in imperfect economies", *Environmental and Resource Economics* 26 (4), 647–685.

Clark, C. (2005) *Mathematical Bioeconomics.* Hoboken NJ: Wiley.

Dasgupta, P. and K.-G. Mäler (2000) "Net national product as a measure of social well-being", *Environment and Development Economics* 5 (12), 69–94.

Dasgupta, P. and K.-G. Mäler (eds) (2004) *The Economics of Non-Convex Ecosystems.* Dordrecht: Kluwer Academic Publishers.

Gordon, Allen-Wardell, Peter Bernhardt, Ron Bitner, Alberto Burquez, Stephen Buchmann, James Cane, Paul Allen Cox, Virginia Dalton, Peter Feinsinger, Mrill Ingram, C. Eugene Jones, Kathryn Kennedy, Peter Kevan, Harold Koopowitz, Rodrigo Medellin, Sergio Medellin-Morales, Gary Paul Nabhan, Bruce Pavlik, Vincent Tepedino, Phillip Torshio and Steve Walker (1998) "The potential consequences of pollinator declines on the conservation of biodiversity and stability of food crop yields", *Conservation Biology* 12, 8–17.

Hein, L., K. van Koppen, R.S. de Groot, E.C. van Ierland (2006). "Spatial scales, stakeholders and the valuation of ecosystem services", *Ecological Economics* 57 (2), 209–228.

Kremen, C. (2007) "Pollination and other ecosystem services produced by mobile-organisms: A conceptual framework for the effects of land-use change", *Ecological Letters* 10, 299–314.

McIntyre, N.E., K. Knowles-Yanez and D. Hope (2000) "Urban ecology as an interdisciplinary field: Differences in the use of 'urban' between the social and natural sciences", *Urban Ecosystems* 4, 5–24.

Mäler, K.-G. (1971) "A method of estimating social benefits from pollution control", *Swedish Journal of Economics* 73, 121–133.

Mäler, K.-G. (1974) *Environmental Economics: A Theoretical Inquiry.* Baltimore: John Hopkins University Press.

Mäler, K.-G. (1985) "Welfare economics and the environment", in A.V. Kneese and J.L. Sweeney (eds), *Handbook of Natural Resource and Energy Economics*, Vol. 1. Amsterdam: North Holland.

Mäler, K.-G., S. Aniyar, C. Casler, E. Weir, J. Fuenmayor, J. Rojas and J. Reyes (1996) "An economic modelling of Los Olivitos mangrove ecosystem", Beijer Reprint Series no. 79. Reprinted from *Boletin del Centro de Investigaciones Biologicas* 2, 99–220.

Mäler, K.G., Chuan-Zhong Li and Georgia Destouni (2008) "Pricing resilience in a dynamic economy–environment system: A capital theoretical approach". Submitted, but available from the Beijer Discussion Paper series 208.

Millenium Ecosystem Assessment (2005) *Ecosystems and Human Well-Being: Synthesis*. Washington, DC: Island Press.

Raiffa, H. and R. Schleifer (1961) *Applied Statistical Decision Theory*. Boston: Harvard University.

Ricketts, T.H. (2004) "Tropical forest fragments enhance pollinator activity in nearby coffee crops", *Conservation Biology* 18 (5), 1262–1271.

Ricketts, Taylor H., Gretchen C. Daily, Paul R. Ehrlich and Charles D. Michener (2004) "Economic value of tropical forest to coffee production", *Proceedings of the National Academy of Sciences of the United States of America* 101 (34), 12579–12582.

Sala, O.E. *et al.* (2000) "Global biodiversity scenarios for the year 2100", *Science* 287, 1770–1774.

Steffan-Dewenter, I., Ute Münzenberg, Christof Bürger, Carsten Thies and Teja Tscharntke (2002) "Scale-dependent effects of landscape context on three pollinator guilds", *Ecology* 83 (5), 1421–1432.

Stockholm Office of Regional Planning and Urban Transportation (2001) *Development Plan for Stockholm County*. Available at: www.stockholmsregionen2030.nu/english/index/html.

Walker, Brian, Leonie Pearson, Michael Harris, Karl-Göran Mäler, Chuan-Zhong Li, Reinette Biggs and Tim Baynes (2009) "Incorporating resilience in the assessment of inclusive wealth: An example from south east Australia", *Environmental and Resource Economics*. Also available in Beijer Institute's Discussion Paper series 209.

Walther-Hellwig, K. and Robert Frankl. (2000) "Foraging habitats and foraging distances of bumblebees, bombus sppp. (hym. apidae) in agricultural landscape", *Journal of Applied Entomomlogy* 124 (7–8), 299–306.

Westphal, Catrin, Ingolf Steffan-Dewenter and Teja Tscharntke (2003) "Mass flowering crops enhance pollinator densities at a landscape scale", *Ecological Letters* 6 (11), 961–965.

Xepapadeas, Anastasios (2001) "Economic growth and the environment", in K.-G. Mäler and J. Vincen (eds) (2001), *Handbook of Environmental Economics*. Rotterdam: North Holland, pp. 1219–1271.

7 Valuation of ecosystem services in coastal ecosystems

Asian and European perspectives

Premachandra Wattage

7.1 Introduction

As of 2007, oceans cover approximately 71 per cent of the surface of the earth and support 44 per cent of the human population living within 93 miles. Therefore, the coastal ecosystem is essential to life on our planet as well as to the support of the livelihood of people living near and dependent on the coastal resources. The abundance of coastal resources of good quality is fundamental to all marine biological processes, for maintenance of biodiversity and ecosystems and for primary and secondary production functions that support human needs. Competition for limited resources has intensified with human population growth in coastal regions, and the diversion of wetlands for economic activities has been experienced globally. It is equally important to underline that such threatened ecosystems can no longer provide their biological functions and regulatory services that sustain coastal economic production and livelihoods. Scientists recognise four categories of ecosystem services in coastal regions: *provisioning services* such as food, mangrove, fibre and water; *regulating services* such as the regulation of climate, coastal erosion, coral bleaching, pollution and disease; *cultural services* including recreational, spiritual and other non-material benefits; and *supporting services* such as nutrient cycling and photosynthesis. There is a global consensus on the need to implement stakeholder management approaches for food security, poverty reduction and the preservation of ecosystems using coastal resources. The reality in most countries is a competition between different groups and sectors for access to coastal resources, other natural resources and water. This is crucial in coastal zones, mainly due to the migration of people from other regions to coastal cities. There is an urgent need, therefore, to reconcile demands for maintaining coastal ecosystem functions and for producing food and services to the people. Finding the right balance is particularly important in developing countries, where the coastal environment is often the principal growth centre of the region. The right balance is difficult to maintain in coastal cities and, as a result, the alleviation of poverty and reduction of hunger rarely arises.

Marine ecosystem services include the provision of seafood, filtration of nutrients coming from the land, recycling of nutrients, control of pests and pathogens, climate regulation, protection of coasts from erosion, and provision of places for recreation, inspiration or cultural heritage, to name a few. Ecosystem services are nearly always undervalued. Among the categories of ecosystem services, provisioning and cultural services are easy to understand and relatively easy to value. Regulating and supporting services are difficult to understand, hence becoming undervalued. Some coastal ecosystem goods, such as water, fish and shellfish have significant economic value as they are exchanged in markets for determined prices. However, most other essential services, especially regulating services, are neither appreciated nor commonly assigned economic worth. Services such as the protection of shorelines from erosion, nutrient recycling, climate regulation, cultural heritage, control of disease and pests, and spiritual benefits are at risk because they are undervalued. These goods are not exchanged in a market place, and present economic systems attach no monetary values to these services. At present, ecosystem management typically ignores the value of these goods in a decision on whether to conserve these resources or convert the area for development. Subsequently, many ecosystems are at risk (Wattage and Mardle, 2005).

7.2 Rationale for valuing the regulating services of coastal ecosystems and issues

Ecosystems provide a wide variety of useful services that improve human welfare. These services are the result of the existence and complex interactions of biotic and abiotic resources. The ecosystem is a complex mixture of plant, animal and other microscopic life and its interactions with the non-living environment. The complexity of the ecosystem deteriorates as a result of the interaction of human activities. Natural ecosystems – such as the forest, freshwater, marine and coastal ecosystems – interact with cultivated ecosystems. The functions of ecosystems which are bio-geophysical in nature result in the flow of various services and benefits for humans and their society. These benefits include provisioning services such as food and water, regulating services such as flood and disease control, cultural services such as spiritual, recreational and cultural benefits and supporting services such as nutrient cycling that maintain the conditions for life on earth. The Millennium Ecosystem Assessment of the UN predicted that 60 per cent of the ecosystem services linked to biodiversity are being exploited in an unsustainable manner or are being degraded. The damage to regulating services is catastrophic and much of the ensuing loss in biodiversity is the consequence of human-induced pressures. The coastal regions of the ecosystems that connect terrestrial and coastal ecosystems are of particular relevance to human activities.

Coastal ecosystems are areas where land and water join to create an environment with a distinct structure, diversity and flow of energy, providing a wide array of goods and services to humankind. They include mangrove swamps, salt marshes, wetlands, estuaries and bays that are home to many different types of plants and animals. They are very sensitive to changes in the environment and there is concern that some areas are now struggling to maintain their diversity due to human activity. In addition, natural phenomenon have been responsible for a significant amount of damage to coastal ecosystems, displacing marine and other wildlife, draining food supplies and disrupting the balance of coastal ecosystems.

The rationale for valuing regulating systems in coastal regions is justified because marine, terrestrial and coastal ecosystems all provide ecosystems that are essential to human survival. This ecosystem generates what is called ecosystem functions, also known as ecological production functions. The ecological production function depends on the initial condition of the ecosystem. The combined human-made and natural force usually causes a shift in the flow of these services. Marginal changes to the ecological production function would indicate the status of the resources. Using economic valuation methods it is possible to assign values to the resources to capture the output of the ecological production function. Policy makers can use these values to design and better manage the ecosystems to improve human well-being.

In addition to valuing coastal ecosystems based on what they provide for human survival, values can also be used in estimating the damage to the resource base. The most significant issue facing coastal areas is runoff from industrial, agricultural and municipal areas, sometimes stemming far from the coastal area affected by the externality. The runoff-related pollution can result in higher nutrient and/or pollutant levels in coastal waters, causing algae blooms that can be dangerous to both humans and marine life. Fish resources will be affected by this change, which has devastating effects for the people dependent on fish stocks. Potential contamination of coastal and ocean waters by runoff waters further damages and diminishes existing fish resources. Existing fishermen attempt to maximise their catch through the utilisation of destructive fishing practices and over-fishing, further threatening both coastal fish populations and their habitats. Aquaculture in coastal areas can reduce pressure on some native stocks. However, the effluent from fish farms can contaminate the surrounding water, introducing a different environmental problem. Also, if farm-bred fish escape they can compete with native fish, potentially becoming an invasive species. In order to regulate and properly manage the coastal areas these resources need to be valued and accounted for. The damage caused by human-induced activities can also be quantified if the total value of the resource is known and obvious to the management and the general public.

The underlying issues in valuing regulating services of coastal ecosystems are very complex. The process of regulating services is difficult to understand, making quantifying benefits complicated. Coastal ecosystems, such as mangrove swamps and marshland, are widely believed to provide a variety of hydrological services, including water quality improvement, as well as reducing erosion and sediment deposits, providing the link between the terrestrial and marine ecosystem. This ecosystem plays a significant role in replenishing various fish populations and provides breeding grounds for fish species for the coastal and lagoon fish industry. Food for marine micro-organisms is provided by the nutrients supplied to the lagoon as detritus from the mangrove ecosystems, which is carried into the coastal waters by the tidal currents. This is the beginning of the marine food chain and also provides services such as refuge and nursery grounds for juvenile fish, shrimps, crabs and molluscs. During the Indian Ocean tsunami, mangroves acted as barriers to reduce the force of the waves in some locations (International Union for Conservation of Nature, 2008). It is difficult to fully elucidate and value the regulatory service of mangroves as prime nesting grounds and migratory sites for bird species.

7.3 Innovative methods of economics usually applied in valuation of coastal resources

The need for plans to address issues such as the protection and sustainable use of coastal ecosystems is a major concern of international organisations, including the Food and Agricultural organisation (FAO), the International Union for Conservation of Nature (IUCN), the UN Commission on Sustainable Development (CSD), the Ramsar Convention of Wetlands and the Convention on Biological Diversity. Sustainable use of coastal resources is governed by the value of coastal resources, and is a key theme of the discussion of international organisations. For example, water use for food production in agriculture and fisheries and water in ecosystems (nature benefits) are important water functions that provide a major contribution to economic growth and poverty eradication, but are not particularly allocated the right price. As such, resources tend to be misused or over-used. In allocating rights to the use of water, judgements must be based on the economic, social, environmental and cultural values, and not the solely face value of water. The need for water for food production is evident and the contribution can be measured in monetary terms. It is less self-evident to enhance food security through more efficient mobilisation and use of water, making its value less clear. Water allocation for agriculture is very apparent and the water value going into agriculture is measurable. However, the contribution of water to ensuring the integrity of ecosystems is less visible and the value of the contribution is more difficult to estimate. The critical importance of proper management of water for food and ecosystems has not been addressed sufficiently, due to the absence of total economic value.

The concept of 'economic value' defined in standard economic theory is the measurement of changes in personal well-being. The theory has been further extended to measure changes in the prices and quantities of marketed goods as well as public and other non-market goods and services. A key concept used in these analyses is the economic surplus, which consists of consumer surplus and producer surplus. Consumer surplus is the difference between the maximum amount that a consumer would pay and the amount that they actually pay, while producer surplus refers to the difference between the revenues received and the cost of production for a commodity. Conceptually, the total economic value (TEV) of a resource consists of its use value (UV) and non-use value (NUV) (or passive-use value). There are several definitions for the TEV of an environmental resource used by several authors. Since Krutilla (1965), the TEV approach has generally been adopted in estimating the value of environmental resources or ecosystems. Environmental economists employ the concept of TEV that focuses on monetising a set of human preferences towards a natural system. UV may be broken down further into direct use values (DUVs), indirect use values (IUVs) and option values (OVs). DUVs of the coastal wetlands include both its consumptive uses such as fish, shellfish and fuel wood, as well as non-consumptive uses of wetland 'services', such as recreation, ecotourism, bird watching, *in-situ* research and education and navigation. It is rather straight-forward to derive values because there is an established market for the provisioning services of the ecosystem. Various functional values of wetland ecosystems are an example of important IUVs. Their values derive from supporting or protecting economic activities such as fisheries via nursery/habitat functions, waste treatment, flood control, storm protection and so on. Values for non-consumptive services such as recreation and ecotourism can be assessed using a revealed-preference type travel cost method (TCM). Part of the OV could also be a potential UV. Therefore, one needs to be careful not to double-count both the value of indirect supporting functions and the value of the resulting direct use. In the economic literature, the OV is a difference between ex ante and ex post valuation due to the uncertainty about a user's future use for a resource and/or its availability as a wetland ecosystem in the future. Although there is a dispute on the categorisation of OV, it is widely included in NUVs in a number of previous studies – for instance, under the collective term of 'preservation values' (Walsh *et al.*, 1985). In particular, the US Federal Court's definition of passive-use values includes 'option value' (Carson *et al.*, 1999). Quasi-OV is potential benefit occurring from delaying exploitation and conversion of the wetland today (Barbier, 1994). Part of IUVs comes under the regulating services such as flood control, carbon storage and water catchment functions of coastal areas. For example, estuaries provide regulating services because they absorb the force of storms in coastal areas and regulate changes in air and water temperature. These functions are difficult to measure and value, mainly because of a lack of an established price. One possible method is estimating the foregone or lost values of goods as a result of damaging the regulating services (flood control). These services are developed over time, and as such they can be estimated using dynamic optimisation approaches using the price of foregone goods.

NUVs are composed largely of bequest values (BVs) and existence values (EVs). BVs are the values that people derive from knowing that others will be able to benefit from the resource in the future. EVs are the perceived values of the environmental asset unrelated either to current or future use, i.e. simply because it exists. Even though there are no conclusive terms associated with NUVs, in general the terms of passive-use value (Arrow *et al.*, 1993; Carson *et al.*, 1999) and preservation value encompass OVs as well as NUVs, including the EV and BV. NUVs in coastal ecosystems are the coastal nature preservation value reflecting the wish to allow descendents to benefit (BV), and preserving coastal biodiversity value attached to the fact that a given good exists (EV). These cultural service values of coastal ecosystems are very difficult to estimate;

recently TEV has been used for this purpose. A variety of innovative economics methods are usually applied in valuation of ecosystem services under the concept of total value. The basic premise underlying all these economic valuation techniques is an individual's willingness to pay (WTP) or willingness to accept (WTA). For an environmental resource under study we estimate the area under the compensated or Hicksian demand curve to quantify the economic values.

The contingent valuation method (CVM) uses a direct stated-preference approach to valuing environmental goods or services, in that it asks people through surveys or experiments what their WTP for the goods or WTA is for the loss of the goods. A demand curve can be traced using the bid values estimated in a CVM study. For these reasons, CVM is widely used to measure EVs, OVs, IUVs and NUVs. Choice experiment (CE) is becoming an increasingly popular stated-preference technique in valuing coastal resources. CE is considered to be both an evolution of, and an alternative to, CVM. According to Adamowicz and Boxall (2001), CEs can be regarded as a variant of CVM because both methods use stated-preference approaches and both are usually based on random utility theory. CEs use attributes and levels under study in an experimental design for the construction of response surfaces from the data, which is a major variant from CVM.

CE is based on the foundation of Lancastrian consumer theory and random utility theory. Further, psychological theories on information processing in judgement and decision making have also played a fundamental role. Lancastrian

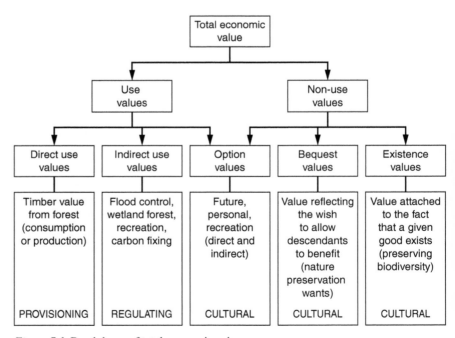

Figure 7.1 Breakdown of total economic value.

consumer theory suggests that utilities for goods can be decomposed into separate utilities for their attributes (Lancaster, 1966), which is a key characteristic of CE. Random utility theory explicitly models the choice among substitute alternatives for a given occasion, considering constraints used in the model. The choice is modelled as a function characterising individuals' decisions when faced with discrete alternatives that are quality differentiated, close substitutes. The random component takes into account, inter alia, the possibility that the analyst may have omitted variables or committed measurement errors, or that the consumer may have been inattentive during the choice process (Adamowicz *et al.*, 1998). Being based on random utility theory, from an economics point of view, CEs have distinct advantages over the alternatives, which has made the elicitation method popular in practice. In the context of unfamiliar environment services, CEs have a further advantage over CVM because CEs are not so constrained. CVM can produce flawed estimates where the resource has never been seen or is difficult to imagine, such that the respondents' preferences in an economic sense for the good cannot be well defined (Carson *et al.*, 2001).

CE does not require any assumptions to be made about the order or cardinality of measurement (Louviere and Woodworth, 1983) and this is one of the major differences compared to CVM. Different sets of alternatives are shown in the questionnaire, and respondents are asked to choose their most preferred option (ibid.), offering a flexibility of choice. The method of CE can also avoid problems such as the un-testable statistical properties of estimated parameters in ranking data and cardinal measurement assumptions in the rating method. It permits the design of choice that imitates real choice environments closely. It is particularly appealing in using the random utility model (RUM), which models the choice of one out of the numerous choices available as a function of the attributes of the good. The RUM implies choices that are logical and that represent many forms of practical welfare questions on a given choice occasion. The choice set is pre-specified in several levels of attributes, which is usually presented to the respondents in a questionnaire format described in an easier form. The alternatives in the set are considered while either holding the attribute levels associated with each alternative constant, or by varying them, within choice sets. The respondent can then select their opinion by making a choice between the different combinations presented. The CE results aim to estimate the relative importance of the individual attributes from the choice set, which can be considered as the trade-offs or marginal rates of substitution that individuals are willing to make between these attributes (Ryan, 1996). The total utility that an individual derives from an alternative is determined by the utility to the individual of each of the attributes.

There are other innovative methods of economics such as TCM, hedonic pricing, dose–effect method and replacement costs which are usually applied in valuation of coastal resources. The objective of this chapter is to reveal problems associated with coastal ecosystem valuation with only CVM and CE using two case studies in Asia and Europe.

7.4 Problems encountered in applying CVM and CE methodology and typical data requirement for coastal ecosystem valuation

The use of two methods in the valuation of ecosystem services of coastal areas will be described using two case studies. One case study was made in a developing country setting in Asia using the CVM approach. CVM has proved to be flexible and is both widely accepted and widely researched (EASAC, 2009). The other case study used the CE approach and was conducted in a developed country setting in Europe.

7.4.1 Case study I[1]

Stakeholder preference for coastal wetland conservation (preservation) in Muthurajawela Marsh and Negombo Lagoon (MMNL) was revealed in Sri Lanka. The TEV of wetland conservation was estimated using CVM. The field study was used to assess individuals' perceptions of conservation of mangroves, clean water and fish stocks, possible uses of the wetlands, respondents' socioeconomic background, and to obtain the individual's WTP measure for having a well-conserved wetland. The study focused on the MMNL area, as well as adjacent villages and towns. These are the areas immediately threatened by development activities and subsequently have the most to gain from conservation (Wattage and Mardle, 2005). Although those who live relatively close to the MMNL would be affected immediately by any developments, the impact of total benefits may be more widespread. However, given time and resource constraints, the study was limited to the MMNL and adjacent areas in which the most significant impact of conservation-related cultural and provisioning ecosystem service benefits might be expected.

Two innovative ideas were used in designing the CVM study in MMNL.[2] In this study a relatively new survey-based method known as one-and-one-half bound (OOHB) was implemented to ask questions on WTP values. Typically, in dichotomous survey formats CVM uses single-bound or double-bound approaches. For example, when using the single-bound elicitation format a WTP question is asked as to whether the respondent would like to pay a given amount, say £5, for a given option, where the answer would be 'yes' or 'no'. In double-bound elicitation format, depending on the response to the first question, a second question will be followed with a different value. A criticism of the double-bound approach is that respondents are not told in advance that there will be a second value. As a result, interviews tend to focus on the first price, with the second price coming as something of a surprise when introduced at a later stage. This surprise may cause discrepancies in the responses to the two prices. The OOHB approach[3] is suggested to avoid the problem. Cooper *et al.* (2002) suggested that eliminating the element of surprise has the potential to remove discrepancies in the responses to the two valuation questions, but that it may prevent being able to ask the second valuation question. That is, the second question will be appropriate half of the time, on average. Due to the advantages of this approach, in this analysis the OOHB has been adopted (Wattage and Mardle, 2008). A series of questions were used in the face-to-face survey to verify a hypothetical conservation programme in the MMNL area and the WTP values. The survey was used to uncover people's perceptions towards conservation of wetlands in the MMNL area and whether they would be willing to pay the local share of the costs. Briefly, the proposed programme considers the setting up of an institution to manage and conserve a good fish stock, clean (unpolluted) water and well-grown mangrove (i.e. 'quality A' type wetland) in MMNL. A question was also asked about individuals' willingness to have a 'quality A' type wetland in the area. For the OOHB dichotomous choice format, the value ranges of bids used were (*25, 75*), (*50, 100*), (*75, 125*), (*100, 150*) and (*125, 175*). Starting bid value was selected randomly from the set of prices. Similarly, the first price from the two values in the bracket was also randomly selected.

A total of 358 out of 379 questionnaires were accepted for analysis. As such, the response rate to the survey was almost 87 per cent. In order to analyse the responses to the OOHB surveys, a normal cumulative distribution function (CDF) was applied to the OOHB data. The chi-squared test for significance of regression is 9.66514, which is significant at $\alpha = 0.05$ level of significance. The income variable was found to be not significant due to the wide variation of income among survey participants. A negative coefficient implies that increases in the parameter have a negative impact on WTP. Data on respondents, such as gender, household size and education level were collected and tested as additional parameters. However, these were found to be not significant, indicating that they are not explanatory variables in the calculation of WTP. Following Cooper *et al.* (2002), a spike model is used to estimate the mean WTP and is calculated by integrating the cumulative density function. The estimated WTP value for the conservation of wetlands in this study amounts to SLRs.287.02 per month for two years, whereas the estimated median WTP value amounts to SLRs.264.26 per month for two years.

Estimating NUV is a controversial issue in valuation studies. The second innovation of this study was the disentanglement of UV and NUV using the method of analytic hierarchy procedure (AHP). The major criticism against the NUV is that it is motivated by a form of altruism termed 'moral satisfaction' or 'warm glow' (Kahneman and Knestch, 1992). Hence, NUV is not an economic value (Carson *et al.*, 2001). By this argument, the ability to measure NUV is contentious. However, in previous attempts to separate NUV from the total value, several approaches have been tested (Wattage and Mardle, 2008). In this approach participants were first asked to reveal the total value for wetland conservation and then used a preference disaggregation approach (AHP) to recognise the NUVs. The nature of the question format involved in the NUV suggests that personal interviews are the best option to elicit preferences. Decomposition of UVs and NUVs is dependent upon some assumptions. It is assumed that subjects valuing environmental resources have value-motives that are related to

UVs, OVs, EVs and BVs. These motives are important in a decomposition approach of a total value. It is also important that subjects know the values associated with each of these motives exclusively in order to separate UVs and NUVs. It is very difficult to evaluate how subjects might differentiate these estimated values for non-use aspects. Available approaches that are suitable for allocation do not have any solid theoretical foundation (Freeman, 1993), and as such the decomposition is very tedious. This leads to the conclusion that there is no accepted method to decompose total value into UVs and NUVs and to further decompose NUVs into motive-related components (Cummings and Harrison, 1995).

AHP could be utilised for this purpose by developing priorities (or weights) for criteria and/or accompanying alternatives. This method was first introduced by Thomas Saaty in the 1970s (Saaty, 1977) and has been used considerably in applications since. The AHP is based on a process of paired comparisons across criteria (or attributes) under analysis. The steps of using the AHP process first include the development of a hierarchy of criteria. A survey is developed for pair-wise comparison of criteria to gain the preferences of individuals towards the criteria selected. Finally, the individual's results are analysed and the aggregate sets of preferences to evaluate the overriding issue are determined. There are several important points that must be ensured during the process. The most important are that the hierarchy developed must be representative of the system and not be biased to the modeller's needs, and that the objectives listed must be clear and convey the same meaning to all individuals (Wattage and Mardle, 2008). On completion of the survey, the analysis can be made using standard software such as Expert Choice.

AHP has been used in the past to study critical situations scientifically in industry, agriculture and the environment (Mardle *et al.*, 2004). However, it has not been used previously to study a situation such as the decomposition of UVs and NUVs. Total value can be disaggregated to NUVs using the weights allocated to the criteria relating to NUVs. It was assumed that preferences of individuals towards these NUVs indicate the relative importance they are perceived to have compared to the resources. The aim of determining 'importance' amongst attributes in the AHP question has clear potential for use as a decomposition method for measuring the impact of the NUVs on the total value. All survey participants who indicated their WTP for wetland conservation were asked to complete the sub-survey of AHP paired comparison to provide preference values for each attribute identified in the analysis (Wattage and Mardle, 2008).

Based on the individual responses, a breakdown of the inconsistency in their responses was attained. Standard AHP practice is to accept responses where inconsistency is less than or equal to 10 per cent. From those who responded in the survey, 101 respondents gave responses to the pair-wise comparison survey with inconsistency less than or equal to 10 per cent, and 99 respondents showed inconsistency between 10 per cent and 20 per cent. Responses with high inconsistency were not included in the analysis as the reliability of their responses could not be ascertained. The aggregated preference towards UV is 0.553 and the NUV is 0.447 in conservation of wetlands in the MMNL area. The implication of this is that a higher stated UV is associated with lower belief of moral responsibility. The total value of wetland conservation in the MMNL area as derived through the OOHB method is SLRs.264.26. So, in this case, TEV can now be split into SLRs.145.34 for UVs and the SLRs.118.92 for NUVs, using the primary results from the AHP (Wattage and Mardle, 2008). The two most important attributes are flood control today (0.254) and future generation use (0.253), where the former is part of the UV and the latter part of the NUV. The range of preference is also given for aggregated UVs and NUVs and shows a particularly insensitive result to changing consistency of responses. The allocation of weights using AHP is a robust method to split total value into UVs and NUVs. Some researchers consider that the OV should be split between UVs and NUVs. If that is the case, then the aggregated preference for the UV is 0.453 and the NUV is 0.547. This implies a stated lower UV, which is associated with higher belief of moral responsibility. So, in this case, TEV would be split into SLRs.119.71 for UVs and SLRs.144.55 for NUVs.

7.4.2 Case study II[4]

This section of the chapter addresses CE, demonstrating the process of marine protected area (MPA) decision making and revealing the findings of its application to the determination of MPAs for deep-water Lophelia reefs off the coast of the Republic of Ireland. The aim of the approach is to estimate an individual's preferences by establishing the relative importance of the different attributes in valuing aspects of coastal ecosystem services. In terms of MPAs, the objective is the determination of the economic benefits of ecosystem protection, which is the difference between the net economic benefits derived from protection and the net economic benefits derived from the resource without protection, with benefits being the net value of costs and including both UVs and NUVs (Dixon and Sherman, 1990; Pendleton, 1995).

The survey, conducted as part of PROTECT, was designed to represent several management scenarios, as presented in Table 7.1. Its main aim was to establish how the Irish public would respond to different attributes of the objectives of managing MPAs. It also incorporated the key features regarded as the most important in the implementation and management of MPAs in Irish deep-sea coral areas. In defining the model structure, care was taken to ensure completeness of the system, such that all major issues related to the deep-sea water corals were incorporated and identifiable at some level. Considerable time was given to clarifying the terms used for the attributes and their underlying implications so that the decision attributes developed were clear and concise. The three main attributes and the associated levels considered in the analysis are shown in Table 7.1. The overriding objective grouping them all was to ensure protection of deep-sea corals while maintaining sustainable fishing practices. While only three attribute groups are employed in this case study, CE models can generally consider more attributes and associated levels.

Table 7.1 Attributes and accompanying management objective levels

Attributes	Level I	Level II	Level III
1 Activity – the fishing activity allowed in the MPA	Status quo (allow all fishing)	Ban trawling (but allow other fishing methods)	Ban all fishing
2 Area – MPA strategy to protect cold-water corals	Status quo (currently identified coral reefs)	All known coral reefs	All coral areas (where coral reefs are thought to exists)
3 Cost – management and monitoring cost	€0 (no additional tax) per person	€1 (additional yearly tax) per person	€10 (additional yearly tax) per person

Source: Final Report, PROTECT Project, CEMARE, University of Portsmouth.

In the context for which the levels were developed, they describe distinct cases that could be prescribed as policy for MPAs. For example, the attribute of the type of fishing activities allowed in MPAs may be followed – accordingly, optimal levels associated with that objective will be maintained. Therefore, the pursuance of this objective will result in a different level of sustainable fishery by controlling fishing activities allowed. In a sustainability sense, and also achieving the maximum benefits of MPAs, banning destructive fishing gear will make a significant contribution. As these values cannot be measured for the multitude of sub-attributes that exist, the state of the fishery relating to the destructive fishing gear as a management objective is considered. The CE study stated the preference of the individual that is measured towards following this objective. Similarly, preferences were stated for the area-related MPA strategy to protect cold-water corals and the associated costs that are involved in management and monitoring of MPAs.

The three attributes and three levels (3^3) in Table 7.1 produce a total of 27 different combinations using a main-effects design. With the ADX Interface for Design of Experiments (SAS 9.1), an orthogonal main-effects design (where all interactions are assumed to be insignificant) was subsequently reduced to nine profiles for use in the study.[5] These nine profiles, with their component attributes and levels, were then incorporated into a postal questionnaire format, using the most popular presentation approach – profile picture cards with a verbal description of the attributes and associated levels. The description of attributes is crucial to ensure that each respondent understands the meaning of each attribute. The questionnaire was designed to include all nine profiles/choices on one card, and respondents were asked to select their most preferred option out of the nine presented to them. The design strategy of presenting all nine choices on the one card was found during piloting to be acceptable without invoking an information overload. It is also easier for respondents to compare the options when they see all the available options on one card rather than separately. The data representation for such single-choice selection consists of one observed choice and eight unobserved subsequent choices. In addition to the behaviour choice questions, a number of socio-economic questions important for the analysis were incorporated into the questionnaire. These were useful in interpretation and validation of the results and were distributed during the latter part of the summer of 2007. A randomly selected sample of 5,000 residents of the Republic of Ireland was selected, ultimately achieving a response rate of just over 500 (1:10), which, with the questionnaire format generating nine choice responses for each respondent, created a robust dataset. It is worth noting that unlike many CE analysis studies, which analyse the responses of a homogeneous survey set, this survey, in targeting the residents of the Republic of Ireland, has dealt with a particularly heterogeneous population.

For the analysis of the model SAS/STAT has been used. The SAS/STAT software does not have a procedure that is specially designed to fit the conditional logit models (CLM). However, with some modification to the data-entry procedure, the PHREG procedure can be used to fit these models. First, the importance of each attribute model was estimated using the PHREG[6] procedure in SAS (SAS Institute Inc., 1999). PHREG was designed to do Cox regression analysis of continuous-time survival data, using the method of partial likelihood to estimate a proportional hazards model. Further, PHREG has the unique option for handling tied data. As such, the range of CLMs estimated are much broader than most Cox regression programs or even programs specifically designed to estimate discrete choices. The result proves that PHREG is one of the best procedures available in statistical tests for handling discrete choice problems.

Several chi-squared likelihood ratio tests were carried out to find out the significance of the model used in the analysis. The first one is the *likelihood ratio chi-square* obtained by comparing the log-likelihood for the fitted model with the log-likelihood for a model with no explanatory variables. The ratio was calculated by taking twice the positive difference in the two log-likelihoods. The *score* is the second test used in the model. This statistic is a function of the first and second derivatives of the log-likelihood function under the null hypothesis. *Wald* chi-squares are the third test reported by the model in this category. These are calculated by dividing each coefficient of the maximum likelihood estimates by its standard errors and squaring the results. The estimated chi-squared values for likelihood ratio, score and Wald statistics indicate that the model is very highly significant (Table 7.2). At a significance level of $\alpha=0.01$, the model rejects the null hypothesis of no relationship between choice and the attributes. In fact, all three model tests indicate a high level of significance with probability <0.0001, indicating that there is a strong relationship between choice and the attributes.

Table 7.2 Model test statistics (global H_0: $\beta=0$).

Test	χ^2	DF	$Pr > \chi^2$
Likelihood ratio	228.4524	6	<0.0001
Score	254.2180	6	<0.0001
Wald	214.6333	6	<0.0001

Source: Final Report, PROTECT Project, CEMARE, University of Portsmouth.

Estimated parameter values of the model and their related statistics are presented in Table 7.3. As shown in the table, some of the parameter values are not significant to at least the $\alpha=0.10$ level. Model descriptive labels for all variables are presented along with the zero coefficients for the reference levels (i.e. status quo of area and activity and the zero cost). Coefficients for the other estimated variables of the model have values relative to the reference level. Under the attribute of 'area', the part-worth utility (i.e. the estimated coefficient) for the variable status quo (currently identified coral reefs) is a structural zero, while the part-worth utility for 'all known corals' is +0.47889 and 'all coral areas' (where coral reefs are thought to exist) is +1.16258. Hence, the protection of all known corals is preferred over the status quo and the protection of all corals is preferred over both the status quo and the protection of known corals. The magnitude of the estimated coefficient indicates which objective is more preferred by the sample respondents. The success of the MPA is dependent on the control of the fishing area and the survey reveals that the Irish public prefers the control of 'all coral areas'. Both parameters tested under this first attribute proved very highly significant as indicated by the *Pr>chi-squared* values. Both values proved significant even at $\alpha=0.01$ levels.

The second management attribute tested in the model was the 'activity', which is the fishing activity allowed in the MPA. These human-induced activities are important in regulating ecosystem services because they alter the natural regulating process. When compared to the status quo (allow all fishing), the trawling ban (with other fishing methods allowed, i.e. netting, lining and potting) and a ban on all fishing were preferred, with the magnitude of the estimated parameter indicating that the trawling ban (+1.27199) was preferred over a ban on all fishing (+0.20468). However, only the trawling ban variable in this attribute proved significant at the $\alpha=0.01$ level, with the part-worth utility for the status quo in MPA management a structural zero. A ban on all fishing was

Table 7.3 Analysis of maximum likelihood estimates for all respondents

Parameter variable	Estimate	Std error	χ^2	$Pr>\chi^2$
Area				
Known corals	0.47889	0.16127	8.8214	0.0030
All corals	1.16258	0.14568	63.6878	0.0001
Status quo	0	–	–	–
Activity				
Ban trawling	1.27199	0.14032	82.1759	0.0001
Ban all fishing	0.20468	0.16372	1.5628	0.2113
Status quo	0	–	–	–
Cost				
One euro	0.11777	0.13737	0.7350	0.3913
Ten euros	−0.05132	0.13727	0.1398	0.7085
Zero euros	0	–	–	–

Source: Final Report, PROTECT Project, CEMARE, University of Portsmouth.

shown to be preferred over the reference objective, allow all fishing (status quo). However, the parameter proved not to be significant, even at the $\alpha = 0.10$ level. While the trawling ban (+1.27199) appears to be the preferred management option, maintaining successful MPAs has been shown to be a general preference of the Irish public. The general consensus of the Irish general public is to ban destructive trawler fishing in MPA-associated fishing grounds. The third management attribute tested in the model was 'cost' (e.g. management and monitoring cost). This willingness to pay (WTP) value was designed as a payment of an additional yearly tax contribution per person towards the maintenance of MPAs.

The status quo was set as €0 (no additional cost) and compared to a €1 additional yearly tax and a €10 additional yearly tax. The results reveal that €1 was favoured over the status quo, with a €10 tax less favourable than both the status quo and a €1 tax. All parameters proved insignificant even at the $\alpha = 0.10$ level, indicating that the attribute of cost was not a significant determinant of preference on this issue.

The parameter estimates in Table 7.3 were used to estimate the probability of each of the nine presented options being chosen. Looking to the consensus of opinion, using the choice probabilities, it is possible to get a crude indication of the importance/preference attached to each of the individual objectives arising out of the consensus. One way of doing this is to take a simple average of probabilities for each attribute, the results of which are shown in Figure 7.2. As shown

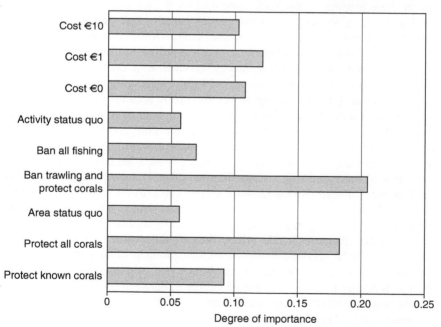

Figure 7.2 Rough estimation of the degree of importance attached to each attribute (derived from the full set of 27 alternatives). (source: Final report, PROTECT Project, CEMARE, University of Portsmouth).

in Figure 7.2, the ranking of attributes and levels suggests that the top two preferences for MPA management are to ban trawling and to protect all coral areas. Payment of €1, €0 and €10 comes as the next preferred options, which can be expressed as the WTP values for the agreed activities. These results are largely as expected, given the results shown in Table 7.3, and confirm the level of importance attached by the Irish public to MPAs in the Irish deep-sea coral areas and the banning of destructive fishing methods such as trawler fishing for the protection of those reefs.

7.5 Problems encountered in this approach in valuation of regulating ecosystem services

As shown in the two case studies, NUVs (passive use) can be derived using appropriate estimation methods. The examples show the values for cultural services that people place on the existence of mangroves and water (case study I) and the deep-sea corals of an MPA (case study II). As shown in case study I, the separation of UVs and NUVs, and to further sub-components of non-use (i.e. option, existence and bequest, as described in Figure 7.1) are also possible using appropriate methods. The provisioning ecosystem service relates to products such as food, materials for construction and energy that can be directly obtained from biodiversity that are controlled by the price system. Any misuse or overuse of these products is naturally controlled by the price mechanism. The cultural services relate to those non-material benefits that people obtain from ecosystems through recreation and aesthetic experiences that can be estimated through revealed-preference techniques such as travel cost and hedonic pricing methods. Biodiversity-related regulating services is a complex concept and attempts to assess the value have proved to be challenging compared to other aspects of value. Price-based approaches are mostly accurate to value provisioning services and this can also be used to assess the costs of environmental degradation of an important habitat by assessing the cost involved in artificially replacing the lost regulating services. A simple example of replacement cost involves estimating the cost of replacing the water filtration services provided by undeveloped watershed with a water filtration plant. Human-built systems could be effective. However, no human-built system can provide all of the ecosystem services of a natural system, and as such the replacement cost is only an approximate value. Supporting ecosystem services relating to those factors can enable all of the three categories to take effect. They are different to provisioning, regulating and cultural services; however, without the help of supporting services, biodiversity will have a substantial detrimental effect on the condition of all of these ecosystem categories and thus on human welfare and livelihood.

One way to protect the regulation of services of the ecosystem processes is to introduce MPAs. This approach cordons off certain areas and restrains the use of available services. One big argument against the MPAs is that they are too small and isolated to sustain the full range of regulating ecosystem services. However, conservation of ecosystems in general is the only solution remaining in order to protect the ecosystems. As noted, the initial approach was a regulatory one, which includes the protected areas and rules that prohibit farming on land slopes and use of pesticides in riparian areas. The use of market instruments to promote conservation has also been introduced more recently (Landell-Mills and Porras, 2002). The success of MPAs or the conservation approach is dependent on the cost and benefits. The cost of conservation includes both the direct cost of implementing conservation measures and the opportunity costs of foregone uses. The benefits of conservation include preserving the services that ecosystem provides, and the only way to quantify such benefits is asking the people who use the service, as discussed in case study II. However, the major problem encountered in this approach to valuation of regulating ecosystem services is allocating total benefits among cultural and regulating services.

7.6 Policy options and recommendations

The concept of coastal ecosystem services is still ambiguous, and valuing ecosystem services is more complex, especially for regulating services. As described above, different methods of economic valuation are applicable to different ecosystem services. With greater difficulty, replacement cost can be used to value some aspects of regulating services. However, it does not encapsulate all of the values consistently provided by an ecosystem. In coastal ecosystems this value can be approximated by applying the avoided cost or replacement cost methods. The avoided cost method calculates the economic value of benefits that are provided by an ecosystem, which may not be robust if the character of the ecosystem was fundamentally different. As such, avoided cost can be calculated by estimating the cost of replacing the existing ecosystem with a restored system (built substitute). Two case studies presented in this chapter demonstrated the use of CVM and CE for valuing aspects of NUVs, i.e. BVs and EVs. Cultural service values are typically NUVs and they can be easily estimated using stated-preference methods. Provisioning services are the easiest service to value among the ecosystem services, mainly because of the established marketplace, and hence prices. Consumer surplus is the widely known approach and the easiest approach to find out the real value. In the absence of marketplace and prices, NUVs are not straightforward to estimate. However, with the available modelling approaches and advances in computer programming over the last few decades, the technology is growing rapidly. By identifying which particular valuation methods would be more appropriate for valuing particular types of services, it might be possible to determine which ecosystem services might be valued relatively rapidly and cheaply. It is the task of the manager to decide what methods are more robust compared to others. It is very important to keep in mind that ease of valuation does not correspond with the importance of a given service. There is an urgent need for research to determine the status of regulating services and how the value can actually be captured and incorporated in decision-making processes in ecosystem management.

As pointed out in the Millennium Ecosystem Assessment, all ecosystems provide multiple services, although the relative importance will vary from system to system. The interaction between different services is complex. A pertinent example is the complementary relationship between some services, such as nutrient cycling (regulating) and primary production (provisioning); enhancing one will enhance the other. Hence, management of an ecosystem for provisioning services, in particular, tends to reduce their ability to provide regulating and cultural services. Unless there is advanced research on biological functions and interactions, the valuation of these services may not be proven successful.

Intensive agricultural development and urban landscape modifications globally have profoundly affected the integrity of ecosystems. The focus of intensive agricultural development is exclusively on the production of food to meet the growing demand from an escalating world population. This is at a huge cost, such as carbon storage for climate regulation through diminishing water quality to cultural services, coined as 'externalities'. The goods produced in provisioning services can easily be valued using market mechanisms; hence the focus of the world towards such goods, as the externality was not entered into the equation. Moreover, other services – such as regulating – lack markets. Therefore, there is little or no attempt to incorporate these methods into economic planning processes. Future actions need to consider this discrepancy and should initiate more policy research on the subject and provide direct support for the maintenance of healthy ecosystems.

Conservation decisions should not only be based on economic criterion. Other criteria such as ethical, cultural and historical factors also play a pivotal role in this connection. Valuation can only provide relevant information highlighting the economic consequences of alternative courses of action. As such, economic valuation of ecosystem services will lead to more informed choices if used correctly in decision-making processes. However, existing economic valuation techniques can provide reliable answers to questions involving relatively small-scale changes in resource use and only become less robust as the scale of the analysis and the magnitude of environmental change increases. Furthermore, economic valuation tends to deal poorly with large-scale ecosystems and long time horizons. Cost–benefit analysis in decision-making becomes more difficult when there is an uncertainty about future benefit flows from ecosystems, and the role of discounting become increasingly detrimental.

Notes

1 This research (Project EMBioC) was funded by the Darwin Initiative of the Department for Environment, Food and Rural Affairs (DEFRA), UK.
2 The focus of this section is based on the paper by Wattage and Mardle (2008).
3 Cooper *et al.* (2002) proposed the OOHB survey design, in which the respondent is given two prices in advance and told that while the exact cost of the item is not known for sure, it is known to lie within the range bounded by these two prices. One of the two prices is then selected at random, and the respondent is asked whether they would be willing to pay this amount.
4 This case study has been produced as an output of the EU 6th Framework-funded, specific-targeted research Project Nu. SSP8-CT-2004-513670 – Marine Protected Areas as a Tool for Ecosystem Conservation and Fisheries Management (PROTECT), www.mpa-eu.net.

5 The nine profiles given using an orthogonal main-effects plan were arrived at by identifying a subset of the full set where each linear combination of attributes of the full set
can be achieved. That is, the subset still enables the analysis of all alternatives to be
made.
6 This procedure fits the Cox proportional hazards model for survival data. The partial
likelihood of Breslow has the same form as the likelihood in a conditional logit model.

References

Adamowicz, W. and Boxall, P. 2001. Future directions of stated choice methods for
environment valuation. Paper presented at the conference: 'Choice experiments: A new
approach to Environment Valuation', London, England.
Adamowicz, W., Boxall, P., Williams, M. and Louviere, J. 1998. Stated preference
approaches for measuring passive use values: Choice experiments and contingent valuation. *American Journal of Agricultural Economics* 80 (1), 64–75.
Arrow, K.J., Solow, R., Portnet, P.R., Leamer, E.E., Rodner, R. and Schuman, H. 1993.
Report on the NOAA Panel on contingent valuation. *Federal Register* 58, 4601–4614.
Barbier, E.B. 1994. Valuing environmental functions: tropical wetlands. *Land Economics*
70, 155–173.
Carson, R.T., Flores, N.E. and Mitchell, R.C. 1999. Theory and measurement of passive-
use value. In: Bateman, I. and Willis, K.G. (eds), *Valuing Environmental Preferences*.
Oxford: Oxford University Press.
Carson, R.T., Flores, N.E. and Meade, N.F. 2001. Contingent valuation: Controversies
and evidence. *Environmental and Resource Economics* 19, 173–210.
Cooper, J.C., Hanemann, M. and Signorello, G. 2002. One and one half bound dichoto-
mous choice contingent valuation. Paper submitted to the *Journal of Review of Eco-
nomics and Statistics* (second review).
Cummings, R.G. and Harrison, G.W. 1995. The measurement and decomposition of
nonuse values: A critical review. *Environmental and Resource Economics* 5, 225–247.
Dixon, J. and Sherman, P. 1990. *Economics of Protected Areas*. Washington, DC: Island
Press.
EASAC. 2009. *Ecosystem Services and Biodiversity in Europe*. European Academies
Science Advisory Council policy report 09, The Royal Society, UK.
Freeman, A.M. 1993. *The Measurement of Environmental and Resource Values: Theory
and Methods*. Washington, DC: Resources for the Future.
IUCN. 2008. *IUCN Policy Brief*.
Kahneman, D. and Knetsch, J.L. 1992. Valuing public goods: The purchase of moral sat-
isfaction. *Journal of Environmental Economics and Management* 22, 57–70.
Krutilla, J.V. 1965. Conservation reconsidered. *The American Economic Review* 57,
776–786.
Lancaster, K.J. 1966. New approach to consumer theory. *Journal of Political Economy*
74 (2), 132–157.
Landell-Mills, N. and Porras, I. 2002. *Silver Bullet or Fools' Gold? A Global Review of
Markets for Forest Environmental Services and their Impact on the Poor*. London:
IIED.
Louviere, J.J. and Woodworth, G. 1983. Design and analysis of simulated consumer
choice or allocation experiments: An approach based on aggregate data. *Journal of
Marketing Research* 20, 350–367.
Mardle, S., Pascoe, S. and Herrero, I. 2004. Management objective importance in fisheries:

An evaluation using the analytic hierarchy process (AHP). *Environmental Management* 33 (1), 1–11.

Pendleton, L.H. 1995. Valuing coral reef protection. *Ocean and Coastal Management* 26 (2): 119–131.

Ryan, M. 1996. *Using Consumer Preferences in Health Care Decision Making: The Application of Conjoint Analysis*. London: Office of Health Economics.

Saaty, T.L. 1977. A scaling method for priorities in hierarchical structures. *Journal of Mathematical Psychology* 15 (3), 234–281.

SAS Institute Inc. 1999. *SAS/STAT® User's Guide*, Version 8. Cary, NC.

Walsh, R.G., Sanders, L.D. and Loomis, J.B. 1985. Wild and scenic river economic: Recreation use and preservation values. Report to the American Wilderness Alliance, Department of Agriculture and Natural Resource Economics, Colorado State University.

Wattage, P. and Mardle, S. 2005. Identifying stakeholder preferences towards conservation versus development for a wetland in Sri Lanka. *Journal of Environmental Management* 77, 122–132.

Wattage, P. and Mardle, S. 2008. Total economic value of wetland conservation in Sri Lanka: Identifying use and non-use values. *Journal of Wetland Ecology and Management* 256 (8), 1517–1572.

8 Valuing the storm protection services of mangroves

Methodological and data challenges

Saudamini Das

8.1 Introduction

According to the Mangroves Action Project, "healthy mangroves are the key to a healthy marine ecology" (www.mangroveactionproject.org). These tropical and sub-tropical swamp forests that grow in saline coastal conditions not only contribute to marine ecology, but by being rich in biodiversity they also provide different ecological or ecosystem services to mankind; their presence adds to the welfare of society. Following the Millennium Ecosystem Assessment approach to categorization of ecosystem services, the different direct and indirect services of mangroves are seen as provisioning, supporting, regulating and cultural services. Of these, the regulating services include flood control, storm protection/wind break, shoreline stabilization, erosion control, and micro-climatic stabilization. The storm protection/wind break is an important regulating (protective) service of the mangroves and it refers to the protection that mangroves provide to the lives and properties lying to the leeward side of the forest during natural calamities such as cyclones.

Mangroves are a threatened ecosystem. While ecosystem service valuation is essential for making any sustainable land-use policy, mangroves are a special case as they form a complex ecosystem representing an intermediate phase between terrestrial and aquatic environment. They combine land and water where the environmental effects are transmitted through water. This special feature makes economic analysis of these systems more complicated than that of a purely terrestrial (aquaculture, field crops) or aquatic (fishery) system (Dixon *et al.*, 1994). However, increasing threats to these systems from different drivers, especially from aquaculture, gave rise to multiple efforts by economists to put an economic value on these systems so the different issues could be suitably resolved. Depending on the threats to the ecosystem, research work on mangroves has focused on different issues. Earlier, when mangrove areas were being converted to different developmental or high-yielding uses like aquaculture, studies tried to evaluate the different direct and indirect use values, or at least the visible services of mangroves to mankind. Consequently, they were no longer considered useless ecosystems and the question of conversion versus conservation could be suitably resolved. In recent years, though mangroves are already degraded and exist in limited pockets in most parts of the world, the focus of the debate is the regeneration of the forest to act as a buffer against natural calamities. The vulnerability of coastal communities to natural calamities such as cyclones and tsunamis, and the fear of increasing frequency and intensity of these events due to climate change, have shifted the emphasis to the protective services of mangroves. Calamities like the super cyclone of October 1999, the Indian Ocean tsunami of 2004 and most recently the havoc unleashed by the cyclone, Nargis, in Burma have given impetus to evaluation of the role of mangroves as a protective structure during such events.

Protective services offered by coastal forests and trees, particularly mangrove forests, against natural hazards have been the subject of intense debate in recent years. Some studies and anecdotal reports have highlighted the effectiveness of mangrove forests in reducing damage from natural hazards such cyclones and tsunamis as they are supposed to dissipate wave and wind energies (Forsberg, 1971; Tynkkonen, 2000; *International Federation of Red Cross and Red Crescent News*, 2002; Badola and Hussain, 2005; UNEP, 2005; Kathiresan and Rajendran, 2005). Strong arguments have been raised against some of these observations (particularly on tsunami and coastal protection) on both statistical and methodological grounds. Though theoretically it is expected that mangroves would reduce cyclone impact as they dissipate normal wind-wave energy (Massel *et al.*, 1999; Mazda *et al.*, 1997, 2006), so far empirical analysis to evaluate the protective services of mangrove forests have been quite limited. International organizations working on coastal planning and rehabilitation have emphasized the need for rigorous assessment of the protective services of coastal vegetation so that successful strategies to counter coastal disasters can be initiated. "A rigorous assessment of the protective roles of coastal forests and trees would provide valuable information for effective coastal forest rehabilitation and management" (FAO, 2006: 1). The Ramsar World Wetlands Day Forum on "Natural Mitigation of Natural Disaster" (Gland, Switzerland, February, 2005) and FAO-supported "Regional Coordination Workshop on Rehabilitation of Tsunami-affected Forest Ecosystem: Strategies and New Directions" (Bangkok, March 2005) have also emphasized the need for "scientific studies on the protective role of coastal forests". A scientific evaluation of the protective services of the coastal forests, or specifically of the mangroves, requires both a sound methodology and the availability of reliable data. The present chapter evaluates the storm protection services of the mangroves by following interdisciplinary approaches where both scientific and socio-economic parameters have been used to define the methodology, and tries to address the above concerns of policy makers by making use of village-level data.

Tropical cyclones bring widespread damage, which includes human casualties, depending on their intensities. Besides cyclone intensity, other factors that play decisive roles in damage occurrences are the socio-economic conditions and the geophysical features such as elevation, topography, bathymetry, hydrology and the nature of the terrain (whether hilly area, forestland, plain agricultural land, etc.) of the affected regions. Hence coastal forests are just one among the many other factors that have a decisive impact on the occurrences of cyclone-related damages. Any empirical work evaluating the protective roles of coastal forests has to consider the role of each factor simultaneously in order to arrive at a conclusive result. This chapter presents a methodology that defines a cyclone-damage function which takes into account the above-mentioned parameters and also presents some results by making use of the data on residential house damage suffered during the super cyclone of October 1999 in the state of Orissa in India, to help estimate the storm protection services of the mangroves of the state.

The roadmap of the chapter is as follows. Section 8.2 gives a review of relevant and related literature; Section 8.3 introduces the study area; Section 8.4 describes the methodology; Section 8.5 gives the data used; Section 8.6 gives the estimated results and the discussion; and, finally, Section 8.7 presents the conclusion of the study.

8.2 Review of literature

Conventional literature has emphasized the role of mangrove forests as a seawall during tropical cyclones (Chan *et al.*, 1993). In recent years, quite a few studies have evaluated this protective service of mangroves using either avoided damages (value equals the value of damages avoided due to mangrove presence); avoided expenditures (value equals the difference in expenditure on maintenance and repair of infrastructure in a mangrove-protected area compared to an unprotected area); expected damage function (EDF) (change in compensating surplus needed to retain the utility level due to change in mangrove area that, in turn, changes the probability of expected coastal hazards); or replacement costs (value equals the cost of installing some infrastructure that can provide the same protective service as mangroves). Both avoided expenditure (Tri *et al.*, 1996) and replacement cost (Sathirathai, 1998) have been used to value a single specific instance of protection of mangroves, whereas the avoided damages approach is being widely used to quantify the protection of mangroves from different types of both cyclonic and tsunami damages.

Tri *et al.* (1996) measured the protection offered by mangroves to coastal infrastructure in the Red River Delta area of Vietnam. They equated this value to the lesser expenditure incurred on maintenance and repair of sea dikes due to both normal and cyclonic wave action in mangrove-protected areas compared to the unprotected areas. The strength of this work was its methodology, which was based on scientifically measured parameters of the mangrove forests in evaluating the protection, although it was limited to the protection of sea dikes only.

Sathirathai (1998) equated the coastline protection and stabilization value of mangroves to the cost of installing breakers on the coastline to protect the coast from being eroded due to wave action in the absence of mangroves. This measure assumes substitutability between mangroves and breakers and could be an overestimate of the actual protection value. As suggested by Barbier (2007), the replacement cost measure should be equal to the cost of the least cost alternative needed to provide that service, and breakers may not be the least cost alternatives.

Barbier (2007) has advocated the use of EDF to measure the storm protection value of coastal wetlands. This methodology is based on the concept of compensating surplus that a representative household requires to maintain its utility level due to the expected increase in the incidence of damaging storm events. The coastal wetlands are assumed to have a direct effect on reducing the production of damaging natural disasters in terms of their ability to inflict damages locally. Barbier assumed that the presence of wetlands in some areas will reduce the occurrences of damaging storm events (as they provide protection) and thus would also reduce the amount of compensating variation needed to be paid to the household to maintain their utility level. Hence, the change in consumer surplus due to change in wetland area will measure the storm protection value of the wetland. However, storm occurrences and their intensities are dependent on climatic conditions, and the damage occurrences due to the storm at a place depend on both the storm features and the physical features of the province. The wetland area of a province may reduce the occurrences of actual damages compared to the potential damages expected from a cyclone, but the presence of wetlands only will have little influence on the ranking of the storm in terms of the damages they caused or the number of damaging storms hitting the province. One has to take into account the storm characteristics as well as the other features of the location. As explained below, storm damages are dependant on multiple factors, and wetland areas are only one among many others. Moreover, such analyses are needed at a micro level, rather than at the level of a province, as the effects of the wetlands are more localized and location-specific.

The use of the avoided damages approach for storm protection started with Farber's (1987) pioneering work in which he used a scientific model of wind velocity and valued the protection value of wetlands from only the perspective of the wind damage from hurricanes. Farber talked about the homogeneity of the population, and this may justify the exclusion of socio-economic factors from damage analysis. But the limitation of his work was that he assumed that wetlands reduce the wind damage, whereas wetlands – unless they have high vegetation – can provide little protection from wind. Of course, wetlands do provide distance as a buffer between the coast and human settlements, which may result in the wind speed being lower by the time the hurricane strikes the settlements. However, if the wetlands are entirely water bodies, then the weakening of the storm becomes less prominent due to moisture supply than it would have been with a more rough surface. Wetlands provide more protection from storm surges and Farber did not account for storm surges in his model.

Costanza et al. (1989, 1997, 2008) talked about the storm protection value of wetlands, but the values used in their earlier papers are taken from elsewhere. The latest study estimates the storm protection value of the coastal wetlands of the United States by using the avoided damages approach. The authors estimated a regression model for 34 major US hurricanes since 1980, with the natural log of damage per unit of gross domestic product in the hurricane swath as the dependent variable, and the natural logs of wind speed and wetland area in the swath as the independent variables. Storm protection value is estimated from the marginal effects. Along with wind speed and wetland area, storm damages depend on multiple other factors and thus the results of the study could be suffering from omitted variable biases.

Among the analytically best studies on the protection of mangroves from cyclone damages has been the well-conceptualized work by Badola and Hussain (2005). Conducting primary surveys for damages in the aftermath of the super cyclone of October 1999, they showed the damages per household to be less in a village sheltered by mangroves compared to the damages per household in a village having a dike nearby but no mangroves, and a village without either mangroves or dikes. Though the authors are given credit for selecting villages as similar as possible – except for the presence or absence of mangroves and dikes – in order to neutralize the impacts of socio-economic factors on storm damages, these impacts are still visible from the summary statistics. However, the attribution of the entire reduced damages by the authors to mangrove presence appears to be a biased overestimate:

1   The study villages are not socio-economically homogeneous – a glance at the general characteristics of the villages shows their economic heterogeneity. Hence, a statistical analysis looking at the effect of all the factors simultaneously on damage occurrences will definitely give different results.
2   The hydrology of the area in the form of distance from rivers, the position of dikes vis-à-vis rivers and the villages, etc. has not been considered.
3   The village Bankual, claimed as having only mangroves and no dikes nearby cannot be true. It is an agricultural village with 70 percent of people being shown as farmers in the mangrove forest area where no agriculture is possible without dikes. The dike could have impacted the damages if it is between the village and the river nearby.
4   Bankual is nearly 65 km away from the cyclone path, whereas both Singidi and Bandhmal are nearly 50 km away. Accordingly, the wind impact would have been less on Bankual. This needs to be taken into account in the analysis.
5   In coastal Orissa, dikes were constructed to facilitate agriculture by stopping the intrusion of salt water during high tide as these areas are extremely low-lying (Ranjit Daniels, 2005), but not as cyclone barriers. Hence, the argument that mangroves are better protectors against cyclones than man-made structures is inappropriate, as these structures were never constructed with that objective in mind.

The avoided damage approach has also been followed to evaluate the protective role of coastal forests in impacting damages during the Indian Oceans tsunami of 2004. The three widely quoted studies are of Kathiresan and Rajendran (2005), Danielson *et al.* (2005) and Dahdouh-Guebas *et al.* (2005). The findings of these studies were criticized on the grounds of methodological and database inadequacy (Kerr *et al.*, 2006; Baird, 2006), though later on the

findings of Kathiresan and Rajendran were reconfirmed and again finally nulli-
fied by Vermat and Thampanya (2006, 2007) after doing some statistical re-
analysis of the original data.

The role of mangrove forests in reducing cyclonic damages and tsunami
damages is likely to be different as the generation and flow of energy in a
storm wave is different from that of a tsunami wave (Cochard *et al.*, 2008;
Baird, 2006), and to that extent the degree of resistance provided by the mangroves to these waves and the provision of protection to inland properties
would be different. However, in analyzing the damages due to these extreme
events, the mangroves or other coastal barriers should never be considered as
the main decisive players. Though the role of elevation, coastal distance and
inundation distances are now recognized as important (Bretschneider and
Wybro, 1977; FAO, 2006; Baird, 2006; Chatenoux and Peduzzi, 2006, 2007;
Dahdouh-Guebas and Nico, 2006), the role of other important factors such as
economic, sociological and hydrological factors in causing damages, particularly in the context of developing countries, are not being talked about at all.
Every unit of analysis (whether hamlet or household) is socio-economically
heterogeneous. Ignoring this aspect will give biased estimates of the role of the
coastal forests, even if they play significant roles in averting damages. Significantly, the most essential point that every researcher seems to have missed out
is the need to control for the unobserved characteristics of the mangrove
habitat areas, in order to identify clearly the impact of the mangrove vegetation on cyclone damages.

The present chapter aims to address these issues and will evaluate the protective role of mangrove forests in the occurrence of cyclone-related damages
by looking at the roles of socio-economic, geophysical and meteorological
factors, including sea elevation (storm surge height) at different coastal points
simultaneously. The study also controls for the unobserved characteristics of
the mangrove habitat areas to isolate the mangrove vegetation effect from
those of the mangrove habitat on storm damages by means of: (1) including a
variable, *Mhabitat*, that measures the width of the mangrove habitat areas
(using the historical mangrove forest map) between a village and the coast in
the model for storm damages; and (2) by limiting the sample to villages that
historically had mangroves located between them and the coast. We do this by
including only those villages in the sample for which *Mhabitat* > 0. The second
part of the control is more important as it is meaningless to talk about the protection value of mangroves in areas where they can't grow (villages with
Mhabitat = 0). Moreover, limiting the sample to villages with *Mhabitat* > 0 will
enable one to interpret the coefficient of the mangrove variable (the width of
the mangrove vegetation at the time of the super cyclone as defined in the
study) as capturing the effect of only the mangrove vegetation, not the unobserved features of the mangrove habitat areas. The effects of the unobserved
features of the mangrove habitat on storm damages are likely to be captured by
the *Mhabitat* variable.

8.3 Study area, the Kendrapada district

The economic values of different protective services such storm protection, shoreline stabilization, etc. is site-specific and country-specific, as well as location-specific. These services could be very important for a coastal area frequently battered by cyclones, but not so crucial for an area with low cyclone probability. Again, these services have added importance if the area is densely populated and the inhabitants are of low economic status. The state of Orissa is one of the most undeveloped states of India, with 47.15 percent of the population below the poverty line (as per the 1999–2000 survey of the National Sample Survey); the coastal districts of the state are densely populated (more than 250 people per square kilometer, whereas the average population density of the state is 202 people per square kilometer). The state faces the fury of cyclones of different magnitude very frequently (Das, 2007). Thus, the storm protection services of mangroves are crucial for the state of Orissa. The present work evaluates the storm protection services of the mangroves of the Kendrapada district of the state.

Ideally, to measure the storm protection services, the choice of the study area should be such that the cyclonic wind as well as the storm surge should be passing through the mangrove forests to reach the inland areas so that the

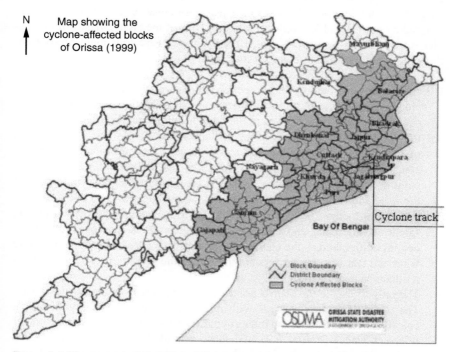

Figure 8.1 The super cyclone affected districts of Orissa and location of Kendrapada district. The path of the cyclone eye is shown by a straight line.

mangroves' impact on storm damages can be assessed. Thus, in the northern hemisphere where the cyclonic wind moves anti-clockwise around the cyclone eye, the ideal study locations are the areas to the north of the cyclone landfall, and in the southern hemisphere, to the south of the landfall. The direction of both wind and surge over these areas is from sea to land, and they would be reaching the interior areas after passing through the mangrove forests. In areas south of the cyclone landfall (or south of eye), the wind and the storm surge would be moving in opposite directions – the cyclonic wind would be blowing from land to sea, the surge from sea to land, and the wind would be pushing the surge water back to the sea. In this situation, even if the mangroves are there on the coast (south of landfall), they can hardly influence the damage occurrences and their impact should not be assessed by analyzing the cyclone damages. Similarly, if the locations north of cyclone landfall are chosen as study areas in the southern hemisphere, the impact of mangroves on storm damages cannot be measured correctly. The Kendrapada district of Orissa was to the north of the landfall point of the super cyclone and it has mangroves on the coast. This is why it is taken as the study area for the present chapter (Figure 8.1).

8.3.1 Reasons for choosing Kendrapada as the study area

The super cyclone of October 1999 had its landfall at a place called Ersama, lying 20 km southwest of Kendrapada district. The entire district was severely battered by both cyclonic wind and rain, and four of the eight tahasils of the district were affected by storm surge. Broadly, there were four main reasons for choosing Kendrapada district as the study area.

1   As mentioned before, the direction of the cyclonic wind being anti-clockwise in the northern hemisphere, the wind direction in Kendrapada district was mainly from the sea to the land during the super cyclone period as the district lies to the north of the cyclone landfall and track. The direction of movement of both wind and storm surge was uniform for the coastal areas of the district. As the wind and surge reached the interior areas after passing through the mangrove forests, it provided a good opportunity to test the wind and surge buffering capacity of the mangroves.
2   According to the 2000 edition of the District Planning Map for Cuttack, Jajpur, Kendrapada and Jagatsinghpur, the entire Kendrapada district is devoid of highlands – the elevation of the district is less than 10 m. The only wind and storm surge barriers are the forest, the sand dunes and the saltwater dikes in coastal areas.
3   The only forests in the district are the mangrove forests in the coastal areas.[1]
4   The district has coastal areas with mangroves and also areas with barren coastlines. The width of the mangrove forests varied from 100 m to 10 km at different places (Figure 8.2). All these provided a basis to compare the cyclone impact both with and without the mangroves and also for different widths of the mangroves.

8.3.2 *Mangroves of Kendrapada*

In the Indian state of Orissa, 48 percent of the population lives below the poverty line. The district of Kendrapada holds the tenth place from among the 30 districts of the state in terms of human development index (HDR, 2004). Lying between 86° 14' to 87° 3' east longitude and 20° 21' to 20° 47' north latitude, this district has a total geographical area of 2,644 km^2 and caters to a total population of 1.3 million. It is a predominantly agricultural district where 78 percent of the population depends on the primary sector and just 5 percent on the secondary sector. Nearly 94 percent of the population lives in the rural areas (HDR, 2004). Except Kendrapada tahasil, which is the district headquarters, more than 50 percent of the population in the remaining tahasils are below the poverty line, the worst being in Derabis (67 percent) followed by Rajnagar (67 percent), the tahasil with the most mangrove forests. The entire district was battered by the super cyclone of October 1999, witnessing massive damages, including 456 human casualties. During the cyclone, except Rajkanika, human casualties were witnessed in all other tahasils, the most (188) being from Mahakalpada (closest to the cyclone landfall) and the second highest (67) from Derabis, the tahasil with the highest population density (740 people per square kilometer) and the highest percentage of people below the poverty line. Only the two coastal blocks witnessed the fury of the severe storm surge, leading to swept away houses and human deaths. Mahakalpada also witnessed maximized other damages due to its proximity to the cyclone landfall.

The only forests found in the district are the coastal mangrove forests present in the Mahakalpada and Rajnagar tahasils. These constituted only 0.43 percent of the total forest area of the state of Orissa[2] in 1999–2000. The district has a 60 km-long coastline and 80 percent of it was covered with mangrove forests nearly 10 km wide in the past (Figure 8.3). Different drivers destroyed these forests over time, particularly between 1952 – when the ownership of these forests was transferred from the *zamindars* (feudal landowners) to the state government – and 1980 – when the Wild Life Division Department was created by the state government and the management of the mangrove forests was entrusted exclusively to this department (Orissa District Gazetteer, 1996). The destruction of mangroves has been very high in the case of Mahakalpada tahasil, where a thin strand of mangroves was left by 1999 when the super cyclone hit the district (Figures 8.2 and 8.3). In contrast, the destruction of mangroves in Rajnagar tahasil has been marginal, which may be due to the presence of ferocious animals in these forests (crocodiles) in the period that state protection was inadequate, and then the declaration of the forest area as the Bhitarkanika Wildlife Sanctuary (672 km^2) in 1975 and then a national park (core area of 145 km^2) on 3 October 1988. The Mahakalpada forests were declared to be reserve forests in 1978 and were brought under the Gahirmatha Marine Wildlife Sanctuary in September 1997. They are protected forests at present. The district has 192 km^2 of mangrove forests as per a 2001 survey[3], more than 93 percent of it being dense and well protected.

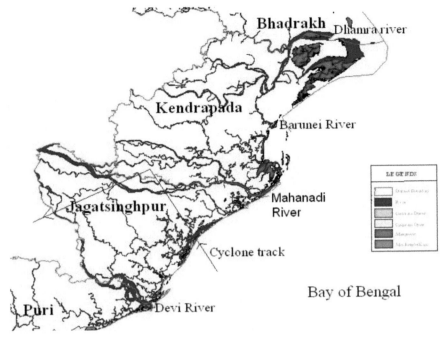

Figure 8.2 Mangroves present in 1999.

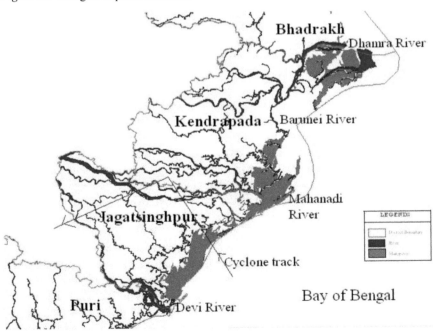

Figure 8.3 Mangroves present in 1950.

8.4 The methodology: the cyclone damage function

We estimate a cyclone damage function to see whether mangrove presence has significantly affected the damage occurrences in areas lying on the leeward side of the forest. We take some types of cyclone damage as the dependant variable and factors including mangroves, which are likely to impact damage occurrences, as independent variables. We describe below the derivation of the cyclone damage function.[4]

Damages including human casualties in any location, i, during a cyclone will depend on the wind velocity, the velocity of storm surge water, the population or property at risk and other socio-economic factors of the location.[5]

$$\therefore D_i = d(V_i, W_i, P_iS_i), \tag{1}$$

where i is the location (villages); D_i is the damage suffered at the ith location; V_i is velocity of wind at the ith location; W_i is velocity of storm surge or the severity of flooding due to surge at the ith location; P_i is population or property at risk at the location; and S_i is the group of socio-economic factors at the location influencing the volume and extent of damages. Micro- or village-level data on wind velocity, storm surge velocity and the socio-economic factors affecting damage occurrences are difficult to get, and thus we approximate them by including their determinants in the damage function.[6] P_i or the property at risk is presented by total population of the village in the year 1999.

8.4.1 Wind velocity

The actual wind velocity at any ith village causing maximum damage would be dependent on the potential wind velocity at the place, which is the wind velocity in the absence of any barriers between the cyclone and the village. This potential wind velocity is approximated by the radial wind[7] of the cyclone at the place (RW_i). Thus, the actual wind velocity at a place would be dependant on the radial wind and other factors such as the minimum distance of the place from the center of the village to the coast line ($dcoast_i$) and the type of wind barriers ($barrier_i$) present within the bounded area of the village and the landfall, etc.

$$\therefore V_i = v(RW_i, dcoast_i, barrier_i) \tag{2}$$

The radial wind over a place during a tropical cyclone will depend on the position of the place vis-à-vis the horizontal structure of the cyclone that consists of four different parts – namely the eye, the eye wall or wall cloud region, the rain/spiral bands and the outer storm area (IMD, 2002). Areas coming under the eye and eye wall face the maximum wind,[8] whereas wind velocity over the other two structures goes on declining with distance away from the cyclone path or from the center of the eye.

The wind profile of a cyclone shows non-linear movements for both maximum wind and radial wind. The maximum wind of cyclones decreases exponentially with distance inland after the landfall (Dube *et al.*, 1981; Basu and Ghose, 1987; Kaplan and Demaria, 1995; Kalsi *et al.*, 2003; Singh and Bandyopadhyay, 2005) due to interaction of the cyclone with rough land surface, or reasons such as reduced moisture supply due to being away from the sea, conversion of heat in the form of rain, etc. In the case of the super cyclone of October 1999, the maximum wind was shown to have declined at an exponential rate of 0.0991 per hour on an average (Kalsi *et al.*, 2003).

However, for explaining the wind profile of cyclones at different radial distances beyond the cyclone eye, both exponential (Holland, 1980; Dube *et al.*, 1981; Basu and Ghosh, 1987) and power functions (Depperman, 1947; Jalesnianski, 1965; Jalesnianski and Taylor, 1973; Das *et al.*, 1974; Roy Abraham *et al.*, 1995) have been used and, accordingly, two different values of radial wind, velocityexp (Dube *et al.*, 1981) and velocitypow (Roy Abraham *et al.*, 1995) have been calculated for every village or gram panchayat for the present work.

$$velocityexp_i = V_{max}\exp(-(dcypath_i - R)/\beta))$$

and

$$velocitypow_i = V_{max}(dcypath_i/R)^{-\alpha}, \tag{3}$$

where, V_{max} is maximum wind at the eye area, $dcypath_i$ is the minimum radial distance of the *i*th village from the center of the eye or cyclone path, R is the radius of the cyclone eye (15 km in the present case) and α and β are the parameters specific to the cyclone. In the present case, α was taken to be 0.6 and β to be 240 km, after consulting the meteorologists and experts. The maximum wind at the eye area was calculated as:

$$V_{max} = 256 \text{ kmh}^{-1} \exp. (-0.0991 * 3) = 190.1622 \text{ kmh}^{-1}, \tag{4}$$

where 256 kmh^{-1} was the landfall wind velocity of the super cyclone, 0.0991 was the average rate of decline of the maximum wind per hour (Kalsi *et al.*, 2003) and the cyclone had taken nearly three hours to reach Garadpur (two hours for the cyclone eye to cross the landfall point (Gupta and Sharma, 2000) and one hour to cover 25 km, the distance between landfall and Garadpur), the location over which the cyclone was stationary and caused maximum damage to the district. Thus, the maximum wind in the entire eye region (areas for which dcypath was ≤15) of the study area was taken to be 190.1622 kmh^{-1}, and the radial winds for different villages were calculated with the help of this maximum wind and the minimum radial distances ($dcypath_i$) of these locations from the cyclone track between landfall and Garadpur, as the study area received maximum damage when the cyclone was on this track.

$$Radial\ Wind(RWi) = \begin{cases} \text{Vmax} (= 190.1622 \text{ kmh}^{-1} \text{ if dcypath}_i \leq 15 \\ \text{Velocitypow (or exp.) if dcypath}_i > 15 \end{cases} \tag{5}$$

The study area is a predominantly agricultural land with all elevation less than 10 m. The only wind barriers present are the mangrove forests (width ranging from 0.1 km to 10 km) or the casuarinas forests (width ranging from 0.2 km to 0.4 km) on the coast line.

$$\therefore Barriers_i = B\,(mangrove_i,\,Mhabitat_i,\,casuarinadumy_i), \tag{6}$$

where $mangrove_i$ is the width of the mangrove forests between the coast and the ith village,[9] $Mhabitat_i$ is the width of the mangrove habitat area and $casuarinadumy_i$ is a dummy variable equal to 1 if the casuarinas forest is present in the coastal distance of the village and equal to 0 otherwise. As the casuarinas forests were nearly uniform in width wherever they were present in the study area, it was represented by a dummy variable.[10] $Mhabitat_i$ is used here to control for any unobserved surface roughness factors of the mangrove habitat area present in the sample area, which can have some impact on wind velocity.

Substituting Equation 5 and 6 into Equation 2, the actual wind velocity at the ith village is defined as:

$$V_i = v[\text{V}_{max}\text{ if }dcypathi_i <15,\,velocitypow_i\text{ (or exp) if }dcypath_i >15,$$
$$dcoast_i,\,mangrove_i,\,mhabitat_i,\,casuarinadumy_i). \tag{7}$$

The actual estimates of wind velocity over different locations not being available, it is approximated by including the five variables of Equation 7 in the main model. Moreover, as the model includes variables $dcoast_i$ and $mangrove_i$, it also implicitly controls for the distance of a village from the mangrove forest boundary that equals $dcoast_i - mangrove_i$.

8.4.2 *Velocity of storm surge*

Storm surge is an abnormal rise of sea level in excess of the predicted astronomical tide and is caused mainly due to the atmospheric pressure variation and the strong surface wind of a cyclone. Along with the wind velocity and pressure variation, other factors that play a decisive role in the generation of the storm surge are the direction (inclination) of the cyclone at landfall, radius of maximum wind, local offshore bathymetry, inland topography, density of sea water, speed of the cyclone, the height of the astronomical tide, etc. (Kalsi *et al.*, 2004). Because of these reasons, there exists no one-to-one relation between the wind velocity at a coastal point and the sea elevation over there. In the case of the super cyclone of October 1999, a very high surge was witnessed only over a coastal stretch of nearly 30 km, whereas nearly 250 km of the coastline was battered by very high surface wind. This explains the necessity of accounting for the sea elevation at different coastal points along with the wind velocity to explain the cyclone damages, especially the cross-section damages of a single cyclone.[11]

The severity of flooding that depends both on the level of water, as well as on the velocity of water at an interior location due to storm surge, will depend on the level of sea elevation (surge height) facing that location and other physical features of the location such as the minimum distance from the coast, the elevation of the place, the topography and the hydrology of the place, the distance of the place from river channels, the presence of natural barriers like mangroves, sand dunes or any other barriers, etc. between the location and the coastline, presence of man-made barriers (dikes) near the village, etc. Taking all these factors into account, the following function was defined for the level of flooding due to storm surge in a place.

$$W_i = w(surge_i, dcoast_i, dmajriver_i, dminriver_i, topodumy_i, Mhabitat_i,$$
$$mangrove_i, casurinadumy_i, roadumy_i), (8)$$

where W_i is the severity of flooding due to storm surge at the ith location inland; $surge_i$ is the surge height or elevation of the sea at the shore nearest to the location (as calculated from the surge envelop curve given in Kalsi *et al.* (2004)); $dcoast_i$ is the minimum distance of the place from the coastline; $dmajriver_i$ is the minimum distance of the place from a major river (directly connected to sea) and $dminriver_i$ is the minimum distance of the place from a minor river (either a tributary of a major river or a drain connected to the tributary). The study area is full of major and minor river channels and their roles during storm surge are different. The major rivers carry away the high velocity surge water to interior areas and, as a result, the surge effects on nearby villages get reduced to a flooding effect. But the opposite happens in the case of minor rivers. Hence, the minimum distance from river channels was divided into two, i.e. minimum distances from a major river (*dmajriver*) and minimum distance from a minor river (*dminriver*).

Topodumy_i is the low elevation dummy that equals 1 if the village is located within a mangrove habitat area (that either historically or in 1999 had mangrove vegetation within its boundary) and equals 0 otherwise. In the absence of elevation data for the villages of the study area, present and historical mangrove forest maps (Figures 8.2 and 8.3) were used to demarcate the low-lying areas. As mangrove forests come up in low-lying vulnerable areas that get inundated regularly during high tides, villages with *topodumy_i*=1 are likely to be low-lying and the ones with *topodumy_i*=0 will be situated at higher elevation levels.

Mhabitat_i is the width of the historical mangrove forests that lay between the village and the coast as seen in Figure 8.3. This variable is likely to capture the effect of the topographic, hydrological and bathymetric factors of the mangrove habitat areas in storm surge inundation as the width of mangrove in an area depends on these factors. The study area had a vast stretch of mangrove forests historically, and different drivers have cleared them to some extent over the years. The physical features of mangrove areas being different from those of the non-mangrove areas, the width of the historical mangrove forest was taken to capture the effect of those special features on cyclone damages. Another reason for including this variable in the damage function was to separate out the effects of mangrove vegetation from those of the mangrove habitat on storm damages.[12]

Mangrove$_i$ is the width of the mangrove forest (vegetation) as existed on 11 October 1999 between the ith village and the coast.

Casurinadumy$_i$, as previously explained, is the dummy variable for the presence of casuarinas forests in between the village and the coast. Lastly, *roadumy$_i$* is the dummy variable for the presence of village roads, as dikes are also used as village roads in the coastal areas.

8.4.3 Socio-economic factors

The cyclone, like any other natural calamity, is presumed to have differential impacts on people depending on their socio-economic status (FAO, 2000) and the coastal poor are likely to be the most vulnerable during cyclones.[13]

Along with economic well-being, institutional, infrastructural and behavioral factors also play decisive roles in averting human death and other damages during cyclones. The efficiency of the meteorology department in providing accurate cyclone warnings, the promptness of the local administration in proper dissemination of the cyclone warning (evacuating people from vulnerable areas), presence of cyclone shelters or some other concrete structures in neighborhoods, community behavior of people in helping each other during the crisis, etc. are some of the important factors that can influence human casualties, as well as livestock losses.

In the absence of a proper economic well-being index for different villages, the differences in socio-economic conditions of different villages are captured by using factors like percentage of literates, as the responsiveness of people to cyclone warning depends on their level of education (FAO, 2000), percentage of different types of workers (earning members), percentage of scheduled caste population (economically and socially most deprived and possess very little assets), percentage of non-workers (who are likely to remain indoor and are less exposed during cyclones), the proximity of villages to metallic roads (better scope of economic prosperity), presence of village road (connectivity to metallic road), dummies for local administration, etc.[14] Thus the socio-economic well-being index influencing the cyclone damages is defined as:

$$S_i = S(tahasildar_i, literate_i, scheduledcaste_i, cultivators_i, aglabors_i,$$
$$hhworkers_i, otworkers_i, margworkers_i, droad_i, roadumy_i), \qquad (9)$$

where S_i is the socio-economic well-being index of the ith village; *tahasildar$_i$* is the dummy variable for the local administration in change of all revenue decisions, including evacuation and relief for the village; *literate$_i$* is the percentage of literate people in the ith village; *scheduledcaste$_i$* is the percentage of scheduled caste people in the village; *cultivators$_i$, aglabors$_i$, hhworkers$_i$, otworkers$_i$, margworkers$_i$* are the percentage of cultivators, agricultural laborers, percentage of workers in own household industries (located either at home or within the village), percentage of other workers (doctors, teachers, engineers, barbers, washer men, priests, etc.), percentage of marginal workers; *droad$_i$* is the minimum distance of the village from the metallic road and *roadumy$_i$* is a dummy variable for the presence of a village road that equals 1 if the village road exists and equals 0 otherwise.

Combining the factors affecting wind velocity, surge velocity and the socio-economic conditions, the following cyclone damage function is obtained for a village:

$$D_i = d(tahasildar_i, velocitypow_i \text{ (or exp)}, surge_i, dcoast_i, topodumy_i,$$
$$mhabitat_i, mangrove_i, casurinadumy_i, dmajriver_i, dminriver_i, droad_i,$$
$$roadumy_i, pop99_i, literate_i, scheduledcaste_i, cultivator_i, aglabor_i,$$
$$hhworkers_i, otworkers_i, margworkers_i), \tag{10}$$

where D_i is the damage suffered in the ith village. The right-hand side variables, though defined above, are explained in Table 8.1.[15] We estimate-tested this model by using the number of fully collapsed houses as the dependant variable.

8.5 Description of data

Four different types of data are needed to estimate the damage function described in Equation 10. The information was either generated through GIS Arc View software from the GIS files or collected from different sources. The sources are mentioned at the end of each category of data as described in Table 8.2.

Though initially the collection of cyclone damage data seemed the most difficult and impossible job, cooperation from the respective officers of the various departments of the Government of Orissa made the work easier. For generating geophysical variables, we combined the GIS files on village boundaries, rivers, roads and coastal forests of Orissa (as existed on 11 October 1999 and in 1950) together with the help of GIS Arc View Software 3.1. The village-level, digitized physical map of coastal Orissa was developed. Then the different location-specific position of the cyclone as described in the NCDM Report (Gupta and Sharma, 2000) was superimposed on the village map and the cyclone track was demarcated at the village scale.[16] The district received maximum damage from the cyclone during the landfall and when it was positioned over Garadpur and, accordingly, this part of the cyclone track has been considered in the analysis to calculate the radial wind for different villages. Different distances as required for the analysis were then calculated with the help of software. As mentioned before, the mangrove variable was defined as the width of the forest along the minimum distance between a village and the coast. The approximate sea elevation at different coastal points is calculated from the surge envelope curve provided by the cyclone warning division of the meteorology department of the Government of India (Kalsi *et al.*, 2004)

The socio-economic variables were calculated for each village by making use of the primary census abstract of Orissa for 1991 and 2001. First of all, the decadal compound rate of growth for the period 1991 to 2001 was obtained for different variables (population, scheduled castes, different types of workers, etc.)

Table 8.1 List of variables

Variables	Definition of variables (all distances in kilometers)
aglabor	Percentage of agricultural laborers in a village
casurindmy	Dummy variable for the presence of casuarinas forest in coastal distance of a village
cultivator	Percentage of cultivators in a village
dcoast	Minimum distance of a village from the coast.
dcypath	Minimum (radial) distance of a village from the path of cyclone
dmajriver	Minimum distance of a village from a major river (directly connected to sea)
dminriver	Minimum distance of a village from a minor river (a tributary of major river)
droad	Minimum distance of a village from a metallic road
hhworker	Percentage of people working in (own) household industries in a village
literate	Percentage of literate people in a village
mangrove	Width of existing mangrove forest in coastal distance of a village
margworker	Percentage of marginal workers in a village.
Mhabitat	Width of the historical mangrove forest (as existed in 1950) in coastal distance of a village or between a village and the coast
otworker	Percentage of other workers (doctor, teacher, engineer, barber, washer man, priest, etc.) in a village
pop99	Total population of a village in 1999
radial wind	The expected wind velocity at different radial distances (*dcypath*) from the cyclone eye
roadumy	Dummy variable for the presence of village road (=1, if village road exists, =0, otherwise)
schdulcaste	Percentage of scheduled caste people in a village
surge	Level of sea elevation (in meters) at different coastal points
tahasildar	Dummy variable for local administration
topodumy	Low elevation dummy (=1 for villages that have or had mangrove earlier and =0 for others)
velocityexp	Approximate radial wind velocity (kmh^{-1}) in a village due to cyclone as given by an exponential function
velocitypow	Approximate radial wind velocity (kmh^{-1}) in a village due to cyclone as given by a power function

and then the 1991 figures were extrapolated for the year 1999 by making use of the respective growth rates.

8.6 Estimation and results

To get an accurate picture of the sheltering capacity of the mangrove forest, we estimated different regressions over different samples. As explained in the review of the literature, including areas that never had mangroves between them and the coast in an exercise that tries to estimate the storm protection value of mangroves makes no sense due to the fact that calculating the storm protection

Table 8.2 Description and sources of data

Data head	Description	Source
Damages due to super cyclone	Number of houses fully collapsed (FC) in each village	Emergency office and Tahasildar Office of Kendrapada and emergency office of Jagatsinghpur
Meteorological information	Landfall wind velocity, radius of cyclone eye, and sea elevation at different coastal points	Cyclone Warning Division, Mausam Bhawan, Government of India, New Delhi
	Track of the cyclone	National Center for Disaster Management (NCDM), Indian Institute of Public Administration, New Delhi
Geophysical information	Distances of different villages or gram panchayats from coastline, cyclone track, river channels, metallic roads and width of present and historical mangrove forests	GIS files on villages, coastline, rivers, drains, roads, village roads, coastal forests, etc. from DCS, Bhubaneswar and GIS software.
Socio-economic information	Total population, percentage of literates, scheduled caste, different types of workers and non-workers in different villages or in gram panchayats before cyclone	Primary Census Abstract of the State of Orissa for the year 1991 and 2001

value of mangrove for a village where mangrove can never be grown is meaningless. Hence, the villages or gram panchayats with *Mhabitat* = 0 have been excluded from the sample and areas that had mangroves historically between them and the coast, i.e. the ones for which the variable *Mhabitat* was positive (*Mhabita* > 0) were included in the sample. Then the sample was restricted further by excluding the areas that came under the cyclone eye from estimation. This was done due to the fact that wind direction inside the cyclone eye area is circular and no forest can provide any sheltering service, particularly from the wind effects. As this sample is expected to provide a more accurate picture of the protective services of the mangrove vegetation, it was further sub-divided to evaluate the effectiveness of mangrove protection for areas lying within different bandwidth from the coastline. Thus regressions were estimated for four different samples as described below.

- Sample 1: areas with *Mhabitat* > 0.
- Sample 2: areas with *Mhabitat* > 0 and wind velocity < 190 kmh^{-1}.[17]
- Sample 3: areas with *Mhabitat* > 0, wind velocity < 190 kmh^{-1} and *dcoast* ≤ 10.
- Sample 4: areas with *Mhabitat* > 0, wind velocity < 190 kmh^{-1} and *dcoast* > 10.

Wind velocity and storm surge are the two main causes of cyclone-related damages, and care was taken to use the most appropriate measures of these variables in the estimating equation. As we had two different measures of wind velocity, one given by a power function ($velocitypow_i$) and the other by an exponential function ($velocityexp_i$), as explained in Equation 3, every equation was estimated twice using each measure of wind velocity once.

The spread of storm surge water after the surge hits the coastline has never been examined. Hence, all the equations were estimated by using the direct measure of sea elevation ($surge_i$) as the independent variable.[18]

We estimate the damage function explained in Equation 10 for the above sample areas using village-level data on the number of houses fully collapsed (FC) during the super cyclone in our study area as the dependent variable. Fully collapsed houses (houses that cannot be repaired) are those that received a very high degree of damage during the cyclone, due to both wind and storm surge.

8.6.1 House damage

The study area, as mentioned earlier, is a poor area with more than 50 percent of the population living below the poverty line, while the residential housing quality is also poor. As per the 2001 Census of India Report, 94 percent of the households in Kendrapada district are in rural areas, and only 15 percent of these households have cemented walls (the rest have mud walls), 10 percent have houses with a concrete roof, and only 2 percent of the households have both a concrete roof and concrete walls. This means that even though 15 percent of households have cemented walls, except for 2 percent, the material used in other households is either raw brick or mud, and their capacity to withstand the super cyclone impact was doubtful. Thus, it is expected that at least 98 percent of the rural households must have suffered some form of house damage depending on the cyclone impact on their location.[19]

House damage was described under three different categories by the state government, namely, fully collapsed houses (either completely or severely damaged), partially collapsed houses (includes all houses with less than 80 percent damage) and swept away houses (both the wall and the roof completely damaged due to water). We could arrange village-level information on house damage for only 451 villages and got gram panchayat-level data for 138 gram panchayats.[20] We used all the explanatory variables explained in Equation 10 except *pop99* and *tahasildar* dummy variable in our estimating equation. We used *Male99* in place of *pop99* to represent properties at risk. The total male population (age>6)[21] ($Male99_i$) has been used as a proxy for properties at risk as no accurate measure of total number of houses at risk was available (particularly due to the joint family system) for the study area. The tahasildars play an important role in cyclone warning dissemination, evacuation and relief, but can in no way impact the damage to static properties like houses. As we estimate the cyclone damage function for house damage, the *tahasildar_i* dummy is not used.

Table 8.3 gives the summary statistics and, as evident from the table, the study area lies between 0.22 km and 72.83 km from the cyclone path and within 0.65 km and 51.23 km of the coastline. The width of the mangrove forest varies from 0.1 km to 10 km at different places. Nearly 70 percent of the population are non-workers and agriculture is the main occupation; owner-farmers (cultivators) constitute 11 percent and agricultural laborers 5 percent of the population. Some of the explanatory variables were significantly correlated with each other, but to ensure that the significance of the mangroves is not due to the variables it is correlated with, we compared the results by dropping the variables correlated with mangroves one by one from the estimation and did not see any change in the significance of mangroves.

Taking fully collapsed houses as a dependant variable and rearranging terms by putting mangrove-related variables first, we write the estimable Equation 10 as:

$$FC_i = \alpha_0 + \alpha_1 mangrove_i + \alpha_2 mhabitat_i + \alpha_3 topodumy_i + \alpha_4 casuarinadumy_i +$$
$$\alpha_5 velocitypow_i + \alpha_6 surge_i + --- + \alpha_{19} m \arg wor \ker s_i + v_i$$

$$(11)$$

where v_i is the error term. Other variables have been explained earlier. The error was heteroskedastic (Breusch–Pagan Chi^2 = 527.47 (P=0.00)). Ordinary least-square estimates with robust standard errors have been used for this model. Regressions were estimated for the four sample areas to see whether the entire district or a part of it received storm protection from mangroves. Table 8.4 gives

Table 8.3 Descriptive statistics of house damage model for sample area 1

Variables	Mean (std dev.)	Min (Max)
fully collapsed	229.31 (297.81)	0 (1885)
mangrove	0.46 (0.91)	0 (10)
Mhabitat	4.58 (1.85)	0.5 (13.7)
topodumy	0.13 (0.33)	0 (1)
casurindumy	0.37 (0.48)	0 (1)
dcypath	19.20 (10.98)	0.22 (72.83)
velocitypow	163.19 (23.80)	73.64 (190.16)
surge	3.14 (2.04)	0.7 (5.9)
dcoast	26.65 (14.67)	0.65 (51.23)
dmajriver	4.01 (3.32)	0.06 (16.66)
dminriver	3.21 (3.21)	0.08 (15.23)
droad	2.21 (2.57)	0.02 (15.68)
roadumy	0.80 (0.39)	0 (1)
Male-99	768.27 (863.8)	3 (5340)
literate	0.66 (0.09)	0.19 (1)
schedulecaste	0.21 (0.17)	0 (1)
cultivator	0.12 (0.05)	0 (0.42)
aglabor	0.04 (0.08)	0 (0.25)
hhworker	0.004 (0.007)	0 (0.07)
otworker	0.06 (0.04)	0 (0.36)
margworker	0.08 (0.08)	0 (0.57)

Note
Number of observations: 516.

Table 8.4 Ordinary least-squares estimates with robust standard errors for fully collapsed houses

Equation/variable	Exp. signs	Sample 1: areas with Mhabitat > 0	Sample 2: part of sample 1 beyond cyclone eye	Sample 3: part of sample 2 within 10 km of coast	Sample 4: part of sample 2 beyond 10 km from coast
mangrove	(−)	−84.27*** (3.83)	−60.11*** (3.12)	−40.39 (1.19)	−56.11*** (3.48)
Mhabitat	(?)	20.83*** (3.17)	11.14* (1.87)	−16.21 (0.73)	21.00*** (3.15)
topodumy	(+)	−27.86 (0.70)	2.70 (0.10)	−33.50 (0.75)	−13.42 (0.36)
casurinadumy	(−)	−45.22 (1.19)	−9.77 (0.27)	−37.96 (0.87)	−61.09 (1.22)
velocitypow	(+)	1.70** (2.55)	2.78*** (3.55)	14.30*** (4.58)	3.04*** (3.62)
surge	(+)	13.17 (1.34)	1.09 (0.11)	−29.97* (1.97)	7.59 (0.52)
dcoast	(−)	0.54 (0.59)	−1.28* (1.69)	−31.69** (2.06)	0.64 (0.72)
dmajriver	(−)	−6.32** (2.41)	−8.09** (2.71)	−15.12 (0.87)	−8.17*** (3.10)
dminriver	(−)	−8.46*** (2.73)	−5.92* (1.68)	−29.50* (1.84)	−3.14 (0.85)
droad	(+)	−7.37 (1.23)	−0.20 (0.04)	7.40 (0.92)	−0.95 (0.15)
roadumy	(−)	28.43 (1.41)	9.20 (0.41)	96.87* (1.68)	−12.65 (0.59)
male99	(+)	0.26*** (10.38)	0.21*** (6.87)	0.22*** (6.55)	0.25*** (7.38)
literate	(−)	−49.35 (0.53)	−63.7 (0.89)	−27.28 (0.17)	65.07 (0.73)
schedulecaste	(+)	59.77 (1.22)	17.05 (0.41)	42.94 (0.20)	47.06 (1.08)
cultivator	(−)	35.47 (0.21)	−260.90* (1.88)	−20.21 (0.07)	−161.66 (0.89)
aglabor	(+)	−127.96 (0.62)	−1.29 (0.01)	−388.85 (0.80)	2.01 (0.01)
hhworker	(−)	−622.63 (0.56)	−583.11 (0.76)	6923.27 (1.27)	−441.69 (0.59)
otworker	(−)	−495.70** (2.13)	−497.08** (2.40)	−1564.66*** (3.65)	−699.03** (2.53)
margworker	(+)	64.59 (0.58)	9.61 (0.08)	−232.05* (1.66)	84.82 (0.52)
Constant	(?)	−245.98* (1.79)	−218.92* (1.68)	−1256.18*** (3.52)	−507.93*** (2.80)
		N=516,R²=0.55, F(19,496)=12.56 Pro=0.00	N=338,R²=0.54, F(19,318)=7.61, Pro=0.00	N=61,R²=0.77, F(19,41)=4.93 Pro=0.00	N=277,R²=0.58, F(19,257)=7.14, Pro=0.00

Notes
* significance at 10 percent level of significance.
** imply significance at 5 percent.
*** imply significance at 1 percent.

the expected signs, as well as the estimated coefficients of the four regressions by using the *velocitypow* measure of wind velocity. The results from using the *velocityexp* measure of wind velocity are not shown as the two measures of wind were highly correlated[22] and results were similar for both.

8.6.2 Expected signs

The *mangrove* variable is expected to reduce the degree of damage to houses and hence is expected to have a negative coefficient with FC, and so should also be the coefficient of *casurinadumy*. Negative coefficients are also expected for the variables *dcoast* (being away from the coast means less intensity in the cyclone), *dmajriver*, *dminriver* (closeness to river will increase the cyclone impact), *roadumy* (villages having village road are usually more well-off and have better-quality houses) and also for *cultivators, hhworkers and otworkers* (they are the most well-off people in the study area). The variables *velocitypow* and *surge* are expected to have positive coefficient (high values indicate more intensity of cyclone) and so are the variables *droad* (proximity to metallic road means economic well-being), *Male 99* (property at risk), *topodumy* (low-lying areas are more vulnerable and poor), *schedulecaste, aglabor and margworker* (very poor people). The sign of the coefficient of *Mhabitat* is uncertain, as this variable is likely to capture the effects of unobserved topographic and bathymetric factors in house damage.

8.6.3 Discussion

The coefficients shown in Table 8.4, wherever significant, have the appropriate sign. As expected, the wind velocity is seen to be the main cause of fully collapsed houses. The surge variable is insignificant except for areas within 10 km of the coast, as expected. The housing quality, as captured by the percentage of economically well-off people (cultivators and other workers) is seen to have reduced the house damage. The proximity to coast and to rivers has increased the damage. The mangrove variable is significant with a negative sign for sample 1, 2 and 4, but not for areas within 10 km of the coast (sample 3). Thus mangroves seem to have reduced the number of fully collapsed houses. The insignificance of mangrove for sample 3 may be because of the fact that these areas witnessed swept away houses and there were very few fully collapsed houses. Thus, in spite of this limitation, we cannot reject the hypothesis that mangroves reduced the number of fully collapsed houses in Kendrapada district of Orissa during the super cyclone of October 1999.

8.6.4 Elasticity of mangroves in reducing house damage

The unit of measurement of different explanatory variables being different, the elasticity rather than the marginal effects of these variables on fully collapsed house damage is compared. The elasticity[23] shown in Table 8.5 is for the coeffi-

Table 8.5 Elasticity of mangroves and other variables on fully collapsed houses for the sample 2 area (cyclone outer eye area with *Mhabitat* > 0) (wind measure = velocitypow)

Variables\equations	Fully collapsed houses, number of observation = 338
velocitypow	**2.409***
surge	0.0027
dcoast	**−0.212***
topodumy	−0.004
hmangrove	**0.301***
mangrove	**−0.221***
casurindumy	−0.008
dmajriver	**−0.203***
dminriver	**−0.101***
droad	0.003
roadumy	0.052
Pop-99	**0.789***
literate	−0.342
schedulecaste	0.029
cultivator	**−0.746***
aglabor	−0.255
hhworker	−0.026
otworker	**−0.423***
margworker	−0.426

Note
***, ** and * indicate the level of significance to be 1 percent, 5 percent and 10 percent respectively.

cients of sample 2, the cyclone outer eye areas with historical mangroves between the villages and the coast.

The mangrove effect in reducing fully collapsed houses is significant, but not very substantial as measured by the elasticity of mangrove width on house damages. A 10-percent increase in mangrove width will reduce the number of fully collapsed houses by 2.2 percent, but this effect is significant. Using the coefficient of mangroves from Table 8.4, we calculated the number of fully collapsed houses for the sample 1 area if the district had no mangroves before the cyclone and the number of averted fully collapsed houses came out to be 20,007. This area witnessed 118,323 fully collapsed houses during the cyclone, which without mangroves would have been 138,330. The cost of repairing a fully collapsed house being Rs.53,800 at 1999 prices (price quoted by HUDCO for constructing a one-room dwelling unit in rural Orissa), the value of damages averted by mangroves in the form of fully collapsed houses comes out to be Rs.1,076,376,600 ($25,628,014) at 1999 prices for Kendrapada district.

8.7 Conclusion

This chapter analyzed the storm protection services of mangrove forests of Orissa using village- and gram panchayat-level data on fully collapsed houses in the Kendrapada district of the state. An inter-disciplinary methodology was used to analyze the data and different variables were used to control for the cyclone intensity and physical features, as well as the socio-economic features of the study area. Mangrove forests were found to have significantly reduced the number of fully collapsed houses in areas lying on the leeward side of the forest. In the absence of mangroves another 20,007 houses would have fully collapsed in these areas, increasing the number of fully collapsed houses to 138,330 from 118,323, the number actually witnessed.

Acknowledgments

Data used for the chapter was collected for the South Asian Network for Development and Environmental Economics (SANDEE) project, "Economic Valuation of Storm Protection Function: An analysis of Super Cyclone of 1999 in Orissa". Financial and academic support from SANDEE is very sincerely acknowledged. I am grateful to Priya Shyamsunder, Kanchan Chopra, Enamul Haque, M.N. Murthy, Jeff Vincent and other SANDEE colleagues for their useful ideas, suggestions and comments. I would like to thank the Emergency Officer and staff of the emergency offices and Tahasildar offices of Kendrapada and Jagatsinghpur districts of Orissa for their varied support. I also sincerely acknowledge the infrastructure and academic facilities received from the Institute of Economic Growth., Delhi.

Notes

1 A few patches of casuarinas plantation were also present in the coastal areas before the cyclone, but the width of these plantations everywhere was 200–400 m and the main forests were the mangroves.
2 District Statistical Handbook (2001), Kendrapada (Directorate of Economics and Statistics, Bhubaneswar, Orissa).
3 The survey, *Forest Survey of India*, was carried out by the Ministry of Environment and Forest.
4 In the present methodology, the cyclone type is ignored as the data used is for a single super cyclone.
5 Flooding due to torrential rain as a cause of damage has been ignored here, as in the study area it rained almost the same amount everywhere and there were not much spatial differences in rainfall over the locations. Getting village-specific rainfall data was also difficult. Moreover, as the variation in rainfall is expected to be correlated with distance from coast and distance from cyclone path, we have implicitly controlled for it by including these variables in the model.
6 Different variables used in the methodology section are all explained Table 8.1.
7 Radial wind is wind velocity at different horizontal distances from the center of the eye of the storm (the cyclone path in the present case) and is dependant on the maximum wind at the cyclone eye wall.
8 Maximum wind is the wind speed at the eye wall region of the cyclone.
9 The present mangrove forests, as mentioned earlier, are in nearly uniform health.
10 The entire coastline of the study area was planted with casuarinas trees after a very severe cyclonic storm hit the area in 1972. Casuarinas grow on sandy beaches and on sand dunes that are more elevated than the areas where mangroves grow, and don't get inundated during high tides. The study area being mostly swampy and low-lying,

casuarinas could survive only in some limited pockets and whenever they survived, the width of the forest is nearly uniform (0.2–0.4 km). Hence, the casuarinas dummy was used to capture the effect of the casuarinas vegetation as well as the special topography of the casuarinas forest area.

11 During a cyclone, storm waves also play a critical role in bringing damage near to the shore area. However, there being some proportional relation between storm waves and surge height, the surge height is likely to capture the storm wave's effect also.

12 Probably because of the random clearing of the mangroves in the study area (some areas witnessing complete destruction of the forest and some with marginal increase in forest cover compared to the past), mangrove vegetation present and the width of the mangrove habitat were not found to be highly correlated.

13 A wealthy household has a good-quality house, vehicle to escape, a transistor or television set to listen to cyclone warnings. Also, some members being educated, they are quick to react to cyclone warnings, etc. In contrast, a poor household has bad-quality houses, their houses are likely to be in low-lying, vulnerable areas. The members are uneducated and less informed, have no vehicle to escape, have poor health, etc., because of which they are more likely to die and suffer more loss than the well-off people.

14 In the absence of data on availability of mass media (TV, radio) at the village level, the percentage of other workers (*otworkers*) that include people with high education, high mobility and in occupations other than agriculture and household industries (doctors, teachers, engineers, barbers, washer men, priests, etc.) are taken as proxies for availability of this commodity.

15 Factors like time and season of occurrence of the cyclone, number of hours before the landfall when the cyclone warning was broadcast, etc. have been ignored as the analysis is for the damage data of a single cyclone.

16 The cyclone was an extremely slow moving one with an average speed of 22–25 kmh^{-1}. It moved northwest after landfall and then lay centered over the Garadpur tahasil of Kendrapada (the center of a triangle formed by joining Kendrapada, Paradeep and Jagatsinghpur) for three hours before moving in southwest away from Kendrapada district. It then lay centered near Bhubaneswar, the state capital, for nearly 35 hours (IMD, 2000; Gupta and Sharma, 2000).

17 The wind velocity or V_{max} was 190.1622 kmh^{-1} in the cyclone eye area (Equation 4) and less in the outer eye area.

18 Three alternative measures of flooding due to storm surge were also tried to see if it brings any change in the results. The alternative measures were:

> Flooding 1 = *surge* × *exp*(−*dcoast*),
> Flooding 2 = *surge*/*dcoast*,
> Flooding 3 = *surge* + a *dcoast* − b (*dcoast*)^2.

Only the use of flooding 1 in place of *surge* gave better results and expected signs of the coefficients, but we don't report these results as flooding 1 is crudely defined.

19 This study analyzes only the village level or the rural household data.

20 To have a dataset with uniform units, we tried to group the villages according to the gram panchayats they belonged to, but the number of observations reduced to 132 for sample 1 and to 89 for sample 2. Many villages had to be dropped as we didn't have data for other villages belonging to that gram panchayat. Regression results with only 132 and 89 observations did give similar results as the larger dataset, but the level of significance was comparatively lower. The coefficient of the mangrove variable was significant for both the samples (−56.87* and −71.26**). However, results for sample 3 and 4 could not be tried due to very few observations. Hence, in spite of the heteroskedasticity problem, the larger dataset was used.

21 The primary census abstract (the source used for population statistics) gives both total

male and female population as well as those less than six years old. Accordingly, *Male99* is the male population in the 6+ age group.

22 The correlation coefficient between *velocitypow* and *velocityexp* measures are 0.95 (sample 1), 0.95 (sample 2), 0.94 (sample 3) and 0.95 (sample 4).

23 Elasticity is calculated by the formulae $\partial \log y / \partial \log x_i$, where y is the dependant variable and x_i is the ith independent variable. In a linear model it equates to the estimated coefficient of th ith variable times the ratio of the average value of the ith variable to that of the dependent variable.

References

Badola, Ruchi and S.A. Hussain, "Valuing ecosystem functions: an empirical study on the storm protection function of Bhitarkanika mangrove ecosystem, India", *Environmental Conservation*, 32 (2005), 1–8.

Baird, Andrew H., "Tsunamis: myth of green belts", SAMUDRA Report No. 44, 14–19 July 2006.

Barbier, Edward B., "Valuing ecosystem services as productive inputs", *Economic Policy*, 22 (49) (2007), 177–229.

Basu, B.K. and S.K. Ghosh, "A model of surface wind field in a tropical cyclone over Indian seas", *Mausam*, 35 (1987), 183–522.

Bretschneider, C.L. and P.G. Wybro, "Tsunami inundation prediction", in C.L. Bretschbeider (ed.), *Proceedings of the 15th Coastal Engineering Conference*, 1006–1024, (New York: American Society of Civil Engineers, 1977).

Chan, H.T., J.E. Ong, W.K. Gong and A. Sasekumar, "The socio-economic, ecological and environmental values of mangrove ecosystems in Malaysia and their present state of conservation", in B.F. Clough (ed.), *The Economic and Environmental Values of Mangrove Forests and Their Present State of Conservation in South-East Asia/Pacific Region*, 41–81 (Okinawa, Japan: International Society for Mangrove Ecosystems, International Tropical Timber Organization and Japan International Association For Mangroves, 1993).

Chatenoux, B. and P. Peduzzi, "Analysis of the role of bathymetry and other environmental parameters in the impacts from the 2004 Indian Ocean tsunami", UNEP/DEWA/GRID Europe, (2006). Available at: www.grid.unep.ch/product/publication/download/environment_impacts_tsunami.pdf.

Chatenoux, B. and P. Peduzzi, "Impacts from the 2004 Indian Ocean tsunami: analyzing the potential protecting role of environmental features", *Natural Hazards*, 40 (2007), 289–304.

Cochard, R., S.L. Ranamukhaarachchi, G.P. Shivakoti, O.V. Shipin, P.J. Edwards and K.T. Seeland, "The 2004 tsunami in Aceh and Southern Thailand: a review on coastal ecosystems, wave hazards and vulnerability", *Perspectives in Plant Ecology, Evolution and Systematics*, 10 (2008), 3–40.

Costanza, R., R. d'Arge, R. de Groot, S. Farber, M. Grasso, B. Hannon, S. Naeem, K. Limburg, J. Paruelo, R.V. O'Neill, R. Raskin, P. Sutton and M. van den Belt, "The value of the world's ecosystem services and natural capital", *Nature*, 387 (1997), 253–260.

Costanza, R., S. Farber and J. Maxwell, "Valuation and management of wetland ecosystem", *Ecological Economics*, 1 (1989), 335–361.

Costanza, R., O. Pérez-Maqueo, M.L. Martinez, P. Sutton, S.J. Anderson and K. Mulder, "The value of coastal wetlands for hurricane protection", *Ambio* 37 (2008), 241–248.

Dahdouh-Guebas, F. and Koedam Nico, "Coastal vegetation and Asian tsunami", *Science*, 311 (2006), 37.

Dahdouh-Guebas, F., L.P. Jayatisa, D. Di Nitto, J.O. Bosire, D. Lo Seen and N. Koedam, "How effective were mangroves as a defense against the recent tsunami?" *Current Biology*, 15 (2005), R443–R447.

Danielson, F., M.K. Sorensen, M.F. Olwig, V. Selvam, F. Parish, N.D. Burgess, T. Hiralshi, V.M. Karunagaran, M.S. Rasmussen, L.B. Hansen, A. Quarto and N. Suryadiputra, "The Asian tsunami: a protective role for coastal vegetation", *Science* 310 (2005), 643.

Das, P.K., M.C. Sihna and V. Balasuburamanyam, "Storm surges in Bay of Bengal", *Quarterly Journal of Meteorological Society*, 100 (425) (1974): 437–449.

Das, Saudamini, "Storm protection values of mangroves in coastal Orissa", in P. Kumar and B. Sudhakara Reddy (eds), *Ecology and Human Well-Being*, 197–212 (New Delhi: Sage Publications, 2007).

Depperman, C.E., "Notes on the origin and structure of Philippine typhoons", *Bulletin of American Meteorological Society*, 28 (1947), 391–406.

Dixon, John A. *et al.*, *Economic Analysis of Environmental Impacts*, 2nd edn (London: Earthscan Publication in Association with the Asian Development Bank and the World Bank, 1994).

Dube, S.K., P.C. Sihna and A.D. Rao, "The response of different wind stress forcing on the surge along the east coast of India", *Mausam*, 32 (1981), 315–320.

FAO, "Reducing agricultural vulnerability to storm related disasters", COAG 01/6, FAO Corporate Document Repository, Annexure, XI, APDC/01/7 (2000).

FAO, "Coastal protection in the aftermath of the Indian Ocean tsunami: what role for forests and trees?" Concept Note, Conclusion and Policy Recommendation, Regional Technical Workshop, Khao Lak, Thailand, 28–31 August 2006.

Farber, S., "The value of coastal wetlands for protection of property against hurricane wind damage", *Journal of Environmental Economics and Management*, 14 (1987), 143–151.

Fosberg, F.R., "Mangroves verses tidal waves", *Biological Conservation*, 4 (1971), 38–39.

Gupta, M.C. and V.K. Sharma, *Orissa Super Cyclone, 99* (New Delhi: New United Press, 2000).

Human Development Report. Prepared by Nabakrushna Choudhury Centre for Development Studies, Planning and Co-ordination Department, Government of Orissa, Bhubaneswar (2004).

Holland, G.H., "An analytical model of tropical and pressure profiles in hurricanes", *Monthly Weather Review*, 108 (1980), 1212–1218.

IMD, *Tracks of Cyclones in Bay of Bengal and Arabian Sea, 1890–1990* (Indian Meteorological Department, Government of India, 2000).

IMD, *Damage Potential of Tropical Cyclones* (Indian Meteorological Department, Government of India, 2002).

International Federation of Red Cross and Red Crescent News, 19 June 2002.

Jalesnianski, C.P., "A numerical calculation of storm tides induced by a tropical storm impinging on a continental shelf", *Monthly Weather Review*, 93 (1965), 345–358.

Jalesnianski, C.P. and A.D. Taylor, "NOAA Technical Memorandum", ERLWMPO, 3 (1973), 33pp.

Kalsi, S.R., N. Jayanthi and S.K. Roy Bhowmik, *A Review of Different Storm Surge Models and Estimated Storm Surge Height in Respect of Orissa Supercyclonic Storm Of 29 October, 1999* (Indian Meteorological Department, Government of India, 2004).

Kalsi, S.R., S.D. Kotal and S.K. Roy Bhowmick, "Decaying nature of super cyclone of Orissa after landfall", *Mausam*, 54 (2) (2003), 393–396.

Kaplan, J. and M. Demaria, "A simple empirical model for predicting the decay of tropical cyclone wind speed after land-fall," *Journal of Applied Meteorology*, 34 (1995), 2499–2512.

Kathiresan, K. and Rajendran, N., "Coastal mangrove forest mitigate tsunami", *Estuarine, Coastal and Shelf Sciences*, 65 (2005), 601–606.

Kerr, A.M., A.H. Baird and S.J. Camphell, "Comments on coastal mangrove forest mitigate tsunami by K. Kathiresan and N. Rajendran", *Estuarine, Coastal and Shelf Sciences*, 67 (2006), 539–541.

Massel, S.R., K. Furukawa, R.M. Brinkman, "Surface wave propagation in mangrove forests", *Fluid Dynamics Research*, 24 (1999), 219–249.

Mazda, Y., M. Magi, Y. Ikeda, T. Kurokawa and T. Asano, "Wave reduction in a mangrove forest dominated by Sonneratia Sp.", *Wetlands Ecology and Management*, 14 (2006), 365–378.

Mazda, Y., M. Magi, M. Kogo and P.N. Hong, "Mangroves as a coastal protection from waves in the Tong King Delta, Vietnam", *Mangroves and Salt Marshes*, 1 (1997), 127–135.

MEA (Millennium Ecosystem Assessment), *Ecosystems and Human Well-being: A Framework for Assessment* (Washington, DC: Island Press, 2003).

Ministry of Environment and Forest, Government of India, *Forest Survey of India* (Dehradun, 2001).

Orissa District Gazetteer, *Cuttuck* (The Gazetteers Unit, Department of Revenue, Bhubaneswar, Government of Orissa, 1996).

Ranjit Daniels, R.J. "The Mangroves' last stand", in background material compiled by Care Earth, Chenai for Pre-Conference Workshop on Ecosystem Services in Coastal and Marine Systems, organized by the Indian Society for Ecological Economics, 2 June 2005, Mumbai, India.

Roy Abraham, K., U.C. Mohanty and S.K. Dash, "Simulation of cyclones using synthetic data", *Proceedings of the Indian Academy of Sciences, Earth and Planetary Sciences*, 104 (4) (1995), 635–666.

Sathirathai, Suthawan, "Economic valuation of mangroves and the role of local communities in the conservation of natural resources: a case study of Surat Thani, south of Thailand", EEPSEA Research Report (1998).

Singh, Charan and B.K. Bandyopadhyay, "Decaying characteristics of severe cyclonic storms after landfall over east coast of India," *Mausam*, 2 (2004), 395–400.

Tri, N.H., N. Adger, M. Kelly, S. Granich and N.H. Nimh, "The role of natural resource management in mitigating climate impact: mangrove restoration in Vietnam", Center for Social and Economic Research on Global Environment Working Paper, GEC 96-06 (1996).

Tynkkonen, O., "Orissa cyclone: a natural phenomenon or a sign of things to come?", Report of Friends of Earth (Finland, 2000).

UNEP, "After the tsunami: rapid environmental assessment", Report of UNEP Asian Tsunami Task Force (2005).

Vermaat, J.E. and U. Thampanya, "Mangroves mitigate tsunami damage: a further response", *Estuarine, Coastal and Shelf Sciences*, 69 (2006), 1–3.

Vermaat, J.E. and U. Thampanya, "Erratum to 'Mangroves mitigate tsunami damage: a further response'", *Estuarine, Coastal and Shelf Sciences*, 75 (2007), 564.

9 European forests and carbon sequestration services

An economic assessment of climate change impacts

Helen Ding, Paulo A.L.D. Nunes and Sonja Teelucksingh

9.1 Introduction

It has been proven that climate change has significant impacts on the natural environment and human health (MEA, 2005). This, in turn, has led to an increasing number of scientific studies focusing on the mapping and identification of the scale of climate change impacts on ecosystem performance and the respective provisioning of ecosystem goods and services. More recently, accompanying studies on the assessment of the role of ecosystems with respect to their contribution to the economy and human well-being were made well known by the Millennium Ecosystem Assessment (MEA). However, to the authors' knowledge, few studies have put an emphasis on the estimation of human welfare losses related to climate-driven changes of biodiversity and ecosystem services. In fact, the costs of climate change impacts on biodiversity are not well mapped due to the complex (and not fully understood) interactions between climate change, ecosystems and the respective impacts on human well-being (both in utility and productivity/employment terms). For this reason, the present chapter attempts to contribute to this line of research by undertaking an empirical valuation of the European forest ecosystems, addressing the role of biodiversity as 'the foundation of the vast array of ecosystem services that critically contribute to human well-being' (MEA: 18). More specifically, we propose a three-step approach to valuing climate change impacts on biodiversity and forest ecosystems. The first step is the characterization of the climate role in the creation of relevant forest ecosystem services. The second step is the calculation of the reduced quantity and quality of these ecosystem services that result in a loss to human welfare under alternative IPCC scenarios. The third step is the (monetary) valuation of that loss.

We begin the analysis with a conceptual DPSIR (OECD, 1999) framework that has been applied to the capture of the causal relationship between climate change, biodiversity, forest ecosystems and human well-being (see Figure 9.1). Scientific evidence has demonstrated that climate change is one of the main drivers that directly alter ecosystem functioning and cause biodiversity loss. The shift of climate conditions can change species distribution, population sizes, the timing of reproduction or migration events, and can increase the frequency of pest and disease outbreaks (MEA, 2005: 10). As a consequence, increases in global temperature and greenhouse gas concentrations may be detrimental to the health of forest ecosystems and, ultimately, human well-being, both through the disturbance of existing biodiversity and through a negative influence on the ability of an ecosystem to deliver goods and services. These damages are directly caused by climate change, and are therefore associated with particular costs to human society. Yet it is important to note that forest ecosystems also cause feedback effects in climate change due to their important contribution to the stock of CO_2 emissions. These are important benefits that ecosystems provide to society. Therefore, monetizing the respective costs and benefits associated with climate change impacts on ecosystems has practical sense in guiding cost-effective climate change policy. Finally, while mitigation and adaptation policy measures can reduce losses – which are translated to a welfare gain – the policies themselves also imply economic costs. Therefore, both costs and benefits need to be considered in the specific valuation strategies.

Following these steps, the chapter is organized as follows. Section 9.2 presents a systematic overview of the current European forest ecosystem and its interaction with climate change impact through a new geo-climatic lens. Section 9.3 discusses the assessment of climate change impacts on forest regulating services using an ecosystem-based valuation approach, which we adopt as the

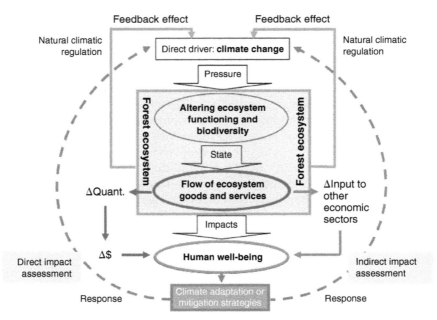

Figure 9.1 A conceptual model for climate change, forest biodiversity and human well-being interactions.

cornerstone of the present valuation exercise. Section 9.4 presents the economic valuation exercise, and corresponding monetary estimation results of forest sequestration services in the context of climate change. Section 9.5 concludes.

9.2 An overview of the regulating services of European forests

9.2.1 A geo-climatic map of European forests

This study covers 34 European countries[1] previously classified as *Western Europe* and *Eastern Europe* sub-regions in the *European Forest Sector Outlook Study 1960–2000–2020 Main Report* (UNECE/FAO, 2005). We regroup these countries into four geo-climatic groups in order to address the spatial effects of climate change impacts:

1   Mediterranean Europe (latitude N35–45°);
2   Central-Northern Europe (latitude N45–55°);
3   Northern Europe (latitude N55–65°); and
4   Scandinavian Europe (latitude N65–71°). The new geographical groupings are presented in Table 9.1.

We adopt this grouping on the basis of the assumption that each country's particular forest types are closely determined by the specific climate conditions. We are therefore able to identify the predominant tree species as well as the respective contributions to the local economy at both the national and the larger

Table 9.1 Geographical groupings of the 34 European countries

Geographical groupings	Latitude classification	Countries included
Mediterranean Europe	Latitude N35–45°	Greece, Italy, Portugal, Spain, Albania, Bosnia and Herzegovina, Bulgaria, Serbia and Montenegro, Turkey, TFYR Macedonia
Central-Northern Europe	Latitude N45–55°	Austria, Belgium, France, Germany, Ireland, Luxembourg, Netherlands, Switzerland, Croatia, Czech Republic, Hungary, Poland, Romania, Slovakia, Slovenia
Northern Europe	Latitude N55–65°	Denmark, United Kingdom, Estonia, Latvia, Lithuania
Scandinavian Europe	Latitude N65–71°	Finland, Iceland, Norway, Sweden

regional scales. From an ecological viewpoint, different tree species can play different roles in ecosystem regulation and life-supporting functions, which will ultimately influence the provision of forest ecosystem goods and services. Alternatively, from an economic perspective, different tree species may deliver very different flows of ecosystem goods and services in terms of economic importance and related welfare impacts. Finally, from a geo-climatic perspective, this classification may also allow us to explore the sensitivity of different tree species to climate changes, in particular to increases in temperature and precipitation rates in the countries under consideration.

Forest areas and forest type distributions

Data collected from the Food and Agriculture Organization (FAO) show a total forest coverage of 185 million hectares over the selected 34 European countries, accounting for about 32.7 per cent of the territory (FAO, 2005) (see Table 9.8 in the Appendix for more information). If we divide the forest areas by latitudes, we observe an uneven distribution of forest types across the four classified geo-climatic regions of Europe, as shown in Table 9.2. In Mediterranean Europe, most of the forests are coniferous and broadleaved evergreen, which account for 30 per cent of the total forest area in the region. The Central-Northern and Northern European regions are home to most of the temperate forests, which account for 35 per cent and 19 per cent of the total forests, respectively. Finally, in Scandinavian Europe, forest area accounts for the remaining 16 per cent of total forest, in which the predominant forest biomes are mainly boreal.

Due to the diverse climatic conditions across latitudes, species diversity and dynamics of forest ecosystems differ considerably throughout Europe, as reflected in the numbers and composition of tree species. For example, the Ministerial Conference on the Protection of Forests in Europe (MCPFE) (2007) reported that approximately 70 per cent of the forests in Europe are dominated by mixed forest consisting of two or several tree species, with the remaining 30 per cent dominated mainly by conifers. In addition to the natural conditions, forest species compositions of the current European forest structures have been heavily influenced by anthropogenic interventions such as past land use and management (Ellenberg, 1986). In particular, the forest protective management strategy in Europe has resulted in a 1.0-per cent annual expansion in the area of

Table 9.2 Distribution of forest ecosystems in Europe

Geographical groupings	Latitude classification	Major forest types
Mediterranean Europe	Latitude N35–45°	Coniferous and broadleaved evergreen forests
Central-Northern Europe	Latitude N45–55°	Temperate forests
Northern Europe	Latitude N55–65°	Temperate forests
Scandinavian Europe	Latitude N65–71°	Boreal forests

mixed forests over the last 15-year period (MCPFE, 2007). This may be partly due to the widely acknowledged scientific evidence that mixed forests composed of several tree species are usually richer in biodiversity than forests dominated by one tree species.

Climate change and European forests

With respect to the sensitivity of tree species to temperature changes, this has been studied in terms of specific forest types located in different geo-climatic regions of Europe. In Mediterranean Europe, most forests consist of *sclerophyllous* and some deciduous species that are adapted to soil water deficits experienced in the summer. Temperature changes may allow the expansion of some *thermophilous* tree species (e.g. *quercus pyrenaica*) when water availability is sufficient (IPCC, 2001). Similarly, Garcia-Gonzalo *et al.* (2007) find that in Scandinavian Europe, where growth of boreal forests is currently limited by a short growing season, low summer temperature and short supply of nitrogen, climate change can be associated with an increase in forest productivity in terms of carbon stock. This is because an increase in temperature can prolong the growing season, enhance the decomposition of organic matter in the soil and thus increase the supply of nitrogen. In turn, these changes may have positive impacts on forest growth, timber yield and the accumulation of carbon in the boreal forests (Melillo *et al.*, 1993; Lloyd and Taylor, 1994; Giardina and Ryan, 2000; Jarvis and Linder, 2000; Luo *et al.*, 2001).

9.2.2 Defining forest regulating services

A concise mapping of ecosystem goods and services (EGS) is the basis of high-quality ecosystem assessment studies. For this reason, we adopt the MEA approach (MEA, 2003), which provides a practical, tractable and sufficiently flexible classification for the categorization of the various types of EGS. In this context, all EGS can be generally classified into four main categories: provisioning, regulating, cultural and supporting services (see Table 9.3).

Table 9.3 A general classification of ecosystem goods and services for European forests

Types of ecosystem services		Examples
Supporting services	Provisioning services	Food, fibre (e.g. timber, wood fuel), ornamental resources.
	Regulating services	Climate regulation, water regulation, erosion regulation
	Cultural services	Recreation and ecotourism, aesthetic values, spiritual and religious values, cultural heritage values

Source: adapted from MEA 2003.

According to the MEA, products obtained from ecosystems are defined as provisioning services. These include food, fiber, fresh water and genetic resources. Cultural services are the non-material benefits obtained from ecosystems through aesthetic experience, reflection, recreation and spiritual enrichment. Regulating services include benefits obtained from the regulation of ecosystem processes, including air-quality regulation, climate regulation, water regulation, erosion regulation, pollination and natural hazard regulation. Supporting services are those that are necessary for the production of all other ecosystem services, such as soil formation, photosynthesis, primary production, nutrient cycling and provisioning of habitat (MEA, 2003). The present chapter focuses on the economic valuation of European forests in terms of carbon regulating services. In particular, the valuation exercise will assess the magnitude of these services as carbon sinks. The methodologies adopted shall be discussed and elaborated in the following section.

9.3 An ecosystem-based economic valuation of global climate change

9.3.1 Climate change and the IPCC storylines

Over the last 30 years, the world has experienced significant temperature increases, particularly in the northern high latitudes (IPCC, 2001). The research results of the IPCC show that the average temperature in Europe will increase from 2.1°C to 4.4°C by 2050, varying across latitudes, with the strongest warming consistently in the higher latitudes. In addition, model simulations also suggest a decrease in precipitation in the south of Europe, particularly in the summer, and an increase in precipitation over much of northern Europe (Schröter *et al.*, 2005). In order to quantify the climate change impacts on forest ecosystems, both quantitative and qualitative data are needed to describe the ability of the ecosystems to provide the necessary goods and services, both in the present time period and in future scenarios of climate change. Moreover, to specify these scenarios, we adopt the four major storylines that are developed by the IPCC, coupling the global circulation models (e.g HadCM3[2]) with socio-economic storylines (Nakicenovic and Swart, 2000; Schröter *et al.*, 2004; Schröter *et al.*, 2005). This enables us to describe the change in flows of ecosystem services under future states of the world or scenarios.

A special report published by the IPCC in 2000 provided a narrative description of four alternative futures, each associated with specific attributes in terms of population growth, CO_2 concentration, degree of temperature changes and change of precipitation. These attributes are the major elements driving future climate changes (Nakicenovic and Swart, 2000) – see a synthesis in Table 9.4.

More importantly, efforts have been made towards the development of a general circulation model – HadCM3 – so as to directly relate socio-economic changes to both climatic changes and land-use changes through climatic drivers (Schröter *et al.*, 2004). As a consequence, the IPCC presents four brief 'future

Table 9.4 The specifications of the four IPCC storylines

Indicator	Climatic model – HadCM3 (scenarios by 2050)			
	Storyline A1FI	Storyline A2	Storyline B1	Storyline B2
Population (10^6)	376	419	376	398
CO_2 concentration (ppm)	779	709	518	567
Δ Temperature (°C)	4.4	2.8	3.1	2.1
Δ Precipitation Europe (%)	−0.5	0.5	4.8	2.7
Socio-economic dimensions	High savings and high rate of investments and innovation	Uneven economic growth, high per capita income	High investment in resource efficiency	Human welfare, equality, and environmental protection

Source: Schröter *et al.*, 2005; IPCC, 2001.

stories' that differ in economic, technical, environmental and social dimensions (Nakicenovic and Swart, 2000). According to the IPCC specifications, A1FI, A2, B1 and B2 storylines are distinguished in terms of four future development paths, i.e. 'global economic' oriented, 'regional economic' oriented, 'global environmental' oriented and 'regional environmental' oriented, respectively. The two economic-oriented scenarios (A1FI and A2) focus on 'material consumption', but A1 scenarios also consider different combinations of fuel, expressed as A1FI. The two environmental-oriented scenarios (B1 and B2) mainly concentrate on the concepts of 'sustainability, equity and environment'. It is important to point out that, among all others, the storyline A2 describes a very heterogeneous world that is characterized by high population growth, regional-oriented economic development and fragmented and slow per capita economic growth and technological changes (in fact mirroring current socio-economic development patterns). For this reason, A2 is frequently used by the European Commission as the baseline scenario, with the remaining scenario analyses conducted relative to this storyline. In particular, our focus is mainly on the comparison of A1 versus A2, in an assessment of the movement to a more economically focused world. Alternatively, we may also consider B1 and B2 versus A2, in an assessment of the movement to a more sustainability-oriented world.

9.3.2 Estimation of the physical changes of ecosystem services due to climate change

As previously discussed, climate plays a significant role in influencing the provision of forest carbon sequestration services. The magnitude of the impact is, however, dependent upon the forest type, as well its distribution across Europe. We shall quantify the potential reduction of carbon stocked in European forests under possible climate change scenarios proposed by the IPCC. It is important to note that our work heavily relies on the previous research results derived from the Advanced Terrestrial Ecosystem Analysis and Modelling (ATEAM) project[3] in terms of its projections of quantitative changes in both forest area and carbon stocks due to climate change. This project provided percentage changes of forest area and stocked carbon for each of the EU-17 countries under four IPCC storylines. For the remaining 17 countries of interest, the changes of forest areas and carbon stocks in the future climate change scenarios are calculated based on the results delivered by an IMAGE 2.2 program (IMAGE, 2001). The projection delivers point estimates for the years 2005 and 2050.

Changes in forest area

In the A1FI and A2 scenarios, forest areas decrease by approximately 21 per cent and 9 per cent by 2050, respectively (see Table 9.8 in the Appendix for more details). The A1FI scenario shows the strongest impact due both to the more severe climate change assumption (Δ temperature of 4.4°C) as well as the no-migration assumption (Thuiller *et al.*, 2005). By contrast, scenarios B1 and B2 demonstrate 6 per cent and 10 per cent increases in forest area, respectively. The higher increasing rate of forest area in the B2 scenario may benefit from both a hypothetical aforestation as well as an assumed higher level of precipitation (Schröter *et al.*, 2005). In addition, we can also observe a significant spatial effect of climate change impacts on the forest land-use pattern across latitudes. For example, Mediterranean Europe (N35–45°) is facing a general negative forest growth in scenario A1FI and A2, but a significant expansion in scenario B1 and B2. Central-Northern Europe (N45–55°) and Northern Europe (N55–65°) regions face negative growth only in the A1FI scenario, in correspondence with the more severe climatic conditions. One should note that the projections for these regions in the A2 scenario are also embedded in a historical trend of forest area increases. Finally, Scandinavian Europe (N+65°) always experiences a decrease in forest growth, which implies a shrinking forest extension under both current conditions and future scenarios.

Changes of carbon stock

The carbon cycle connects forests and climate change. The total carbon stored in forests has a very important role in determining any climate stabilization path. In fact, the quantity of carbon stocked in tree biomass approximately corresponds to 77 per cent of the carbon contained in the global vegetation, while forest soil stores 42 per cent of the global 1 m-top-soil carbon (Bolin *et al.*, 2000). Forests exchange large quantities of carbon in photosynthesis and respiration, contributing to the global carbon cycle as a source of carbon when they are disturbed, and as a sink when in recovery and regrowth after disturbances. In turn, climate change may also influence the future carbon-storage capacity of forest ecosystems. We therefore construct projections for carbon sequestration in forests for all the European countries across the four IPCC storylines (see Table 9.9 in the

Appendix for more details). Our findings show that the average carbon stock tends to increase in all scenarios, but the respective magnitudes differ. For example, in the A1FI scenario, representing a world oriented towards 'global economic' growth together with the highest CO_2 concentration and temperature, the total carbon sequestrated by forests appears to be the lowest. This result is consistent with results reported by Schröter *et al.* (2005), who highlighted that for most ecosystem services the A1FI produces the strongest negative impacts. On the other hand, B-type storylines, which are sustainable development oriented, contribute to an increase in forest area and a consequently large quantity of carbon stock. These figures, in turn, will be the basis of the economic valuation exercise, which shall be discussed in detail in the following sub-section.

9.3.3 The monetization of climate change impacts: the application of a hybrid economic valuation method

In the context of the MEA classification of provisioning, regulating and cultural ecosystem goods and services (see Table 9.3), it is not difficult to agree that no single valuation method will deliver a full range of the forest value components under consideration. A flexible, systematic and integrated straightforward approach is therefore needed to estimate the costs of climate change through each of the value components. In Figure 9.2, we summarize all valuation techniques, both market and non-market, used for the assessment of the value of forest ecosystem goods and services. These include market price analysis methods, cost assessment methods and valuation methods based on meta-analysis. These techniques are most appropriately applied in the context of

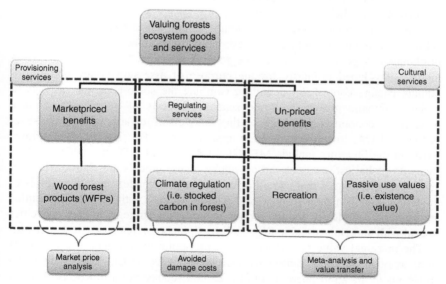

Figure 9.2 A hybrid economic valuation methodology.

regional- or national-scale climate change impacts, disaggregated by sector or market. In the present chapter, we shall focus on the monetary value assessment of forest regulating services.

9.4 Economic valuation of stocked carbon in European forests under future IPCC scenarios

9.4.1 The Integrated Assessment Models and the marginal value of carbon

Despite significant scientific investigation, the economics of climate change is still not well understood due to the high uncertainties of climate change impacts in the long run (Kelly and Kolstad, 1999). More ambitious and controversial approaches of cost–benefit analysis require additional information about the monetized value of climate impacts, which is necessary to calculate the 'optimal' policy, or to determine whether a particular policy is 'worthwhile' (Ackerman and Finlayson, 2005). Moreover, another major drawback of the existing literature on climate change impacts is that most of the impact studies take a static approach (Tol, 2002a; Watson *et al.*, 1996; Pearce *et al.*, 1996; Tol *et al.*, 2000), whereas climate change is rather a long-term dynamic process, involving the complexity of interface between physical and economic dynamics, such as increasing CO_2 concentration, growing world population and economy, and evolving technologies and institutions (Tol, 2002b). More precisely, the consequences of climate instability and rapid large-scale shifts in global climate may interfere with the economic production function in many sectors (e.g. forestry and tourism), whereas socio-economic development is always the embedded driving force behind climate change.

The current literature provides a significant amount of research on the application of economic modelling to the estimation of socio-economic damage costs of climate change, also known as Integrated Assessment Models (IAMs). These models, developed primarily for the purpose of assessing policy options for climate change control, by definition combine the socio-economic aspects of global economic growth with the scientific aspects of geophysical climate dynamics. Economists have been putting more effort towards moving the state-of-the-art IAMs towards a dynamic approach (e.g. Tol, 2002b). Well-known IAMs in the literature include MERGE,[4] IMAGE,[5] FUND[6] and DICE,[7] with a focus on global estimates of carbon stocks. These models are characterized by significant differences that can all affect the final estimates, including levels of modelling detail in their respective capacities to deal with climate–economic–atmospheric complexity and the economic modelling strategy, in their capacities to deal with uncertainty and in their abilities to incorporate economic responses.

The marginal value of carbon storage or carbon price refers to the benefits from avoided damages caused by incremental CO_2 or CO_2-equivalent GHG emissions in the atmosphere due to the carbon sequestration functions of forest ecosystems. The avoided damage costs assessment method has been widely used in the literature (Cline, 1992; Nordhaus, 1993a, 1993b; Merlo and Croitoru, 2005; CASES, 2008) to indirectly calculate the benefits from carbon sequestrated in forests. While it is important to note that the concept is different from the market price of carbon (obtained via the emission trading scheme) and the marginal abatement cost (which involves the costs of technological R&D for facilitating the emission abatement), under certain restrictive assumptions the three measures would be broadly equal (DEFRA, 2007). The estimation of carbon price in our chapter is built on an existing project, 'Cost Assessment for Sustainable Energy Systems' (CASES),[8] a worldwide study funded by the EU. One of the main features of CASES is that it is built upon the IAMs, to estimate the cost of GHG emissions under different energy evolution paths in 2020, 2030 and 2050. The CASES study adopted the estimates of the UK Department for Environment, Food and Rural Affairs (DEFRA) (2005) with respect to the social costs of carbon. As a consequence, the CASES project was able to obtain three levels of estimates of marginal damage costs, i.e. lower, upper and central estimates,[9] respectively. For example, as reported in the CASES final report, the lower estimates of marginal damage costs range from €4/tCO$_2$ in 2000 to €8/tCO$_2$ in 2030; the upper estimates range from €53/tCO$_2$ in 2000 to €110/tCO$_2$ in 2030; and the central estimate ranges from €23/tCO$_2$ in 2000 to €41/tCO$_2$ in 2030.

In the present chapter, we adopt the CASES central estimate and calculate the respective economic values in 2050. The future values are then converted to 2005US$ using Purchasing Power Parity (PPP) and the necessary time adjustments. Final economic valuation results are presented and discussed in the following sub-section.

9.4.2 Estimation results

Table 9.5 presents the economic valuation of stocked carbon in European forests under future IPCC scenarios. These estimation results depend not only on the IPCC scenarios under consideration, but also on the European geographical areas under consideration. For example, the forests in Central-Northern Europe contribute to the largest portion of benefits from the carbon regulating services in Europe, but this result depends both on acreage and the type of forests present.

Table 9.5 Projection of total benefits of carbon storage in European forests (million $, 2005)

Scenario	Mediterranean Europe	Central-Northern Europe	Northern Europe	Scandinavian Europe	Europe
A1 2050	37,176	117,241	11,489	32,817	198,722
A2 2050	45,790	159,453	17,362	32,605	255,210
B1 2050	66,575	190,755	22,679	46,310	326,320
B2 2050	63,609	190,341	23,546	35,733	313,229

In addition, the productivity value of climate regulating services ($/ha) is also calculated based on the projected forest areas under different future scenarios (see Table 9.6 and/or Table 9.10 for disaggregated data). The results clearly show the marginal benefit of carbon regulating services provided by different forest lands. Moreover, different forest management schemes may also influence these values. For instance, *ceteris paribus*, the B1 scenario shows the highest marginal value of regulating services provided by European forests.

To better interpret the results, we undertake a comparative study among all four IPCC scenarios. Table 9.7 shows the comparative results of three IPCC scenarios (i.e. A1, B1 and B2) with respect to the A2 (BAU) storyline, which is characterized by a high population, strong economic growth and high income per capita. This scenario is today interpreted by the European Commission as the benchmark scenario, so as a reference point in the evaluation of the (comparative) welfare changes due to climate change.

From these results, one can clearly see that the countries within Mediterranean Europe (Greece, Italy, Portugal, Spain, Albania, Bosnia and Herzegovina, Bulgaria, Serbia and Montenegro, Turkey and Yugoslav) will benefit from the highest welfare gain in a movement towards the B1 or B2 storyline. In fact, this geo-climatic zone can experience welfare gains with increases in the value of the carbon sequestration services of up to 45 per cent. In other words, the 'no adoption' of a B2 storyline, and a movement towards an A2 scenario, will be associated with a high welfare loss in Mediterranean Europe due to the reduced quantity and quality of the forest ecosystem services under consideration.

Alternatively, moving from an A2 towards an A1 scenario will always involve a welfare loss for Mediterranean Europe. In short, for Mediterranean Europe, the A-type scenarios will always be associated with reduced quantity and quality of forest ecosystem services and the resultant lowering of human welfare levels. On the other hand, storyline B1 is ranked as the most preferred scenario for this geo-climatic area. The region of Scandinavian Europe (including Finland, Norway and Sweden) presents mixed results. First, moving from an A2 towards an A1 scenario will not involve any welfare loss; on the contrary, small welfare gains can be registered. Furthermore, in a movement towards a B-type scenario, Scandinavian Europe will also experience significant welfare gains in the provision of carbon sequestration services. The respective welfare

Table 9.6 Projection of the productivity value of carbon sequestration ($/ha/year, measured in 2005)

Scenario	Mediterranean Europe	Central-Northern Europe	Northern Europe	Scandinavian Europe	Europe
A1 2050	927	2,712	1,563	748	927
A2 2050	950	2,795	1,625	763	950
B1 2050	1,093	2,879	1,913	992	1,093
B2 2050	990	2,684	1,720	836	990

Table 9.7 Projection of total benefits of carbon storage in European forests

Benchmark A2 Scenario		Mediterranean Europe	Central-Northern Europe	Northern Europe	Scandinavian Europe	Europe
Absolute value difference (million $, 2005)	A1 vs A2	−8,614	−42,212	−5,874	212	−56,489
	B1 vsA2	20,785	31,303	5,317	13,705	71,109
	B2 vs A2	17,819	30,888	6,183	3,128	58,018
Percentage change	A1 vs A2	−18.8%	−26.5%	−33.8%	0.6%	−22.1%
	B1 vs A2	45.4%	19.6%	30.6%	42.0%	27.9%
	B2 vs A2	38.9%	19.4%	35.6%	9.6%	22.7%

gains are, however, much lower when compared to Mediterranean Europe, *ceteris paribus*. If we consider Mediterranean and Scandinavian Europe as two 'corner situations' in terms of the respective welfare change magnitudes, we can observe that Central-Northern Europe and Northern Europe each presents an intermediate state of affairs. In any case, it is important to note that a movement from an A2 to an A1 scenario will always be associated with high welfare losses in regulating services, with the highest losses registered among the Northern Europe countries (Denmark, United Kingdom, Estonia, Latvia and Lithuania). Finally, both Central-Northern Europe and Northern Europe show a similar profile in terms of carbon sequestration values: any B-type scenario is characterized by a welfare gain, results that are in accordance with what is also registered in Mediterranean and Scandinavian Europe.

9.5 Conclusions

This chapter reports an original economic valuation of the impact of climate change on the provision of forest regulating services in Europe. To the authors' knowledge, the current chapter represents the first systematic attempt to estimate human well-being losses with respect to changes in biodiversity and forest regulating services that are directly driven by climate change. The valuation exercise is anchored in an ecosystem service-based approach, involving the use of general circulation models and integrated assessment models. The modelling and economic assessment is performed in the context of climate change, with a particular focus on the carbon sequestration services provided by European forests.

In order to value climate change impacts, we first identify four different climate scenarios, corresponding to the four IPCC storylines, referred to as A1FI, A2, B1 and B2 scenarios. Second, we proceed with the analysis and evaluation of climate change impacts on the total forest area (for each country), as well as on the quantities of carbon stored in forests (in biophysical terms). We project future trends of forest areas and stocked carbon in 2050 for the four IPCC scenarios, through the construction and simulation of global circulation models such as HadCM3.

Moreover, considerable impacts of differentiated latitudes on the variability of forest EGS are taken into account by regrouping the 34 selected countries by their different latitude intervals. As a consequence, we are able to identify the dominant forest types, assess their respective efficiency in terms of carbon sequestration and compare their sensitivities to climate change impacts. Finally, we apply a central estimate of carbon price derived from CASES, to combine the dynamics of global economic growth with the dynamics of geophysical climate dynamics.

Figures 9.3 summarizes the economic valuation of regulating services provided by forest ecosystems in Europe across the four IPCC scenarios. As we can see, the value of stocked carbon in the Mediterranean European region varies from $37.2 billion in the A1 scenario to $45.8 billion in the A2 scenario, to $63.6 billion in the B2 scenario, and $66.6 billion in the B1 scenario. Therefore, the B1 scenario is ranked as the one with the highest level of provision. The same ranking holds also for Central-Northern Europe and Scandinavian Europe, where the B1 scenario is associated with the provision of $190.8 billion and $46.3 billion in stocked carbon value, respectively. Finally, for the Northern Europe countries, the highest benefits from carbon sequestration services are again registered in the B-type scenarios, but with the B2 scenario corresponding to $23.5 billion of benefits, slightly higher than in the B1 scenario.

In summary, we address two dimensions in the evaluation of climate impacts on European forests.

First, future projections yield different states of the world depending upon the IPCC scenario adopted. In particular, our results suggest a loss of benefits of carbon stocks from forests to all of Europe in the A1 scenario, when compared to the A2 scenario. This may be the result of intensive harvesting of forest products to meet the rapid progress of the economic development path, represented by the A1 scenario. In contrast, a focus on sustainable development and environmental protection in the B-type scenarios may lead to the extension of protected forest area and thus consequent welfare gains from carbon sequestration in most of the geo-climatic regions.

Second, spatial issues matter in an assessment of the distributional impacts of climate change, as these impacts are not distributed in a uniform way across the European countries under consideration. With carbon sequestration defined as a global public good, an analysis of the distributional aspects of welfare gains and losses is crucial in signalling the potential for international negotiations. The implied transaction costs are beyond the scope of the present analysis, but are an important direction for future research.

Acknowledgements

The current research is part of the ongoing University Research Sponsorship Programme financed by the European Investment Bank. The authors are grateful

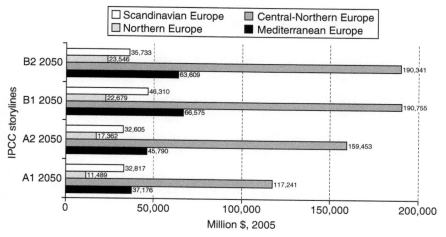

Figure 9.3 Total value of carbon stored by forests in different European regions by 2050.

for its financial support. The authors also thank Carlo Carraro, Francesco Bosello, Ramiro Parrado, Renato Rosa, Mateu Turrò, and Peter Carter for their valuable comments and suggestions on a previous version of this chapter. In addition, the authors thank Silvia Silvestri for valuable research assistance, data management and suggestions on an earlier version. Finally, the authors thank the research group, Advanced Terrestrial Ecosystem Analysis and Modelling, Potsdam Institute for Climate Impact Research (PIK), Germany, and in particular Dagmar Schröter, scientific coordinator. Finally, the authors also thank Jeannette Eggers at the European Forest Institute.

Appendix: projections of the forest EGS in 2050 in both physical and monetary terms

Table 9.8 Projection of European forest area (estimates in 1,000 ha)

Latitude	Country	2005[a]	2050 A1FI[b]	2050 A2[b,c]	2050 B1[b]	2050 B2[b]
35–45	Greece	3,752	2,292	2,360	3,762	3,598
	Italy	9,979	8,346	8,253	11,677	11,893
	Portugal	3,783	2,170	2,174	3,254	3,283
	Spain	17,915	12,052	11,969	17,389	17,633
	Albania	794	519	835	918	991
	Bosnia and Herzegovina	2,185	1,476	2,372	2,609	2,817
	Bulgaria	3,625	2,279	3,664	4,030	4,351
	Serbia and Montenegro	2,694	1,789	2,876	3,163	3,415
	Turkey	10,175	6,788	10,912	12,002	12,959
	TFYR Macedonia	906	612	984	1,082	1,168
	Regional total	55,808	38,324	46,399	59,885	62,108
45–55	Austria	3,862	5,298	5,177	5,199	5,471
	Belgium	667	526	545	698	842
	France	15,554	15,094	16,056	20,080	21,926
	Germany	11,076	10,049	10,075	12,696	14,033
	Ireland	669	442	379	638	656
	Luxembourg	87	80	78	103	94
	Netherlands	365	151	421	333	413
	Switzerland	1,221	1,985	1,913	2,113	2,121
	Croatia	2,135	1,438	2,311	2,542	2,745
	Czech Republic	2,648	1,781	2,863	3,149	3,400
	Hungary	1,976	1,288	2,070	2,277	2,458
	Poland	9,192	6,118	9,834	10,816	11,679
	Romania	6,370	4,299	6,911	7,601	8,207
	Slovakia	1,929	1,297	2,085	2,294	2,477
	Slovenia	1,264	837	1,345	1,479	1,597
	Regional total	59,015	50,682	62,064	72,017	78,118
55–65	Denmark	500	414	677	434	839
	United Kingdom	2,845	1,986	2,145	2,780	3,476
	Estonia	2,284	1,515	2,435	2,678	2,892
	Latvia	2,941	1,948	3,132	3,445	3,719
	Lithuania	2,099	1,364	2,193	2,412	2,604
	Regional total	10,669	7,227	10,582	11,749	13,530
65–71	Finland	22,500	18,224	17,999	16,517	17,079
	Iceland	46	30	29	28	28
	Norway	9,387	6,478	6,277	5,141	5,761
	Sweden	27,528	22,704	22,198	25,884	22,704
	Regional total	59,461	47,435	46,503	47,569	45,572

Notes

a data from FAO.

b projections by ATEAM and CLIBIO on the basis of the Integrated Model to Assess the Global Environment (IMAGE), developed by Netherlands Environmental Assessment Agency.

c interpreted by the European Commission as the baseline scenario, i.e. the scenario characterized by policy inaction.

Table 9.9 Projection of carbon stock in European forest (estimates in Mt/year)

Latitude	Country	1990[a]	2005[b]	2050[d] A1F1	2050[d] A2	2050[d] B1	2050[d] B2
35–45	Greece	293.23	305.53	190.46	201.11	368.57	319.44
	Italy	1,315.59	1,389.67	1,186.02	1,200.24	1,826.60	1,770.73
	Portugal	161.08	170.08	99.55	101.92	218.21	169.31
	Spain	987.42	1,076.28	738.83	758.43	1,224.48	1,162.31
	Albania	62.62	64.66	43.15	71.14	89.95	88.03
	Bosnia and Herzegovina	177.93	177.93	122.61	202.14	255.58	250.11
	Bulgaria	274.83	295.19	189.39	312.23	394.78	386.33
	Serbia and Montenegro	215.71	219.38	148.65	245.07	309.86	303.23
	Turkey	818.55	828.57	564.07	929.94	1,175.81	1,150.64
	TFYR Macedonia	73.78	73.78	50.84	83.82	105.98	103.71
	Regional total	4,380.75	4,601.05	3,333.57	4,106.03	5,969.82	5,703.84
45–55	Austria	937.51	943.37	1,454.04	1,440.26	1,549.25	1,562.36
	Belgium	72.87	72.87	64.56	67.19	97.03	103.55
	France	1,702.22	1,724.73	1,880.61	2,135.35	3,134.30	3,099.40
	Germany	1,257.57	1,257.57	1,281.98	1,395.33	2,233.45	2,130.37
	Ireland	71.30	78.33	58.13	51.71	99.80	94.39
	Luxembourg	23.50	23.50	24.40	24.53	31.68	27.03
	Netherlands	52.10	52.82	24.57	69.80	61.58	71.22
	Switzerland	294.63	300.04	547.99	540.40	653.70	620.48
	Croatia	575.06	576.68	436.35	722.68	779.21	788.89
	Czech Republic	712.27	715.24	540.47	895.12	965.14	977.12
	Hungary	515.09	533.73	390.85	647.32	697.96	706.63
	Poland	2,446.89	2,482.82	1,856.69	3,075.03	3,315.58	3,356.76
	Romania	1,719.50	1,720.58	1,304.75	2,160.91	2,329.95	2,358.88
	Slovakia	518.87	521.03	393.72	652.07	703.08	711.81
	Slovenia	334.66	341.41	253.94	420.57	453.47	459.10
	Regional total	11,234.04	11,344.72	10,513.04	14,298.25	17,105.17	17,068.00

	55–65					
Denmark	60.92	62.68	53.44	91.68	71.13	121.77
United Kingdom	409.39	417.01	300.10	334.64	498.37	568.02
Estonia	304.98	310.55	212.33	354.77	459.44	446.08
Latvia	392.27	399.88	273.10	456.31	590.95	573.76
Lithuania	274.66	285.40	191.22	319.50	413.77	401.73
Regional total	1,442.21	1,475.52	1,030.20	1,556.89	2,033.65	2,111.36
65–71						
Finland	1,040.16	1,041.32	869.50	903.69	1,219.41	991.76
Norway	786.34	793.61	564.61	560.76	511.91	535.89
Sweden	1,770.79	1,774.27	1,508.58	1,459.27	2,421.32	1,676.58
Regional total	3,597.29	3,609.20	2,942.69	2,923.71	4,152.64	3,204.23

Notes

a data from Karjalainen et al. (2003) and Advanced Terrestrial Ecosystem Analysis and Modelling (ATEAM), PIK.

b EIBURS projections.

c projections by Karjalainen et al. (2003); [d]projections by ATEAM and EIBURS needed to add the Finland study.

Table 9.10 Economic value of carbon sequestration (Estimates in $/ha/year, $2005)

Latitude	Country	2005	2050 A1FI[b]	2050 A2[b,c]	2050 B1[b]	2050 B2[b]
35–45	Greece	1,629	927	950	1,093	990
	Italy	2,785	1,585	1,622	1,744	1,660
	Portugal	899	512	523	748	575
	Spain	1,202	684	707	785	735
	Albania	1,629	927	950	1,093	990
	Bosnia and Herzegovina	1,321	927	950	1,093	990
	Bulgaria	1,629	927	950	1,093	990
	Serbia and Montenegro	1,629	927	950	1,093	990
	Turkey	1,629	927	950	1,093	990
	TFYR Macedonia	407	927	950	1,093	990
	Regional average	1,476	927	950	1,093	990
45–55	Austria	4,885	3,061	3,102	3,323	3,185
	Belgium	2,185	1,369	1,374	1,551	1,371
	France	2,218	1,389	1,483	1,741	1,576
	Germany	2,271	1,423	1,544	1,962	1,693
	Ireland	2,342	1,467	1,523	1,744	1,605
	Luxembourg	5,402	3,385	3,487	3,418	3,205
	Netherlands	2,894	1,813	1,851	2,065	1,923
	Switzerland	4,915	3,079	3,150	3,450	3,263
	Croatia	5,402	3,384	3,487	3,418	3,205
	Czech Republic	5,402	3,384	3,487	3,418	3,205
	Hungary	5,402	3,385	3,487	3,418	3,205
	Poland	5,402	3,384	3,487	3,418	3,205
	Romania	5,402	3,384	3,487	3,418	3,205
	Slovakia	5,402	3,385	3,487	3,418	3,205
	Slovenia	5,402	3,385	3,487	3,418	3,205
	Regional average	4,328	2,712	2,795	2,879	2,684

55–65	Denmark	2,507	1,441	1,510	1,827	1,618
	United Kingdom	2,932	1,685	1,740	1,999	1,822
	Estonia	2,719	1,563	1,625	1,913	1,720
	Latvia	2,719	1,563	1,625	1,913	1,720
	Lithuania	2,719	1,563	1,625	1,913	1,720
	Regional average	2,719	1,563	1,625	1,913	1,720
65–71	Finland	926	532	560	823	648
	Norway	1,691	972	996	1,111	1,037
	Sweden	1,289	741	733	1,043	824
	Regional average	1,302	748	763	992	836

Note
a projections by CLIBIO based on CASES.

Notes

1 Three EFSOS sub-regions are presented in the Appendix.
2 HadCM3, Hadley Centre Couplet Model Version 3 is a coupled atmosphere–ocean GCM developed at the Hadley Centre and described by Gordon *et al.* (2000).
3 ATEAM's main objective is to assess the vulnerability of human sectors relying on ecosystem services with respect to global change. For more information, see: www.pik-potsdam.de/ateam.
4 MERGE – Model for Estimating the Regional and Global Effects of GHG policies.
5 IMAGE – Integrated Model to Assess the Greenhouse Effect.
6 FUND – Climate Framework for Uncertainty Negotiation and Distribution model.
7 DICE – Dynamic Integrated Climate Economy model.
8 CASES, Project No. 518294 SES6, (2006–2008). Project official website: www.feem-Project.net/cases.
9 The values are based on full *Monte Carlo* runs of the FUND and PAGE models, in which all parameters are varied to reflect the uncertainty surrounding the central parameter values in both models. The lower and upper bounds are the 5 per cent and 95 per cent probability values of the PAGE model, while the central guidance value is based on the average of the mean values of the FUND and PAGE models. A declining discount rate is used as suggested by the UK government's *Green Book*. The equity weighting of damages in different regions is applied to an aggregation of the regional damage costs to global damages; in other words, lower and higher weights are applied to damages in richer and poorer regions respectively.

References

Ackerman, F. and Finlayson, I. (2005) 'Monetized Impacts of Climate Change: Why are the Numbers So Small?', Evidence submitted to the Stern Review, 8 December.

Bolin, B. *et al.* (2000) 'Global Perspective: Land Use, Land-use Change, and Forestry'. In: Watson, R.T. *et al.* (eds). *A Special Report of the IPCC*. Cambridge: Cambridge University Press, 23–51.

CASES (2008) CASES Project No. 518294 SES6, (2006–2008). Project official website: www.feem-Project.net/cases.

Cline, W.R. (1992) *The Economics of Global Warming*. Washington, DC: Institute for International Economics.

DEFRA (2005) *The Social Cost of Carbon Review: Methodological Approaches for Using SCC Estimates in Policy Assessment*. London: AEA Technology Environment.

DEFRA (2007) *The Social Cost of Carbon and the Shadow Price of Carbon: What they Are, and How to Use them in Economic Appraisal in the UK*. Economics Group of the Department for Environment, Food and Rural Affairs.

Ellenberg, H. (1986) *Vegetation Mitteleuropas mit den Alpen*, 4th ed. Stuttgart: Ulmer.

Garcia-Gonzalo, J., Peltoa, H., Gerendiain, A.Z. and Kellomäki S. (2007) 'Impacts of Forest Landscape Structure and Management on Timber Production and Carbon Stocks in the Boreal Forest Ecosystem under Changing Climate', *Forest Ecology and Management*, 241: 243–257.

Giardina, C.P. and Ryan, M.G. (2000) 'Evidence that Decomposition Rates of Organic Carbon in Mineral Soil do not Vary with Temperature', *Nature*, 404: 858–861.

Gordon, C., Cooper, C., Senior, C.A., Banks, H., Gregory, J.M., Johns, T.C., Mitchell, J.F.B. and Wood, R.A. (2000) 'The Simulation of SST, Sea Ice Extents and Ocean Heat Transports in a Version of the Hadley Centre Coupled Model without Flux Adjustments', *Climate Dynamics* 16: 147–168.

IMAGE (2001) Integrated Model to Assess the Global Environment, Netherlands Environmental Assessment Agency. Available at: www.rivm.nl/image.

IPCC (2001) *Climate Change 2001: The Scientific Basis*. Cambridge: Cambridge University Press.

Jarvis, P.G. and Linder, S. (2000) 'Botany-constraints to Growth of Boreal Forests', *Nature*, 405: 904–905.

Karjalainen, T., Pussinen, A., Liski, J., Nabuurs, G.J., Eggers, T., Lapvetelainen, T. and Kaipainen, T. (2003) 'Scenario Analysis of the Impacts of Forest Management and Climate Change on the European Forest Sector Carbon Budget', *Forest Policy and Economics*, 5: 141–155.

Kelly, D.L. and Kolstad, C.D. (1999) 'Integrated Assessment Models for Climate Change Control'. In Flmer, H. and Tietenberg, T. (eds), *International Yearbook of Environmental and Resource Economics 1999/2000: A Survey of Current Issues*. Cheltenham: Edward Elgar.

Lloyd, J. and Taylor, J.A. (1994) 'On the Temperature Dependence of Soil Respiration', *Functional Ecology*, 8: 315–323.

Luo, Y.Q., Wan, S.Q., Hui, D.F. and Wallance, L.L. (2001) 'Acclimatization of Soil Respiration to Warming in a Tall Grass Prairie', *Nature*, 413: 622–625.

MCPFE (2007) *State of Europe's Forests 2007: The MCPFE Report on Sustainable Forest Management in Europe*. Ministerial Conference on the Protection of Forests in Europe, Liaison Unit Warsaw, Poland.

MEA (2003) *Ecosystems and Human Well-being: A Framework for Assessment*. Washington, DC: World Resources Institute

MEA (2005) *Ecosystems and Human Well-being: Biodiversity Synthesis*. Washington, DC: World Resources Institute.

Melillo, J.M., McGuire, A.D., Kicklighter, D.W., Moore III, B., Vorosmarty, C.J. and Schloss, A.L. (1993) 'Global Climate Change and Terrestrial Net Primary Production', *Nature*, 363: 234–239.

Merlo, M. and Croitoru, L. (2005) *Valuing Mediterranean Forests: Towards Total Economic Value*. Wallingford, UK: CABI Publishing-CAB International.

Nakicenovic, N. and Swart, R. (2000) *IPCC Special Report on Emission Scenarios*. Cambridge: Cambridge University Press.

Nordhaus, W.D. (1993a) 'Optimal Greenhouse Gas Reductions and Tax Policy in the "DICE" model', *American Economic Review, Papers and Proceedings*, 83: 313–317.

Nordhaus, W.D. (1993b) 'Rolling the "DICE": an Optimal Transition Path for Controlling Greenhouse Gases', *Resources and Energy Economics*, 15: 27–50.

OECD (1999) *Environmental Indicators for Agriculture: Volume 1: Concepts and Frameworks*. Paris: OECD.

Pearce, D.W., Cline, W.R., Achanta, A.N., Fankhauser, S., Pachauri, R.K., Tol, R.S.J. and Vellinga, P. (1996) 'The Social Costs of Climate Change: Greenhouse Damage and the Benefits of Control'. In Burce, J.P., Lee, H. and Haites, E.F. (eds), *Climate Change 1995: Economic and Social Dimensions – Contribution of Working Group III to the Second Assessment Report of the Intergovernmental Panel on Climate Change*. Cambridge: Cambridge University Press, pp. 179–224.

Schröter, D. *et al.* (2004). *ATEAM (Advanced Terrestrial Ecosystem Analyses and Modelling) Final Report*. Potsdam Institute for Climate Impact Research.

Schröter, D., Cramer, W., Leemans, R., Prentice, I.C., Araùjo, M.B., Arnell, N.W., Bondeau, A., Bugmann, H., Carter, T.R., Gracia, C.A., de la Vega-Leinert, A.C., Erhard, M., Ewert, F., Glendining, M., House, J.I., Kankaanpää, S., Klein, R.J.T.,

Lavorel, S., Lindner, M., Metzger, M.J., Meyer, J., Mitchell, T.D., Reginster, I., Rounsevell, M., Sabaté, S., Sitch, S., Smith, B., Smith, J., Smith, P., Sykes, M.T., Thonicke, K., Thuiller, W., Tuck, G., Sönke, Z. and Bärbel, Z. (2005) 'Ecosystem Service Supply and Vulnerability to Global Change in Europe', *Science*, 310: 1333–1337.

Thuiller, W., Lavorel, S., Araùjo, M.B., Sykes, M.T. and Prentice, I.C. (2005) 'Climate Change Threats to Plant Diversity in Europe', *Proceedings of the National Academy of Sciences*, 102 (23): 8245–8250.

Tol, R.S.J. (2002a) 'New Estimates of the Damage Costs of Climate Change: Part I. Benchmark Estimates', *Environmental and Resource Economics*, 21 (1): 47–73.

Tol, R.S.J. (2002b) 'New Estimates of the Damage Costs of Climate Change: Part II. Dynamic Estimates', *Environmental and Resource Economics*, 21 (1): 135–160.

Tol, R.S.J., Frankhauser, S., Richels, R.G. and Smith, J.B. (2000) 'How Much Damage Will Climate Change Do? Recent Estimates', *World Economics*, 1 (4): 179–206.

UNECE/FAO (2005) *European Forest Sector Outlook Study, 1960–2000–2020, Main Report*. United Nation Publications.

Watson, R.T., Zinyowera, M.C. and Moss, R.H. (eds) (1996) *Climate Change 1995: Impacts, Adaptation, and Mitigation of Climate Change: Scientific Technical Analysis Contribution of Working Group II to the Second Assessment Report of the Intergovernmental Panel on Climate Change*. Cambridge: Cambridge University Press.

10 Valuing the services of coral reef systems for sustainable coastal management

A case study of the Gulf of Kachchh, India

Arun M. Dixit, Lalit Kumar, Pushpam Kumar and Kinjal Pathak

10.1 Introduction

Management of ecosystem services is a priority matter given that their provision by natural ecosystems worldwide is declining, primarily due to human intervention. For example, more land was converted to cropland since 1945 than in the eighteenth and nineteenth centuries combined; 25 per cent of the world's coral reefs were badly degraded or destroyed in the last decades; 35 per cent of mangrove area has been lost in this time; the amount of water in reservoirs quadrupled and withdrawals from rivers and lakes doubled since 1960 (MA, 2005a, 2005b). Valuation of ecosystem services has been sought as an effective tool to enable decision makers to design the cost-effective response policies for management of ecosystems towards alleviating the poverty, especially in economically poor regions like South Asia. The unique feature of most of the services emanating from ecosystems is that they – although acknowledged by people – are unaccounted for and unpriced, and therefore remain outside the domain of the market. Such problems are treated as externalities, where the market fails and decision makers try to correct the market failure by creating market-like situations. Subsequently, they obtain the value of services through various valuation techniques based on the stated preferences of the people. In the case of regulating services of ecosystems such as climate regulation, waste treatment capacity, nutrient management and various watershed functions, classic situations of market failure occur. The missing market for the ecosystem services adds to the problem because most of the vulnerable section of society in Bangladesh, Bhutan, India, Nepal and Pakistan depends on those services directly or indirectly for their livelihood. Therefore, any decision proves to be inefficient and unfeasible from the social perspective, causing problems for sustainability and human well-being. In recent years, there have been attempts to develop methods and tools to capture some of the services of ecosystems (Costanza *et al.*, 1997; Balmford *et al.*, 2002; Maler *et al.*, 2008; Ansink *et al.*, 2008; Daily *et al.*, 2009, Rouquette *et al.*, 2009).

10.1.1 Rationale of valuation

Diverse natural systems provide a range of benefits such as food, wood, clean water, healthy soil, energy, protection from floods, carbon storage, etc. across generations. Costanza *et al.* (1997) emphasize that well-being and survival of human beings is dependent upon the continuous flow of various ecosystem goods (such as food, medicines) and services (such as waste assimilation, climate stabilization, etc.). It is also recognized that biological diversity of any system is an ecological capital that performs three major functions (Pearce and Turner, 1990):

•   provision of goods and services for human activity;
•   absorption of waste from production;
•   environmental functions/services such as ecosystem stability and other amenity services.

Increasing human population and rapid economic growth put pressure on the fragile environment and ecosystem, creating situations of conflicts between population growth and production demands on one side, and the environment on the other. These conflicts downgrade the functions and values of ecosystems and undermine the ultimate goal of providing sustainable livelihood to millions of people around the globe. Actually, the deterioration of the environment may be defined as the occurrence of the loss of functions and economic goods, and thus regarded as costs to human society. Such degradation of the environment has brought into focus the need to value the scarce natural resources available to the mankind for various needs.

In an economic sense, most ecosystem benefits fall into the category of 'public goods' and hence have no direct price. As a matter of fact, while the values are assigned to the private goods and services, markets tend not to assign economic values to the largely public benefits of conservation. On a day-to-day basis, nature is the source of much value to human well-being, and yet it mostly bypasses markets, escapes pricing and defies valuation. It is well understood, now, that this lack of valuation is an underlying cause for the degradation of many of the ecosystems and associated loss of biodiversity. This actually generates a lot of interest among economists as well as environmentalists to develop and practise valuation works in a wide range of economic and ecological systems. Furthermore, of late, in the process of developing different tools that facilitate management of natural resources by taking appropriate trade-off-related decisions, economic valuation of ecological systems had gained tremendous popularity amongst researchers, managers and policy makers.

Economic valuation is used to construct monetary measures of welfare (functions, goods and services) arising from changes in the environment. Valuation has particular importance in the context of social welfare-based public policy. Dixon (2002) describes five areas of political decision making that can benefit from natural resource valuation:

- raising the profile of environmental concerns in setting national or regional sectoral priorities for the budget allocations;
- intervening in the market with taxes, regulations and incentives to correct the under-provision of public goods;
- providing information for cost–benefit analysis to help include environmental concerns into the decision-making process;
- full cost accounting in government statistics;
- evaluating the true impact of projects, programmes and policies.

Since many of the environmental goods and services do not enter the market, valuation requires special approaches and methods which account for the values beyond market demand functions. Generally, in order to obtain the total economic value of any given natural ecosystem, different use and non-use values are considered for their measurement (Table 10.1).

10.1.2 Economic values of coastal systems

Coastal and marine ecosystems are among the most diverse and productive systems in the world and are constituted by a mosaic of natural ecosystems such as mangroves, lagoons, rocks, sea-grass bed, estuaries and marsh, coral reefs, etc. There is worldwide recognition of the benefits of management for sustainable use and conservation of the coastal and marine ecosystems (MA, 2003). The value of coastal and marine systems almost always refers to the socio-economic values, i.e. various goods and services provided by marine ecosystems (Table 10.2). Logically, the value also attempts to attach a monetary value to the goods and services (de Groot *et al.*, 2002; Turpie *et al.*, 2003).

Table 10.1 Types of economic values and their definitions

Value	Type	Description
Use values	Direct use	Arise from the direct exploitation of the environment, and are generally demand-driven goods, e.g. fisheries
	Indirect use values	Benefits which are derived from the environment, without the intervention of man, e.g. climate regulation
	Option use value	Value associated with an individual's willingness to pay to safeguard the option to use a natural resource in the future, when such use is not currently planned
Non-use values	Bequest value	Value an individual places on ensuring the availability of a natural resource to future generations
	Existence value	Value placed on simply knowing that a natural resource is there, even if it is never experienced

Table 10.2 Relative significance of goods and services across coastal and marine ecosystems

Goods and services	Estuaries and marsh	Mangrove	Lagoons and salt ponds	Intertidal	Rock and shell reefs	Sea grass	Coral reefs
Food	+++	++	+	++	++	+	++
Fibre, timber, fuel	+++	++++	++				+
Medicines	+	+	+				
Biodiversity	+++	+++	++	++++	++++	++	++++
Biological regulation	+++	+++	++	+	+		++
Freshwater storage and retention	+		+				
Biochemical	+	+					+
Nutrient cycling and fertility	+++	+++	++	+	+		+++
Hydrological	+		+				
Atmospheric and climate regulation	+++	+++	++	+	+	+	++
Disease control	+++	+++	+++	++	+	+	+
Waste processing	++++	++++	++		+	++	+++
Flood/storm protection	++	+++	+	+	++	++	+++
Erosion control	++	++++	+			+	+
Cultural and amenity	++++	+	++	++++	++	++	++++
Recreational	+++	+	+	++++			++++
Aesthetic	+++	+	++	+++			++++

Source: MA, 2005.

Coral reefs are three-dimensional, shallow-water structures dominated by hard, reef-building (Scleractinian) corals and are the most biologically diverse of shallow-water marine ecosystems. Coral reefs cover an estimated 284,300 km², or about 1.2 per cent of the world's continental shelf area (Spalding *et al.*, 2001). Australia and Indonesia are the two most reef-rich areas: each has about 50,000 km² of reef and account for nearly 35 per cent of the world's reefs. Coral reefs represent about 0.25 per cent of total ocean area, but support over 25 per cent of marine life and also more species per unit area than any other ecosystem (Ahmed *et al.*, 2004). The high productivity of coral reefs within otherwise unproductive surrounding waters makes coral reefs critical to the survival of the coastal marine ecosystems. It is important to understand that coral reef and its associated life forms are part of a large ecological system and thus linked at various levels with other ecological systems (e.g. with mangroves). While they are important for ecological integrity, they also have a significant role in providing livelihoods to the vast majority of coastal communities, especially fishermen.

Coral reefs represent crucial sources of income and resources through their role in tourism, fishing, building materials, coastal protection and provision of new drugs and bio-chemicals (Moberg and Folke, 1999; Spalding *et al.*, 2001; Carte, 1996). Globally, many people depend in part or wholly on coral reefs for their livelihood, and around 8 per cent (0.5 billion people) of the world's population live within 100 km of coral reef ecosystems (Pomerance, 1999). Estimates of the total number of people reliant on coral reefs for their food resources range from 500 million (Wilkinson, 2004) to over one billion (Whittingham *et al.*, 2003). Some 30 million of the world's poorest and most vulnerable people in coastal and island communities are totally reliant on reef-based resources as their primary means of food production, sources of income and livelihoods (Gomez *et al.*, 1994; Wilkinson, 2004). Due to increasing population size, the reliance on reef resources is set to increase in the future.

Due to these characteristic, coral reefs are ecosystems with enormous value, including the intrinsic, ecological, economic, cultural and aesthetic. Sadly, 27 per cent of the world's coral reefs have already been lost. Present rates of destruction will cause 60 per cent of the remaining reefs to be destroyed over the next 30 years (Cesar, 2003). Thus, an informed and concerted conservation effort of these precious ecosystems is urgently required.

10.1.3 *Context and ecological profile of the site*

Gujarat is a maritime state endowed with a 1,650 km-long coastline (over 21 per cent of the Indian coastline of 7,517 km), which makes it strategically important, serving as a natural gateway to India. The coastline of Gujarat has two indentations, the Gulf of Kachchh (GoK) and Gulf of Khambhat, covering about 60 per cent of the state coastline. According to the 1991 Census, about 549 villages with a total population of about one million are situated along the Gujarat coast.

The GoK is very rich in terms of biodiversity values. It supports varied habitats including coral reefs, mangroves, creeks, mud flats, islands, rocky shore, sandy shore, etc., which, in turn, provide suitable environment for a wide range of flora and fauna. Of these habitats, coral reefs are quite unique in terms of their isolation and survival in extreme oceanographic and climatic conditions. While, these coral reefs and associated systems provide a range of goods and services to human beings, they are also vulnerable to various resource-extraction activities like fishing, mangrove cutting, etc. In addition to the above, anthropogenic activities like rapid industrialization and large coastal infrastructure development projects like ports and oil terminals, etc. damage the natural capital of coral reef and its associated systems, jeopardizing both ecological and livelihood securities in the region.

In the context of coral reef systems at the GoK, where the industrial and other human-generated pressures are mounting day by day, resource managers seek answers that could help them take better decisions for sustainable development and conservation of coral reef systems. The research for the chapter is limited in terms of tenure and is being undertaken from November 2008 to April 2009. The chapter attempts to value various goods and services provided by coral reef systems in the GoK. It also aims to identify key issues and knowledge gaps in measuring the total economic value of coral reef systems.

The chapter runs through three questions: What are the key benefits of the coral reefs in the GoK in terms of their economic value? How can the limited ecological data available in the GoK be used for valuing the coral reef systems? How can these quick valuations of coral reefs be used in the decision-making processes of coastal zone management?

10.2 Valuation of coral reefs: evidence across the world

Coral reefs are highly productive, diverse and attractive ecosystems that provide a wide range of benefits or 'ecosystem goods and services' that are of high value and critical importance to local and national economies (Table 10.3). Coral reefs provide coastal recreation and habitats for commercially valuable fish, and they reduce the impact of waves on the shore, slowing erosion and beach loss and lessening damage from storms. In addition, coral reefs harbour a vast range of genetic diversity with unknown potential uses.

Valuation of goods and services generated by coral reef systems has widely been attempted by researchers in different parts of the world. Thus, while Costanza *et al.* (1997) estimated a total global value of coral reef systems as $6,075 per hectare per year (the total extent of coral reef systems was 62 million hectares), Cesar *et al.* (2003) estimated total net benefit per year of the world's coral reefs to be $29.8 billion. Of this amount, tourism and recreation account for $9.6 billion, coastal protection for $9.0 billion, fisheries for $5.7 billion and biodiversity for $5.5 billion. However, at regional levels the values ranged widely, mainly due to the variations in type and extent of the coral reef systems and also the underlying socio-economic state of the beneficiaries. Accordingly,

Table 10.3 Goods and services provided by coral reefs

Provisioning services (products obtained from ecosystems)	Regulating services (benefits obtained from regulation of ecosystem processes)	Cultural services (non-material benefits obtained from ecosystems)	Supporting services (natural processes that maintain the other services)
• Food (fish and shellfish) • Genetic resources • Natural medicines and pharmaceuticals • Ornamental resources • Building materials	• Erosion control • Storm protection	• Spiritual and religious values • Knowledge systems/educational values • Inspiration • Aesthetic values • Social traditions • Sense of place • Recreation and ecotourism	• Sand formation • Primary production

Source: Adapted from MA, 2003.

in Southeast Asia, the total potential sustainable annual economic net benefit per km^2 of healthy coral reef is estimated to range from \$23,100 to \$270,000, arising from fisheries, shoreline protection, tourism, recreation and aesthetic value (Burke *et al.*, 2002). In the Caribbean, the annual net benefits provided by coral reefs in terms of fisheries were estimated to be about \$300 million (Burke and Maidens, 2004).

At the site-specific level, utility values associated with coral reef biodiversity were estimated at Phi Phi, Thailand. The mean willingness to pay (WTP) per visit was estimated at \$7.17 for domestic visitors and \$7.15 for international visitors, or \$147,000 per year for domestic visitors and \$1.2 million per year for international visitors. The study also calculated the mean WTP of vicarious domestic users at \$15.85. The total value of the reefs was estimated to be \$497.4 million per year, or \$15,118 per hectare per year (Seenprachawong, 2004). Similarly, the total economic value for Guam's reefs was estimated at \$127.3 million per year, with tourism accounting for approximately 75 per cent of this value (\$94.6 million per year), diving and snorkelling for \$8.7 million per year, fisheries for \$4.0 million per year, biodiversity for \$2.0 million per year, and coastal protection for \$8.4 million per year (Van Beukering *et al.*, 2007). The total economic value of coral reefs in Indonesia's Wakatobi National Park in Southeast Sulawesi was estimated to be \$308,000 or \$12,100 per square kilometre (Samonte-Tan and Armedilla, 2004). A summary of economic values (adjusted to 2007 price) of various goods and services of coral reef systems in different parts of the world is presented in Table 10.4.

Table 10.4 Summary of economic values of various goods and services of coral reef systems

Values	Range (\$ per ha/ year)	Range in 2007 (\$ per ha/year)	% of total value
Marketable			
Recreational values (including non-market)	45–8,295	~100–37,000	30–75
Fisheries	32–700	~80–90	1–25
Ornamental fish	1–4	~1–10	
Aquaculture	1–60	~1–65	
Building materials	5–270	~10–270	
Non-marketable			
Coastal protection	55–14,000	~80–40,000	15–50
Education and research	2–186	~6–184	0–2
Biodiversity	1–660	~1–660	1–20
Water purification	58	~75–100	1–5
Existence value, option value	2–120	~3–160	
Total economic value	\$1,000–17,100 (Costanza: 6,075)	~1,000–17,700 (Costanza: ~10,000)	

10.3 Study site: Gulf of Kachchh and coral reefs

In India the total coral reef area is 5,790 km², distributed between four major regions: Lakshadweep, Gulf of Mannar, Andaman and Nicobar Islands, and the GoK. Reef structure and species diversity vary considerably between the areas due to differences in the reef extent and geo-environmental conditions. Of the 793 reported coral species in the world, India has more than 208 species, which is far less than the 581 species reported to exist in the neighbouring Indo-Pacific's centre of diversity.

The GoK lies N22°15'–23°40' latitude and E68°20'–70°40' longitude, and is aligned approximately east to west in direction, and bound between northern and southern lips. The northern side of the gulf shares the boundary with Kachchh district, while the southern border touches with Rajkot and Jamnagar districts (Figure 10.1). The GoK encompasses an area of about 7,350 km² and a volume of about 220,000 Mm³. The depth ranges from a maximum of about 60 m at the mouth to less than 20 m at the head of the gulf, with an average depth of about 30 m. The geomorphology of the area shows that sandy beaches characterize the northern part of the coast, while the southern coastal region is demarcated by mudflats in the inter-tidal zones. The GoK has characteristic oceanographic features, especially those related to the tidal currents, sedimentation, sea-water salinity and temperature, which varied spatio-temporally (for a detailed description of these parameters, see Sen Gupta and Deshmukhe, 2000).

Importantly, these features play a critical role in supporting a diverse natural habitat and ecosystem, which is considered as one of the biologically richest marine habitats along the west coast of India. It is important to reiterate that the GoK has quite distinct physical characteristics on its northern and southern sides.

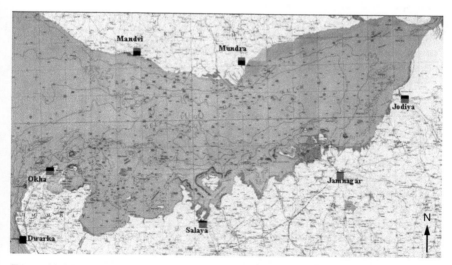

Figure 10.1 Location of the Gulf of Kachchh. The northern side of the Gulf is part of Kachchh district, while the southern side is part of Jamnagar district.

Thus, one of the most striking features of the southern side of the GoK is the presence of many islands and records of coral reefs and mangroves. Realizing the importance of conservation of the southern part of the GoK, a total of 457.92 km² area was designated as a marine national park and sanctuary (MNPS).

An estimate of the actual extent of coral reefs in the GoK is yet not final, mainly due to inadequate surveys of coral reefs in the sub-tidal zone. Nevertheless, satellite imagery-based assessment (Bahuguna and Nayak, 1998) delineated an area of about 277 km² under coral reefs which constitute reef flats, sand over reefs and mud over reefs. Thus, in the context of the present study, the extent of coral reefs in the GoK was considered to be about 277 km². In the GoK, coral reefs are patchily distributed in shallow water and grow on sandstone platforms that surround 34 islands. As a matter of fact, the coral reefs of the GoK are one of the most northerly reefs in the world. Importantly, these reefs survive in extreme environmental conditions like high salinity, frequent emersion, high temperature fluctuations and relatively high sedimentation. In a sense, coral reefs in the GoK are quite distinct from those recorded in the Gulf of Mannar, Lakshadweep and the Andaman and Nicobar Islands in terms of their prolonged exposure to the air atmosphere, mainly due to high tidal amplitude. Thus, in general terms, coral species are settled differently in the GoK. For example, coral species are recorded on inter-tidal rocks, in shallow puddles (where they can be considered as miniature atoll), in knee-deep lagoons and in sub-tidal waters.

Compared to other Indian sites, the diversity of coral species is quite low in the GoK, mainly because of geographical isolation and the extreme environmental conditions (e.g. the temperature range of 15–35°C, salinity range of 25–40 ppt), strong tidal currents and heavy sediment load. Researchers explored coral species diversity in the GoK during different periods, thus adding new species to the list of GoK coral (e.g. Patel, 1976, 1985; Pillai and Patel, 1988; Pillai *et al.*, 1979; Chavan, 1984; Scheer, 1985; Singh *et al.*, 2006). A compilation of coral species from the existing literature confirmed a list of 68 coral species from the GoK – 45 hard corals and 23 soft coral species.

In the GoK, the fringing reefs are found in three distinct situational types: contiguous to mainland, along the aerial islands and along the submerged islands. These three types, due to different locations and positional arrangements, carry out different functions and generate different values. Each type is further divided into different sub-categories based on minor alterations in their positions and thus the inundation patterns. Coral species are differentially distributed among the different types and sub-types.

The coral reef systems in the GoK are facing threats from various natural and anthropogenic forces, such as development of industries related to oil and petrochemicals, fertilizer, cement, ship-breaking, etc.; infrastructure projects such as the construction of ports, jetties, thermal power plants; destruction of mangrove forests; over fishing; climate change; and sedimentation.

Interestingly, globally observed phenomena of coral bleaching due to anomalous high sea-surface temperatures in 1998, recorded that compared to the Gulf of Mannar (89.2 per cent) and Lakshadweep islands (81.8 per cent), bleaching of coral reefs was quite restricted (10.7 per cent) in the GoK (Arthur, 2000). This is attributed to the fact that coral species in the inter-tidal reefs are well adapted to a higher degree of temperature fluctuation (Gates, 1990).

10.4 Approach and methodology

We mainly focus on the fringe reefs of the GoK that are lying in both inter-tidal and sub-tidal areas. As per existing knowledge, a total of about 277 km^2 of coral reefs exists in the GoK, especially along the coasts of Jamnagar district. Therefore, in the present context, the coral reefs of Jamnagar district were considered for valuation purpose.

Based on preliminary surveys and discussions with various stakeholders, many values of coral reefs – with specific reference to the GoK – were identified. However, in the context of the present study of economic valuation, focus was given mainly to five major goods and services provided by coral reef systems in the GoK. These include: fisheries, recreation and tourism, protection of coastal aquifers (against salinity ingression), protection of coastal lands (against erosion) and biodiversity. Notably, in the context of the GoK, the above goods and services were selected for valuation purpose mainly because of their importance to local economies.

As discussed earlier, the aim of this study was to rapidly measure the economic value of various goods and services of coral reefs in the GoK, at least at a gross level of approximation, using data that are already available from different agencies and institutions. However, for validation of these data, field-based assessment was also conducted by use of primary surveys. Collated data were used in valuing different goods and services by applying different valuation approaches. Importantly, while the values for fisheries, tourism and protection of coastal aquifers against salinity ingression were measured using direct values, the coastal protection against erosion and biodiversity were measured by applying benefit transfer method (BTM). BTM is used when values derived and used in other comparable studies are transferred and adjusted to find and estimate the values in the current study. The logic of BTM is that a study carried out in similar circumstances and locations can be used as a substitute and a proxy for another area, especially if the data are inadequate for the study site and the time for the study is also limited. The data-gathering scheme and valuation approach for different valuation themes is presented in Table 10.5.

Finally, each of the selected goods and services was presented in terms of annual values per unit area of coral reefs in GoK. For better comprehension, each of these values was further elaborated in terms of Present Value (PV) for 20 years and for the annuity.

Table 10.5 Data collection scheme and adopted valuation techniques during the study

Valuation theme	Secondary data	Primary surveys	Adopted valuation technique
Fisheries	• Time series data on fish production in 17 centres or 23 villages of Jamnagar district • Species-wise quantity of fish that are being exported and their price in Jamnagar district • Listing of fish species likely to be associated with coral reefs in the GoK	Sample survey of fishing villages and meetings with fishermen of different categories (pagadias, boat owners, etc.). Survey of fish traders and market middlemen	Financial analysis approach. Market value of fisheries at landing site and additional values from export market
Recreation and tourism	• Number of tourists visiting MNPS and coral reef sites in Jamnagar district over the years	Sample surveys among the tourists visiting the coral reefs in MNPS to measure expenditure pattern	Extrapolation of expenditure pattern of tourists
Protection of coastal aquifer (against salinity ingression)	• Well monitoring (groundwater salinity) data in coastal villages of Jamnagar district • Crop/land productivity data • Government interventions (like Bandharas, sub-surface dikes, tidal regulators, etc.) and their costs in coastal villages of Jamnagar district	Sample villages to conduct problem analysis and to understand the loss of crop productivity due to salinity ingression	Defensive or preventative expenditure by government agencies; change in crop productivity
Protection of coastal areas (against coastal erosion)	• Identification of vulnerable areas along the coast of Jamnagar district • Technical and financial details of various schemes of the Irrigation Department to halt the coastal erosion	Sample villages to conduct problem analysis	Defensive or preventative expenditures by government agencies; benefit transfer method
Coral reef biodiversity	• Listing of all the species associated with coral reefs in the GoK with conservation status • Compilation of existing state of bio-prospecting in Indian marine waters		Benefit transfer method

10.5 Summary of estimates

10.5.1 Fisheries

In the context of coral-reef-associated fisheries in the GoK, this study limits its focus to those of Jamnagar district. Marine fishing is a key economic activity for about 10,000 active fishermen from the 26 fishing centres of Jamnagar district. The coral reefs and mangrove forest in the GoK constitute important breeding and nursery grounds for the large varieties of fish and prawns. A total of 144 fish, 27 prawn, four shrimp, 21 crab and one lobster species are reported in the GoK waters (Singh *et al.*, 2006). Catches of prawns, jewfish, thread fin, pomphret, mullet and crabs are the dominant forms of fishing in the GoK. In addition to this, fishermen are also engaged in molluscan shell fishing, which includes pearl oyster, window pane oyster, chanks and bivalves. While collection of shells is banned after the designation of the MNPS, collection of smaller bivalves and other shells is still in practice.

On average, the fish catch of Jamnagar district contributes about 10 per cent of the total fish catch of the Gujarat state. The fish catch data from 1982–1983 to 2005–2006 recorded a mean annual fish catch of about 53,500 tons, with values fluctuating between 25,238 and 102,846 tons. There are 16 fish-landing centres in Jamnagar district. The catch in these centres fluctuates widely. Among these sites, Okha is the largest, followed by Bet Balapur and Dwarka. However, in order to estimate the total fish catch from coral reef areas, two levels of data correction were considered: (1) exclusion of the few centres that are not fishing within GoK waters; (2) use of coralline areas varied for different fish species. Accordingly, fishermen assigned appropriate weights to each fish species.

During the present study, the value of coral-reef-associated fisheries was estimated using a financial analysis approach that involves calculating the revenue generated from fisheries of Jamnagar district within the limits of the GoK. Three major streams of fishery-related revenue were considered: (1) net revenue of fisheries at the landing centre (a major part of this revenue is distributed among the fishermen); (2) revenue generated from value-added fisheries, i.e. the export-based revenue (a major part of this revenue is distributed among fish traders and fish-processing units); and (3) net revenue generated from pagadia fisheries. (Pagadia fishing literally means the practice of fishermen venturing into intertidal areas on foot and fishing using basic fishing tackle. In a strict sense, this kind of fishing is subsistence fishing.)

At fish-landing centres, the gross revenue of fisheries was estimated based on species-wise fish catch between 2002–2003 and 2005–2006 and their sale price. From this, the net revenue was also estimated by subtracting operating costs. Thus, while average annual gross revenue of Rs.1,431 million was generated from commercial fisheries over this period, the net annual revenue from was estimated at Rs.1,074 million. Furthermore, it is estimated that from the study area, a total annual revenue of Rs.135 million was generated as value addition by export. In addition to the above, the fish catch of about 1,500 pagadia fishermen from the study area had a net annual worth of Rs.75 million.

Accordingly, a total annual fish value of Rs.1,284 million could be linked to coral reef and its associated systems in the GoK. The above value is also defined in terms of value per unit area of coral reef in the GoK. Due to the $277\,km^2$-extent of the coral reef in the GoK, coral-reef-associated fish value was found to be Rs.4.64 million per year per square kilometre of coral reef area. To make a comparison to other nearby areas, it was found that the value of coral-reef-associated fisheries in Sri Lanka was about Rs.2.46 million per year per square kilometre.

10.5.2 Tourism

In the context of the present study, the economic value of tourism and recreation related to coral reefs in the GoK was assessed by using a simplified 'financial revenue' approach and focused on the gross revenue transaction (mainly the expenditure pattern of tourists) associated with coral tourism. Also, in the present case the expenses incurred by students who attended nature education camps in the MNPS were also considered and included as educational tourism. While the estimate of numbers of tourists in the MNPS was provided by park managers, to record the expenditure pattern of tourists and students who visited different coral reef locations, a questionnaire-based primary survey was conducted. Thus, during the study, opportunistic interviews of 20 tourists (five foreigners and 15 Indians) were conducted.

Globally, key tourism activities associated with coral reefs include scuba diving, snorkelling, reef walking, etc. In the GoK, however, tourism of coral reefs areas is not yet promoted to the level at which it can generate good revenues. Nevertheless, the last few years' data suggest that the total number of tourists visiting MNPS is gradually increasing. Within MNPS, Pirotan Island and Narara Bet are the two main tourist destinations, where tourists mostly go 'reef walking'. According to official records, a total of 14,272 tourists (including 141 foreigners) visited MNPS in 2007–2008. In addition to this, in the same year, a total of 6,830 students visited the MNPS as part of nature education camps.

The results of the primary survey highlight that the per-person expense related to coral-associated tourism varies from site to site. Also, the expense pattern varies between Indian and foreign tourists. Accordingly, based on the feedback from the respondents and assuming that each tourist visits the site once per year, per-head expenses for Pirotan was estimated to be Rs.1,144 per year. For the Narara Bet site, the same was estimated to be Rs.982 and Rs.3,672 for Indian and foreign tourists, respectively. In addition, students who visited the MNPS as part of nature education camps incurred per-head expense of about Rs.300 for a one-day camp. Thus, by applying the expenditure method, the annual value of tourism and recreation in the GoK was estimated to be around Rs.17.8 million. This value was used to estimate the tourism function value in terms of per unit area of coral reefs in the GoK. Considering the total coral reef area in the entire

GoK is about 277 km², the coral-reef-associated tourism value of the GoK was found to be Rs.64,203 per square kilometre per year. However, it is important to state here that since reef walking is not an eco-friendly practice and may cause coral reefs to die, the tourism value may decline in the long run. Therefore, MNPS authorities need to promote other sustainable tourist activities.

10.5.3 *Protection of coastal aquifers against salinity ingression*

According to a recent study, in 127 out of 250 coastal villages of Jamnagar district (i.e. almost half of the villages) groundwater has already turned fully saline. The problem is mainly due to salinity ingression into groundwater aquifers. Salinity ingression is the lateral sub-surface intrusion of sea water as a result of lowering groundwater levels and percolation of sea water far within the inland region due to over-withdrawal of fresh water from the land adjoining the coastal strip. In natural conditions, the problem is controlled by some form of physical barrier (such as thick, impervious rocky layers) which restrict the lateral movement of saline water towards mainland aquifers.

In this context we attempt to explore the role of coral reef health in prevention of salinity ingression. Considering the physical processes involved in causing salinity ingression, the coral reefs that are located close to the mainland and form rocky layers along the coast assume greater significance in restricting the lateral movement of saline water and thus controlling the problem of salinity ingression, at least to certain extent. The function of the coral reef in this case is just a separation between the fresh water/groundwater in coastal aquifers and the saline groundwater in the seabed. Interestingly, this function can be performed by dead coral reefs, so while it does not necessarily give much argument for maintaining the health of the coral reef, the logic of coastal area conservation still holds true for not allowing large-scale mining or dredging of age-old, dead coralline rocks. A review of the global literature suggests that there is hardly any work that focuses on this functional aspect of coral reef systems.

During the present study, data regarding groundwater salinity for 1980 and 2008 was collected for 36 coastal villages of Jamnagar district from the relevant government department. Also, the status of coral reefs and mangroves were ascertained for each of these 36 villages. Analysis of the above data suggests that between 1980 and 2008 the groundwater salinity was increased by about 123 per cent in those villages where both coral reefs and mangroves were absent. In contrast, there was just a marginal increase in groundwater salinity (21 per cent) in those villages where both corals and mangroves were present. Similarly, in the two villages where only coral reefs were present the salinity increase was only 5.6 per cent. The above findings, although not conclusive, strongly indicate that coral reefs have some impact on the control of salinity ingression in coastal villages.

Keeping the above findings in mind, the cost of salinity ingression was measured in two terms: (1) decreased land productivity; and (2) increased preventive expenditures (through salinity-control measures). Finally, we attributed some portion of these costs as a proxy for coral value within this function.

The survey recorded a decline in productivity of groundnut crop (a traditional crop) in the six sampled villages. Farmers correlated this loss in productivity to a rapid increase in groundwater salinity. Thus, on average, a loss of 2,108 kg/ha of groundnut crop was recorded in the six sample villages. Further, the study clearly suggests that due to salinity ingression problems between 1990 and 2000, farmers lost about 1,350 ha (i.e. about 36 per cent of the total) of irrigated land in 23 salinity-affected villages. Based on the above, an annual monetary loss of Rs.56.9 million was associated with salinity-ingression-linked decline in productivity in groundnut crop in 23 salinity affected villages. It is important to note that the entire estimated value of monetary loss cannot be attributed to the health of coral reefs. Thus, for the present purpose, we used a conservative value of 15 per cent as the linkage between coral health and value of land productivity. The 15-per cent contribution of coral reefs is just a notional value (as no empirically derived value is available). Thus, in monetary terms, the annual value of coral reefs in controlling salinity ingression will be in the region of Rs.8.54 million per year.

In addition to the above, between 1999 and 2008 a total expenditure of about Rs.120 million was made under the Salinity Ingression Prevention Scheme (SIPS) by the Irrigation Department in the coastal villages in Jamnagar district. Thus, on average, Rs.12 million was spent annually on construction of various physical structures to prevent salinity ingression problems along the Jamnagar coast. However, all of the above mitigation expenditures cannot be ascribed to replacement for the coral reef function, because most of the mitigation measures are simply to deter excessive pumping of groundwater to facilitate groundwater recharge. Considering that the value of coral reefs in preventing the salinity ingression was 15 per cent (see above), an annual value of Rs.1.8 million preventive expenditure can be attributed to coral reef systems.

Thus, in the present case, the presence of coral reefs along the coast would have produced additional crop output of Rs.8.54 million per year and would have saved Rs.1.8 million annually in preventive expenditure costs. This implies an annual net worth of Rs.10.34 million assigned to coral reefs for the function of controlling salinity ingression in coastal areas of Jamnagar district. Considering that the total coral reef area in the entire GoK is about 277 km², the annual salinity ingression prevention value of coral reefs in the GoK was found to be Rs.37,329 per square kilometre.

10.5.4 Protection against coastal erosion

The landward displacement of the shoreline caused by the forces of sea waves and currents is termed *coastal erosion*. The process of stabilization of the coast is very expensive and, if not tackled properly, usually provides temporary solutions. Literature on the issues related to coastal erosion in the GoK is almost non-existent. Also, discussions with key stakeholders like MNPS officials, port authorities, the Gujarat Maritime Board and local farmers, suggested that at present, there is hardly any stretch of coastline in the GoK where the problem of coastal erosion is conspicuous. However, it is generally recognized that due to the presence of rocky shores, mangroves and coral reefs (although quite patchily distributed), the southern side of the GoK is well protected from the problem.

Keeping the above in mind, and also in wake of the paucity of data related to coastal erosion in the GoK, the coastal protection prevention function of coral reefs was valued by applying BTM. To use BTM in the present case, coastal protection values of coral reef systems in two neighbouring regions (Southeast Asia and the Indian Ocean) were considered separately and then appropriately adjusted, initially by applying the GDP deflator index and subsequently by using four parameters: (1) the ratio of reef flat to coastal margin; (2) population density; (3) per capita income; and (4) contribution of agriculture production to GDP. Importantly, due to a lack of data for a local site like the GoK, the values were estimated using data for the Gujarat state. The key values used for this estimation is given in Table 10.6.

Thus, by applying the parameters, we estimated two values of the coastal erosion prevention function of coral reefs for the GoK with respect to (1) Southeast Asian regions ($75,560 per square kilometre) and (2) Indian Ocean country of Sri Lanka ($44,674 per square kilometre). An average of these two values ($60,117 per square kilometre) was considered as the coastal erosion prevention value of coral reefs in the GoK. As the total coral reef area in the GoK is about 277 km², the total annual coastal erosion prevention value of coral reefs would be around Rs.799.31 million ($1=Rs.48). In per unit area terms, the coastal

Table 10.6 Parameters used for benefit transfer method in coastal protection and biodiversity values of coral reefs

Parameters	Unit	Southeast Asia*	Indian Ocean*	Gujarat (GoK)
GDP deflator index (2007)	–	115	124	–
Estimated coastal erosion prevention value (2003)	Million $	5,047	1,595	–
Adjusted coastal erosion prevention value (2007)	$ per sq. km	71,269	44,666	–
Estimated biodiversity value (2003)	Million $	458	199	–
Adjusted biodiversity value (2007)	$ per sq. km	6,696	5,574	–
Length of shoreline	km	95,680	1,340	342
Ratio of reef area to coastal margin (shoreline)	Sq. km/km	0.79	0.51	0.81
Population density	No. per sq. km	159	307	258
Per capita income	$	2,250	1,540	1,334
Value added in agriculture	% of GDP	12	17	12

Notes
*Countries considered for Southeast Asia estimates include the Philippines, Indonesia and Malaysia. Sri Lanka was considered for the Indian Ocean.

erosion prevention value of coral reefs in the GoK was estimated as Rs.2.886 million per square kilometre.

10.5.5 *Maintenance of biodiversity*

It is well recognized that biodiversity and, to a larger extent, the community structure, control ecosystem functioning. Furthermore, it is also understood that high diversity leads to greater community stability and productivity and makes the system less vulnerable to external pressures and eventualities. Being repositories of ancient phyla, as well as more recent specialized taxa, coral reefs are among the most spectacular, productive, diverse (per unit area) and threatened ecosystems on earth. Despite the biological, cultural and economic value of coral reefs and, at the same time, wide range of threats causing their global decline, it is realized that there are serious gaps in knowledge about the patterns of diversity of coral reefs.

The GoK is considered as one of the biodiversity hotspots of India. Specifically, the southern coast of the gulf is known for its rich biodiversity, mainly due to the presence of coral reefs, mangroves and other associated habitats such as sea grass, rocky inter-tidal areas, etc. No comprehensive and authentic list of flora and fauna is available for the GoK in general or for the coral reefs in particular. A compilation of flora and fauna from different sources was attempted on many occasions, but the species list associated with coral reefs is still based on conjecture rather than systematic surveys.

As part of this study, effort was made to prepare a comprehensive list of species under different taxa within the GoK. Accordingly, the following was recorded in the GoK: 174 species of algae; ten species of mangrove; 365 species of fish; 129 species of aquatic bird; eight species of reptile; five species of marine mammal; 69 species of sponge; 102 species of coelenterate, which includes 68 species of coral; 357 species of molluscan; 115 species of arthropod, including 71 species of crab and 33 species of prawn; 35 species of echinoderm, including ten species of sea cucumber and six species of star fish; and 58 species belonging to minor phyla. Thus, colourful sponges, corals, reef fish, prawns, lobsters, pearl oyster, window pane oyster, sea horse, giant sea anemone, sea hare, puffer fish, sharks, cat fish, ray fish, star fish, sea urchin, *Bonellia*, *Sabella*, dugong, sea turtle, dolphin, etc. are the species having high conservation values, both locally and globally.

In the context of the present study in the GoK, the bio-prospecting value of genetic diversity of marine flora and fauna was ascertained at least in qualitative terms by compiling the results of screening of various organisms for different biological activities. While going through the literature, it was found that not enough biological materials from the GoK were screened for bio-prospecting. However, with the kind of species diversity the GoK possesses, the future value of these species in deriving various drug and other biosynthetic products for industrial uses may be quite high.

Because limited knowledge exists about the biodiversity pattern of the GoK, its economic valuation is considered a difficult task. However, during the present study maintenance of the biodiversity function of coral reefs in the GoK was valued by applying BTM. For this purpose, a similar approach was adopted as for the coastal protection function. However, in the present case, values were adjusted based on three parameters: (1) ratio of reef flat to coastal margin; (2) population density; and (3) per capita income.

Accordingly, using the above parameters – which are considered to have influence in defining the value of coral-reef-associated biodiversity in two regions (Southeast Asia and the Indian Ocean) – we estimated the values of biodiversity for the GoK. We recorded two values for the GoK – one with respect to Southeast Asian regions ($7,234 per square kilometre) and another with respect to the Indian Ocean country of Sri Lanka ($6,122 per square kilometre). Finally, an average of these two values ($6,678 per square kilometre) was attributed as the biodiversity value for the GoK. Considering the total coral reef area in the entire GoK is about 277 km^2, the total annual biodiversity value of coral reefs would be around Rs.88.79 million ($1 = Rs.48). In per unit area terms, the biodiversity value of coral reefs in the GoK would be estimated as Rs.0.3205 million per square kilometre.

10.5.6 Net present value

In terms of the above-described goods and services, coral reefs in the GoK provide an annual benefit of approximately Rs.2,200 million (Table 10.7). In terms of the net present value of these benefits for the annuity (i.e. perpetuality), the total values turned out to be about Rs.110,000 million and Rs.55,000 million, using the discount rate of 2 per cent and 4 per cent, respectively (Table 10.8).

It is important to mention here that there are many conceptual and empirical problems inherent in producing such an estimate, yet this exercise is important in order to: (1) establish at least a first approximation of the values of ecosystem

Table 10.7 Total estimated annual value of benefits from coral reefs in the GoK

Goods and services	Method	Total annual value (million Rs.)	Value per unit area of coral reefs in GoK (Rs./km²/year)
Fisheries	Financial revenue analysis	1,284.00	4,640,000
Tourism and recreation	Financial revenue analysis	17.80	64,203
Protection against salinity ingression	Productivity change and preventive expenditure measure	10.34	37,329
Protection against coastal erosion	Benefit transfer method	799.31	2,885,628
Maintenance of genetic diversity (biodiversity)	Benefit transfer method	88.79	320,530
Total		2,200.24	7,947,690

Table 10.8 Net present value of different ecosystem functions of coral reefs in the GoK (values in Rs. million)

Coral functions/benefits	Net annual benefit (2007)	20 years		Infinitum	
		2% DR	4% DR	2% DR	4% DR
Fisheries	1,284.00	20,993	17,334	64,200	32,100
Tourism	17.80	291	240	890	445
Biodiversity	88.79	1,452	1,199	4,439	2,220
Protection against salinity ingression	10.34	169	140	517	258
Protection against coastal erosion	799.31	13,069	10,791	39,965	19,983
Total	2,200.24	35,974	29,704	110,011	55,006

Note
DR = discount rate.

services of coral reefs in the GoK; and (2) identify critical research needs. It also needs to be emphasized that the present estimates represent a minimum value, which would certainly increase by adopting better data-gathering systems and accounting for the spatio-temporal dynamics of coral reef systems in the GoK.

10.6 Summary

The coral reefs perform a number of functions that provide a number of benefits to mankind, which are otherwise taken for granted. The benefits of coral reefs will continue to be available to the local population for infinitum, provided they are not degraded. Quantifying these benefits is a starting point for conservation of coral reefs because they provide policy makers with the guidance they need to carry out cost–benefit analysis of proposed actions. The coral reefs provide current and long-term benefits and require greater focus on their management for inter-generational equity. As mentioned earlier, the valuation done here is only a rough guide to the true values of the coral reefs because, first, not all benefits can be quantified and, second, due to inadequacies of the valuation techniques.

The estimation of present value conclusively proves that the coral reefs of the GoK have a very high intrinsic value, which is essential for the survival of the local economy of the coastal belt of Jamnagar (located in the semi-arid zone of Saurashtra in Gujarat, where agricultural productivity is low and is totally dependent upon monsoonal rainfall). Coral reefs also provide inter-linkages with the local economy and consistently prove to be a large income multiplier. In such a scenario, the coral reefs of the GoK provide invaluable resources and income to the local population at no cost. Hence, they must be managed and conserved to sustain economic development at the village level. Already, excess pressure on the coral reefs due to increasing population has resulted in the decline of functional values and benefits derived from them. The cost/value of not conserving would directly hit the food security and livelihood function of the coral reefs. Hence, these first order/rough estimates of the benefits (or cost if not protected) are of great significance in motivating policy makers towards conservation and sustainable management of coral reef systems in the GoK. Any coastal planning in the context of apparent drivers of change in the region must acknowledge this economic significance of coral reefs. These values are at the most conservative and fall in the lower bound, as many other functions have not been accounted for due to limitations in the data. Any decision bereft of this recognition of the economic values of coral reefs might prove inefficient and myopic.

Acknowledgement

We sincerely thank the World Bank (New Delhi) for initiating and supporting this study under the India Integrated Coastal Zone Management Project. We also thank Dr Jack Ruitenbeek for his valuable comments and suggestions on the draft study report. Thanks are also due to the office of the Gujarat Ecology Commission and Marine National Park for providing logistic support for the study. We are grateful to different government departments for providing valuable field data relevant to this study. Special thanks are due to Mr M.I. Patel, who shared his knowledge and understanding about the ecology of the GoK and its coral reef system.

References

Ahmed, M., Chong, C.K. and Balasubramanian, H. 2004. An overview of problems and issues of coral reef management. In: Ahmed, M., Chong, C.K. and Cesar, H. (eds). *Economic Valuation and Policy Priorities for Sustainable Management of Coral Reefs.* Penang, Malaysia: WorldFish Center, pp. 2–11.

Ansink, E., Hein, L. and Hasund, K.P. 2008. To value functions or services? An analysis of ecosystem valuation approaches. *Environmental Values* 17: 489–503.

Arthur, R. 2000. Coral bleaching and mortality in three Indian reef regions during an El Nino southern oscillation event. *Current Science* 79 (12): 1723–1729.

Bahuguna, A. and Nayak, S. 1998. *Coral Reefs of the Indian Ocean.* Ahmedabad: Space Application Centre.

Balmford, A., Bruner, A., Cooper, C., Costanza, R., Farber, S., Green, R.E., Jenkins, M., Jefferiss, P., Jessamy, V., Madden, J., Munro, K., Myers, N., Naeem, S., Paavola, J., Rayment, M., Rosendo, S., Roughgarden, J., Trumper, K. and Turner, R.K. 2002. Economic reasons for conserving wild nature. *Science* 297: 950–953.

Burke, L. and Maidens, J. 2004. *Reefs at Risk in the Caribbean.* Washington, DC: World Resources Institute.

Burke, L., Selig, E. and Spalding, M. 2002. *Reefs at Risk in Southeast Asia.* Washington, DC: World Resources Institute.

Carte, B.K. 1996. Biomedical potential of marine natural products. *BioScience* 46: 271–286.

Cesar, H. 2003. Economic valuation of the coral reefs of Egypt. Report prepared for the MVE-Unit of EEPP, funded by USAID.

Cesar, H., Burke, L. and Pet-Soede, L. 2003. *The Economics of Worldwide Coral Reef Degradation.* Arnhem: Cesar Environmental Economics Consulting.

Chavan, S.A. 1984. Coral adventure. *Sanctuary Club* 1 (3): 12–15.

Costanza, R., d'Arge, R., de Groot, R., Farberk, S., Grasso, M., Hannon, B., Limburg, K., Naeem, S., O'Neill, R.V., Paruelo, J., Raskin, R.G., Sutton, P. and van den Belt, M. 1997. The value of the world's ecosystem services and natural capital. *Nature* 387: 253–260.

Daily, G.C., Polasky, S., Goldstein, J., Karieva, P.M., Mooney, H.A., Pejchar, L., Rickets, T.H., Slazman, J. and Shallenberger, R. 2009. Ecosystem service in decision making: Time to deliver. *Frontiers of Ecology and Environment* 7 (1): 21–28.

De Groot, R.S., Wilson, M.A. and Boumans, R.M.J. 2002. A typology for the classification, description and valuation of ecosystem functions, goods and services. *Ecological Economics* 41: 393–408.

Dixon, B. 2002. Scotland's mountains: Valuing the environmental benefits. MSc thesis, Department of Environmental Science and Technology, Imperial College, London.

Gates, R.D. 1990. Seawater temperature and sublethal coral bleaching in Jamaica. *Coral Reefs* 8: 193–197.

Gomez, E.D., Alino, P.M., Yap, H.T. and Licuanan, W.Y. 1994. A review of the status of Philippines reefs. *Marine Pollution Bulletin* 29 (1–3): 62–68.

MA. 2003. *Ecosystems and Human Well-being: A Framework for Assessment.* Washington, DC: Island Press.

MA. 2005a. *Findings from Responses Working Group.* Washington, DC: Island Press.

MA. 2005b. *Ecosystems and Human Well-being: Biodiversity Synthesis.* Washington, DC: World Resource Institute.

Maler, K.G., Aniyar, S. and Jansson, A. 2008. Accounting for ecosystem services as a way to understand the requirements for sustainable development. *Proceedings of the National Academy of Sciences* 105: 9501–9506.

Moberg, F. and Folke, C. 1999. Ecological goods and services of coral reef ecosystems. *Ecological Economics* 29: 215–233.

Patel, M.I. 1976. Generic diversity of Scleractinians around Poshitra point, Gulf of Kutch. *Indian Journal of Marine Sciences* 7: 30–32.

Patel, M.I. 1985. Patchy corals of the Gulf of Kutch. *Proceedings of the Symposium on Endangered Marine Animals and Marine Parks* 1: 411–413.

Pearce, D.W. and Turner, K.R. 1990. Economics of Natural Resource and the Environment, 1st edn. London: Harvester Wheatsheaf.

Pillai, C.S.G. and Patel, M.I. 1988. Scleractinian corals from the Gulf of Kutch. *Journal of Marine Biological Association, India* 30: 54–74.

Pillai, C.S.G., Rajgopal, M.S. and Varghese, M.A. 1979. Preliminary report on the reconnaissance survey of the major coastal and marine ecosystems in the Gulf of Kutch. Marine Fishery Information Service. CMFRI No. 14: 16–20.

Pomerance, R. 1999. Coral bleaching, coral mortality, and global climate change. Report presented by Deputy Assistant Secretary of State for the Environment and Development to the U.S. Coral Reef Task Force, 5 March, Maui, Hawaii.

Rouquette, J.R., Posthumos, H., Gowing, D.J.G., Tucker, G., Dawson, Q.L., Hess, T.M. and Morris, J. 2009. Valuing nature: Conservation interests on agricultural floodplains. *Journal of Applied Ecology* 46: 289–296.

Ruitenbeek, J. and Cartier, C. 1999. *Issues in Applied Coral Reef Biodiversity Valuation: Results for Montego Bay, Jamaica.* World Bank Research Committee Project RPO# 682–22.

Samonte-Tan, G. and Armedilla, M.C. 2004. Economic valuation of Philippine coral reefs in the South China Sea biogeographic region. National Coral Reef Review Series (3). United Nations Environment Programme (UNEP), Nairobi.

Scheer, G. 1985. The distribution of reef corals in Indian Ocean with a historical review of its investigation. *Deep Sea Research Part A* 31: 885–900.

Seenprachawong, U. 2004. An economic analysis of coral reefs in the Andaman Sea of Thailand. In Ahmed, M., Chong, C.K. and Cesar, H. (eds). *Economic Valuation and Policy Priorities for Sustainable Management of Coral Reefs*. Penang, Malaysia: WorldFish Center, pp. 79–83.

Sen Gupta, R. and Deshmukhe, G. 2000. *Coastal and Maritime Environments of Gujarat: Ecology and Economics*. Vadodara: Gujarat Ecological Society.

Singh, H.S., Yennawar, P., Asari, R.J., Tatu, K. and Raval, B.R. 2006. *An Ecological and Socio-Economic Study in Marine National Park and Sanctuary in the Gulf of Kutch*. Gandhinagar: GEER Foundation.

Spalding, M.D., Ravilious, C. and Green, E.P. 2001. *World Atlas of Coral Reefs*. Prepared by the UNEP-World Conservation Monitoring Centre. Berkeley, CA: University of California Press.

Turpie, J.K., Heydenrych, B.J. and Lamberth, S.J. 2003. Economic value of terrestrial and marine biodiversity in the Cape Floristic region: Implications for defining effective and socially optimal conservation strategies. *Biological Conservation* 112: 233–251.

Van Beukering, P.J.H., Haider, W., Longland, M., Cesar, H.J.S., Sablan, J., Shjegstad, S., Beardmore, B., Liu, Y. and Garces, G.O. 2007. *The Economic Value of Guam's Coral Reefs*. Guam: University of Guam Marine Laboratory.

Whittingham, E., Campbell, J. and Townsley, P. 2003. *Poverty and reefs: A Global Overview*. Exeter: IMM Ltd.

Wilkinson, C.R. (ed.). 2004. *Status of the Coral Reefs of the World*, vols 1–2. Townsville, Queensland: Australian Institute of Marine Science.

Part III
Synthesis

11 Institutions and ecosystem functions

The case of Keti Bunder, Pakistan[1]

John M. Gowdy and Aneel Salman

The evidence is clear. The consequences of biodiversity loss and ecosystem service degradation – from water to food to fish – are not being shared equitably across the world. The areas of richest biodiversity and ecosystem services are in developing countries where they are relied upon by billions of people to meet their basic needs. Yet subsistence farmers, fisherman, the rural poor and traditional societies face the most serious risks from degradation. This imbalance is likely to grow. Estimates of the global environmental costs in six major categories, from climate change to overfishing, show that the costs arise overwhelmingly in high- and middle-income countries and are borne by low-income countries.

(Srinivasan *et al.*, 2008 quoted in TEEB, 2008: 20)

11.1 Introduction: ecosystems, economics and development

A consensus exists among conservation biologists that the earth is experiencing a loss of biodiversity on the scale of the five major extinction episodes that occurred during the past 600 million years of complex life on earth. It is no exaggeration to say that human activity within the past 100 years has drastically altered the course of biological evolution. The International Union for the Conservation of Nature (IUCN) estimates that one-quarter of mammal species face extinction (Gilbert, 2008). At least 12 percent of birds are threatened, together with 30 percent of amphibians and 5 percent of reptiles. Particularly alarming is the state of the world's oceans and coastal areas. Human-caused threats to ocean biodiversity are summarized by Jackson (2008: 11458):

Today, the synergistic effects of human impacts are laying the groundwork for a comparatively great Anthropocene mass extinction in the oceans with unknown ecological and evolutionary consequences. Synergistic effects of habitat destruction, overfishing, introduced species, warming, acidification, toxins and mass runoff of nutrients are transforming once complex ecosystems like coral reefs into monotonous level bottoms, transforming clear and productive coastal seas into anoxic dead zones, and transforming complex food webs topped by big animals into simplified, microbially dominated ecosystems with boom and bust cycles of toxic dinoflagellate blooms, jellyfish, and disease.

The alarm expressed by biologists about the state of the world's ecosystems is in sharp contrast to the attitude of most economists. Dasgupta (2008: 1) puts it bluntly: "Nature has been ill-served by 20th century economics." Economists have frequently been guilty of "misplaced concreteness" (Daly, 1985; Dasgupta, 2007; Georgescu-Roegen, 1971) in assuming that the standard general equilibrium model of the economy can deal adequately with very long-run and dynamically complex issues like biodiversity loss and climate change. In the twenty-first century attitudes among economists are beginning to change as (1) the magnitude of the environmental crisis becomes increasingly apparent; (2) the standard model is enriched by behavioral economics, neuroeconomics and evolutionary game theory; and (3) the current financial crisis has exposed the fragility the world economic system, whose growth has been based to a large extent on transforming natural into financial capital (Gowdy and Krall, 2009; Kallis *et al.*, 2009).

The field of ecological economics was established some 20 years ago in response to the divide between mainstream economics and those economists and biologists concerned about the degradation of the natural world. Today that divide is much smaller for two reasons. First of all, welfare economic theory is undergoing a revolution as economic models increasingly accommodate alternatives to the assumptions of rational economic man and perfect competition. This has broadened the concept of "utility" beyond mere per capita income, and the concept of "production" to include the unpaid services of nature. Second, as traditional models of economic growth are expanded to include the services of nature, the policy recommendations of mainstream and ecological economists are converging. A consensus is emerging among environmental and ecological economists around the belief that, if human economic activity is to become sustainable, the damage to the earth's supporting ecological and physical systems must be reversed.

But even if economists begin to recognize the importance of natural capital, why should the loss of biodiversity and ecosystem integrity be an economic development concern? In the past, economists have argued that only the wealthy have the luxury of being concerned about environmental quality. So the story goes, the best way to protect ecosystems is to encourage economic growth so that the poor can have enough income to become "green." This is the so-called "post-materialist" thesis of Inglehart (1990), Krutilla (1967) and others. Martinez-Alier (1995) points out two flaws in this thesis. First, continued material growth implies continued environmental stress. Second, compared to the wealthy, the world's poorest receive a much larger percentage of their livelihoods directly from ecosystems, and thus they have a much greater incentive to preserve local ecosystems. The "GDP of the poor" (European Communities, 2008) is undervalued because so much of it depends on unpriced inputs from nature. Estimates from India suggest that ecosystem services add to only 7 percent of measured GDP, but comprise 57 percent of the GDP of the country's poorest (Sukdev and Bishop, 2008). Yet, in general it is the rich who decide whether or not to preserve biodiversity and ecosystem functions based on market rates of interest and investment opportunities. And, although the poor have a larger stake in preserving ecosystem functions and the resulting flows of ecosystem services, a large percentage of the world's disadvantaged are in such a desperate position that they must sometimes sacrifice these services for immediate gain.

This chapter explores the value of the services of ecosystems and biodiversity from several perspectives, including market economics, human well-being and ecosystem functioning as a biological process. A major focus is the value of regulating services, those benefits obtained from the smooth functioning of ecosystem processes, including maintaining water quality and quantity, erosion control, water purification, regulation of human disease vectors, provision of biological species, pollination and storm protection.

Preliminary survey results from the village of Keti Bunder on the southeastern coast of Pakistan are used to illuminate the discussion. The next section discusses the functions of ecosystems and biodiversity and surveys various methods used to value them. Section 11.3 discusses the potential impacts of climate change on coastal ecosystems in South Asia; Section 11.4 discusses the relevance of some innovative ideas in development economics to ecosystem valuation; Section 11.5 discusses the current situation in Keti Bunder; Section 11.6 presents some relevant preliminary results from a survey of Keti Bunder conducted by the authors; and Section 11.7 concludes.

11.2 Ecosystem functions and values of ecosystem services

The Millennium Ecosystem Assessment (2005) provides a useful classification of ecosystem services: supporting, provisioning, regulating and cultural. The values of ecosystems and biodiversity can be seen as layers of a hierarchy moving from market value (supporting, provisioning and regulating) to non-market value to humans (cultural and psychological), to the role of biodiversity and complexity in preserving ecosystem resilience. These levels of value point to the need for a pluralistic and flexible methodology to determine appropriate policies for ecosystem use and preserving ecosystem functions (Gowdy, 1997).

11.2.1 The economic value of ecosystems and biodiversity

Economists have used many approaches to place economic value on ecosystem services. One way is to follow the NNP accounting framework and to calculate the "shadow price" of a particular service. This involves using a constrained optimization model to specify the necessary conditions for a social welfare optimum, including the use of environmental goods. This method has been constructively employed to estimate the benefits of environmental services, but it brings with it numerous assumptions including strictly rational behavior by all economic actors, perfect competition, near to equilibrium markets, and so on (see the discussion by Mäler *et al.*, 2008). Another approach is to directly estimate the contributions of funds[2] of ecosystems and biodiversity to economic activity including, for example, eco-tourism, recreation and the value of direct biological inputs such as fisheries and forests. Yet another way is to estimate the costs avoided by preserving an ecosystem – for example, avoiding the costs of flooding if a wetland were destroyed. A classic example is Chichilnisky and Heal's (1998) study of the value of the Catskills watershed to protection of the purity of New York City's drinking water. Augmenting the water purification capacity of the watershed was estimated to cost $1.3 billion, while the cost of building a new water treatment plant was estimated to be $8 billion. Another example of ecosystem service loss is the extinction of bees in Maoxian county, China. Pollination of apple trees must now be done by hand. Formerly, it took two bee colonies to directly pollinate 100 trees, a task that is now done by 20–25 people (Melillo and Sala, 2008).[3]

In a simple system it may be possible to estimate the contribution of a particular ecosystem to a particular economic activity. For example, the value of mangroves to the fishing industry might be estimated by the following equation, where Q is the output (or value of the catch) of fish, S is the area of mangroves, and X_i are the other inputs (Barbier, 2008):

$$Q = F(X_1 \ldots X_i, S) \tag{1}$$

Barbier (ibid.) gives an excellent survey of the value of mangroves as an input to the fishing industries of several countries. Complications exist with this approach due to complex interactions and positive and negative biological and institutional feedback effects in coastal ecosystems. Perhaps the greatest drawback is the existence of large and unpredictable exogenous fluctuations both in fish stocks and market prices.

Although evidence from contingent valuation, hedonic pricing and other economic valuation tools underscores the importance of biodiversity and ecosystem functions, these methods give incomplete, lower-bound estimates of their values (Mäler *et al.*, 2008; Nunes and van den Bergh, 2001). It should also be noted that environmental accounting prices do not value the environment as a whole (Dasgupta *et al.*, 2000). Rather, these estimates place monetary values on specific economic services of specific ecosystem functions. The total value of the earth's environment is infinite and thus is not amenable to economic analysis. If any one of the world's major biophysical systems is perturbed beyond a certain point, the existence of all human life would be threatened.

11.2.2 *The socio-cultural value of ecosystems and biodiversity*

We also know that the biological world contributes to human psychological well-being in ways that can be empirically measured (Kellert, 1996; Wilson, 1994) but not adequately valued in a traditional social welfare framework (Norton, 2005; Orr, 2004). Spiritual, cultural and aesthetic benefits of interacting with nature may be considered in a more comprehensive conception of utility such as the Bentham/Kahneman notion of utility as well-being. This goes back to Georgescu-Roegen's (1971) definition of utility as an "immaterial flux" – the enjoyment of life.

In traditional communities spiritual ties to the land are much stronger than in modern western societies. Hunter-gatherers and traditional agriculturalists depend directly on solar energy – and its immediate conversion to plants and animals – for their day-to-day existence. If the direct services from nature's funds are disturbed, the consequences are immediately apparent. Thus, all traditional societies have strict rules and regulations to protect these funds (see the examples from Gowdy (1998)). Among the inhabitants of the Nicobar Islands, for example, numerous ceremonies and rituals are linked to the regulation of natural resource use (Singh, 2006).

11.2.3 The ecological value of biodiversity and complexity to ecosystems

Evidence suggests that biologically diverse ecosystems are more resilient to environmental shocks than less diverse ones (Tilman and Downing, 1994), though the relationship between resilience and biodiversity is complicated (Robinson, 1992). If a system loses its resilience it can quickly and irreversibly flip to another state (Walker *et al.*, 2004). Furthermore, it is impossible to tell ahead of time what the loss of a species or species relationships will do to the system. In general, removing keystone species from an ecosystem will have significant (and non-marginal) effects. For example, Brock and Kelt (2004) removed kangaroo rats from a plot of land in the southwestern United States. The result was a significant increase in plant cover, significant declines in bare ground, and declines in seed predation. Bromley (1998) refers to this as "functional transparency" – the effects of removing a species or otherwise altering an ecosystem can only be known after the alteration.

11.2.4 The services of mangrove ecosystems

Mangrove ecosystems are one of the most critical natural resources in the tropics. They provide a number of functions, including protection of a pool of biodiversity and provision of a habitat for a diverse community of organisms ranging from bacteria and fungi to fish, shrimps, birds, reptiles and mammals. They are a critical breeding ground and habitat for economically valuable fish and other seafood. Mangroves are a source of fuel wood and fodder for livestock. They protect the coastal zone from wind and tidal action and they reduce siltation and the strength of storm surges. Mangroves dissipate the energy and size of waves as a result of the drag forces exerted by their multiple roots and stems. Wave energy may be reduced by 75 percent during the wave's passage through 200 m of mangrove (Colls *et al.*, 2009). In October 1999, Mangrove forests reduced the impact of a 'super cyclone' that struck Orissa on India's east coast. On 26 December 2004, when the tsunami struck Indonesia, the Andaman and Nicobar Islands, Sri Lanka and the coastlines of Kerala and Tamil Nadu, human settlements located behind the mangrove stands suffered smaller losses compared to other areas (McLeod and Salm, 2006).

Because of their important ecosystem functions, and their direct economic uses in tropical areas around the world, mangrove ecosystems are critical to the well-being of a large portion of the world's poorest people. Mangrove forests are in many ways a major focal point in the intersection between poverty, declining ecosystems and global climate change. Over the last 50 years about one-third of the world's mangrove forests have been destroyed by human activity (Alongi, 2002; McLeod and Salam, 2006). Climate change threats to mangroves include decreased precipitation in some regions, increased storm damage and rapid sea-level rise.

11.3 Climate change and ecosystems in South Asia

A consensus has emerged among scientists and policy makers that global climate change represents a major threat to the well-being of humankind and the biosphere (Stern, 2007; IPCC, 2007). During the past 100 years or so the average global temperature has risen by about 1°C, with much of that increase due to human activity, especially fossil fuel burning and deforestation. The rate of increase has accelerated during the past 20 years as the human impact has begun to dominate natural processes. The real concern is not what has happened so far, but that global temperatures are projected to increase further, by 1.4–5.8°C by 2100, and to continue to rise long after that (Archer, 2009; IPCC, 2007). Scenarios of the likely consequences of such an increase differ substantially among regions, but include sea-level rise, shortages of freshwater, biodiversity loss, increased droughts and floods, more frequent and intense forest fires, more intense storms, more extreme heat episodes, agricultural disruption, the spread of infectious diseases and mass migrations. Evidence from past climate regimes indicate that even if CO_2 emissions were immediately halted, the earth would eventually warm by 2–3°C, solely because of past emissions and the inertia of the climate system (Haywood and Williams, 2005; Jiang *et al.*, 2005). All living species are adapted to particular climate regimes and are most likely in for a rough ride in the coming decades and centuries, even if aggressive mitigation steps are taken soon (Anderson and Bows, 2008; Schneider, 2009).

South Asia is particularly vulnerable to the effects of climate change. About one-quarter of the world's population lives in the four countries of Pakistan, Nepal, India and Bangladesh. Hundreds of millions of people living near the coasts of South Asia will eventually be displaced by rising sea levels, increased severity of storms and shortages of freshwater. Specific physical impacts predicted from climate change models include the following.

Higher average temperatures: analysis of climatic data shows that there has been an increase in average temperature by 0.6–1.0°C in the coastal areas of South Asia since the early 1990s. During 2005, Bangladesh, India and Pakistan faced temperatures 5–6°C above the world average (UNDP-HDR, 2007). Temperature changes in the mountain ranges of the Himalayas have been even more dramatic, resulting in accelerated melting of glaciers from Nepal to the Hindu Kush (Steinbauer and Zeidler, 2008). These higher temperatures bring a variety of risks to South Asia (Munasinghe, 2008).

Changes in rainfall patterns and extreme weather events: the coastal areas of South Asia have suffered from erratic rainfall patterns in recent years. Evidence from the northern mountains is inconclusive due to the lack of significant monitoring in that area, but the area has apparently experienced an increase in rainfall in recent years. In any case, changing rainfall patterns are expected to be an increasingly serious problem as climate change intensifies. All climate change scenarios point to increased flooding in mountainous regions due to glacial melting, and in coastal regions due to sea-level rise and the intensification of tropical storms. These changing physical impacts will have unknown, but likely adverse, consequences on agricultural output, water availability and migration patterns.

Regional water shortages: the drinking water for much of India and Pakistan comes from the Himalayan, Karakoram, and Hindu Kush glaciers that are already beginning to melt from warmer temperatures (Jianchu *et al.*, 2007). Climate models indicate that this melting will accelerate in the coming years with unknown but severe consequences for drinking water, agricultural irrigation and human health. Increasing salinity in coastal regions from rising sea levels and more severe storms has already taken a toll on coastal communities (Rees and Collins, 2004).

The main effects on human well-being from the physical effects of climate change are as follows.

Loss of agricultural production: South Asian economies are heavily dependent on agriculture, meaning the economic sector is most vulnerable to climate change. Crop yields are already declining in the region, possibly due to climate change. According to IPCC Chairman Rajendra Pachuri: "Wheat production in India is already in decline, for no other reason than climate change. Everyone thought we didn't have to worry about Indian agriculture for several decades. Now we know it's being affected now" (quoted in Worstall, 2007). In Pakistan, agricultural yields are also declining and climate change may be the culprit. Changes in the timing of monsoons are already having an adverse effect on agriculture in Pakistan and India.

Climate-induced migration: in recent months tens of thousands of families in India have been displaced by severe flooding. Chandrashekhar Dasgupta (2007) asks: "If a developing country is so vulnerable even to normal seasonal variations, how will it cope with the impacts of climate change – floods and droughts, sea-level rise, changes in rainfall patterns, cyclones or typhoons?" Recent monsoons in India resulted in a major river changing course, resulting in the loss of thousands of human lives and tens of thousands of refugees. Water shortages in the north of Pakistan and sea-level rise along the coast will eventually result in millions of environmental refugees flooding the nation's major inland cities.

Human health: South Asia's health indicators are among the worst in the world. Infant and child mortality are very high. According to a World Bank

(2006) report, environmental health risks contribute to more than 20 percent of the total disease incidence. Environmental health risks will accelerate with climate change, as water shortages become more acute and as more and more environmental refugees seek refuge in inland urban centers. Again, it is the very poor who are most susceptible to the effects of climate change and the resulting disruption of ecosystem functions (Khan, 2002).

11.4 Institutions and adaptation: the economics of sustainable well-being

Including only measured economic output in estimates of ecosystem and biodiversity values grossly underestimates their contribution to human well-being (Banuri *et al.* 2002; Gowdy, 2005; Mäler *et al.*, 2008). While income is a critical factor in human welfare, it is only one of several important ingredients. A growing body of economic research uses measures of subjective well-being as indicators of social welfare (Agrawal, 2008; Frey and Stutzer, 2002; Haq, 1997; Kahneman and Sugden, 2005). These measures show that, above some minimal level, per capita income growth and well-being are frequently only weakly correlated (Frey and Stutzer, 2002). Focusing only on income misses some equally important contributors to well-being and fails to capture many of the cultural and biological resilience contributions of healthy ecosystems and biodiversity to total value.

In the 1990s development economists began to call for approaches that went beyond increasing a nation's GDP. Sen (1999) suggested focusing on increasing the ability to live an informed and full life. Sen and Haq developed a comprehensive measure of human well-being called the Human Development Index (HDI). The HDI measures three basic dimensions of human development – health, education, and income. The HDI spawned a number of related indices that go deeper in measuring the notion of "human capabilities." The "capability poverty measure" (CPM) looks at three basic capabilities – nourishment and health, the capability of healthy reproduction and female illiteracy (Womenaid International, 2007). The CPM measure shows that while 21 percent of the population in developing countries is below the income poverty line, 37 percent are below the minimum standard in terms of capability (ibid.). Nussbaum (2000) called for a focus on "distributive justice," that is, creating the conditions for the realization of a set of central human capabilities. Such policies promise to be more effective than simply relying on aggregate income growth alone to improve the lives of the world's poorest. They also offer more flexibility in adapting to environmental changes and differing cultural worldviews. With a focus on well-being, individual happiness and self-actualization, the developing world may improve its human welfare position without emulating the environmentally and psychologically destructive consumption patterns that drove past economic growth in developed economies.

The research on subjective well-being has important implications for valuing ecosystem functions and formulating policies to protect them. Some evidence indicates that when individuals are more materially secure (not necessary financially wealthier) they are more likely to care about the environment (Rangel, 2003). Development policies focusing on subjective well-being might thus pay a double dividend. People would not only be happier, they would also be more willing to support efforts to conserve environmental services. But even if policies are based on sustainable welfare, it may not ensure the preservation of biodiversity and ecosystems. Examples abound of societies that apparently worked well in satisfying the broad preferences of their citizens but ended in ecological collapse (McDaniel and Gowdy, 1999). Humans get subjective well-being from nature, but this does not ensure that individuals living today will choose to preserve those features of nature that may be essential to future generations. Sound measures of the factors contributing to human well-being are needed, but also needed are indicators of the physical and biological requirements for long-term human survival.

As mentioned earlier, the well-being of the world's poorest depends to a large extent on the direct services of ecosystems and on maintaining ecosystem functions. These functions are under threat both from worldwide environmental changes, as well as from inadequate institutional responses to these changes. Development policies are unlikely to be effective unless these institutional factors are understood and targeted in development initiatives.

11.5 Keti Bunder, Pakistan

Keti Bunder is part of the Thatta district in Pakistan's Sindh province, located 200 km southeast of Karachi.[4] It is part of the Indus Delta and its four major distributaries – the Chan, Hajamoro, Khobar and Kangri. Keti Bunder consists of 42 village clusters (called *dehs*) spread over a total area of about 60,000 ha. The village settlements are built on mudflats between the various channels of the major Indus distributaries. The majority of the people in Keti Bunder are fishermen and belong to more than a dozen castes, most of them engaged in small-scale business and agriculture. Almost all the people speak the *Sindhi* language except for a few *Pathans* and *Punjabis*. The *Punjabis* have lived in Keti Bunder for generations and are now part of the local community.

Keti Bunder's climate is typical of South Asian coastal areas. January is the coolest month, with a minimum temperature of 9.5°C, while in June and July temperatures range from 23°C to 36°C. Mild winters extend from November to February, while the summer season extends from March to October. Average annual rainfall is 220 mm and falls mainly during the monsoon season. The northern part of Keti Bunder is a designated wildlife sanctuary harboring a significant population of migratory and resident water birds. A recent WWF survey recorded five species of aquatic mammals (dolphins and porpoises), three species of large mammals and 15 species of small mammals. A total of 69 bird species were observed, including 25 resident species and 44 migratory species. Additionally, 21 species of reptile and two species of amphibian were recorded. For fish, 63 species of finfish and 24 species of shellfish were observed (WWF-Pakistan, 2008b).

Before 1950, Keti Bunder was a major port and the center of a prosperous fishing and agricultural area. The entire area now faces a number of severe environmental problems and a resulting loss of livelihood opportunities. As a consequence of the construction of dams and other barriers upstream slowing the downstream water flow, as well as rises in sea level, salt water intrusion from the sea has become a major problem. The area is vulnerable to cyclones and tsunamis. The intensity of these cyclones has increased significantly during the last 30 years, possibly due to global warming. Thousands of Keti Bunder residents may be displaced in the next few years due to the impact of storms, rising sea levels and other expected effects of climate change.

Mangroves are the key environmental resource in Keti Bunder. The Indus Delta mangroves represent the largest area of arid climate mangroves in the world. An estimated 95 percent of the mangroves in the Indus Delta belong to the species Avicennia marina. Relatively small patches of Ceriops roxburghiana (from the Rhizophora family) and Aegicerias corniculata (from the Myrinaceal family) are found near the mouth of the Indus at Keti Bunder. Mangroves depend on freshwater discharges from the Indus river, a small quantity of freshwater from runoff, and domestic and industrial effluents from Karachi. Mangrove ecosystems are important for maintaining the many commercial fish species along the Pakistan coast. Despite the benefits provided by mangrove ecosystems, they face continuous pressure from human activities. Water flow into the Indus Delta has declined from 140 million-acre feet to 40 million-acre feet over the last few years and this, together with sea-level rise, has increased the salinity of seawater, which is detrimental to mangrove growth (see Figure 11.1). According to a Space and Upper Atmosphere Research Commission (SUPARCO) study conducted through satellite images in 1988–1989, the mangroves in Pakistan covered 160,000 ha. This cover was reduced by half, to 80,000 ha, when WWF-Pakistan surveyed the mangroves in 2002. Overharvesting of mangroves and dumping of refuse and pollutants by the local communities also contributed to

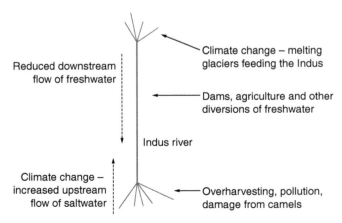

Figure 11.1 Threats of mangroves in Keti border.

this loss. The rate of degradation of mangrove forests in the delta was estimated to be 6 percent per year between 1980 and 1995, and only a small percentage are now considered to be healthy (Wood *et al.*, 2000). Water flows to the delta started declining when the Punjab irrigation system was developed in the 1890s. However, the construction of *Sukkur* (1932), *Kotri* (1955) and *Guddu* (1962) dams resulted in a drastic reduction of water flow to the delta, and a complete shift from agriculture to fisheries, coastal erosion and depletion of mangroves.

Freshwater for farming in Keti Bunder and other coastal regions comes almost entirely from the Indus river and its distributaries. The declining freshwater flow has negatively affected fish and shrimp breeding, and the upstream migration of the once plentiful Palla fish has dramatically declined. There is a water shortage in all villages in the area and water for drinking and cooking must be purchased from sellers in town. The shortage of clean drinking water is the main cause of many illnesses. A lack of health facilities also contributes to the increase in diseases. The common diseases in the community are diarrhea or dysentery, typhoid, hepatitis B, asthma, tuberculosis, malaria, skin and eye infections and other seasonal diseases (WWF-Pakistan, 2005a).

11.5.1 Economic conditions

A few decades ago the people of Keti Bunder had multiple options for economic subsistence, but the decline in freshwater forced a major change from agriculture and livestock to fishing. A growing population has increased the pressure on natural resources, especially the mangrove ecosystems. Fishing is now the main occupation of the inhabitants of all villages and the sole source of income. The indiscriminate use of banned nets and diminishing mangrove forests has reduced the fish catch. Due to inadequate alternate employment opportunities, the pressure on fisheries resources is intense, and the demise of the industry directly affects the livelihoods of everyone in Keti Bunder. The direct economic effect of the loss of freshwater has been the complete loss of the agricultural sector. Indirect effects are the increased incidence of water-borne diseases, another effect of the lack of fresh drinking water, and the disappearance of several fish species. Many of these effects are hard to quantify, much less measure using market values. If only market-measured income losses are considered, the livelihoods of the poor will always be overwhelmed by the monetary gains of the wealthy.

A major internal conflict in Keti Bunder and the surrounding villages involves the *Jaat* community that was previously engaged in agriculture and livestock raising, but has now turned to fishing due to land degradation. In competition with indigenous fishermen, *Jaats* use supposedly banned, small-mesh nylon nets to get the maximum catch in the short run. These nets catch juvenile fish of many species, driving some of them toward extinction (WWF-Pakistan, 2008b). The *Jaats* have also increased the camel population – grazing by these animals is damaging the mangrove forests.

Women have limited roles in decision making because economic resources are owned by men. They do have a significant role in the fishing process. Usually men fish while women dry small fish for domestic use. Women are also involved in making the cotton fishing nets, but use of the fine-mesh nylon nets has crowded out this domestic industry. However, the indigenous fisherwomen of the area enjoy more liberty and freedom as compared to other women of the area. For centuries the fisherwomen have had the greater role in family matters due to the fact that the fishermen are absent for much of the time. Thus, women of the village have to deal with all day-to-day family matters.

In April 2009, together with WWF-Pakistan, we administered a detailed questionnaire to Keti Bunder residents to help understand the perceptions of the community regarding the role of ecosystem services in community well-being, vulnerably to climate change and possible institutional responses to environmental disruption.[5] We believe that these survey results can be generalized to many coastal village communities throughout South Asia. In consultation with WWF-Pakistan, we chose two villages in creeks, Bhoori and Tippun, and one inland village, Haji Musa. Bhoori is the largest village, having 400 households. Tippun has 100 households and is significant because the 2007 cyclone leveled the entire village. Haji Musa is a small inland village with 40 households. All of the villages have common problems, but are also different demographically and physically. To complement the quantitative socio-economic and ecological data collected through questionnaires, we also used in-depth interviews to collect qualitative data. Focus group discussions involving both male and female community members were used to gain deeper insights and to cross-check the survey results. The interviews also provided a detailed intergenerational perspective. The survey used a random sample totaling 55 individuals in Bhoori village (39 males and 16 females), 32 individuals in Tippun village (20 males and 12 females) and 13 individuals in the inland village of Haji Musa (9 males and 4 females).

11.6 Survey results

The results of our survey generally confirm those of the earlier WWF survey and the impressions of the WWF field team. Based on our survey results the main observations of Keti Bunder residents are: (1) a decline in the health of mangroves; (2) the depletion of the stocks of major fish species; (3) reduced rainfall; and (4) an increase in extreme weather events. These negative trends are the result of complex interactions between exogenous physical changes (climate change and the reduced availability of freshwater) and changing patterns of resource use within the villages (overfishing and the destruction of mangroves). Another complicating socio-economic factor is the increased reliance on short-term borrowing by local fishermen, which has led to increased pressure to generate income. It also appears that the decline in ecosystem services has exacerbated ethnic tensions among the various Keti Bunder communities.

Environmental change was analyzed by using a Likert scale ranking (1 = poor, 5 = good for the state of mangroves and rainfall; 1 = less frequent, 5 = more frequent for cyclones) for the state of mangroves, the frequency of cyclones and

Table 11.1 Mangroves, cyclones and rainfall

Village			State of mangroves		Frequency of cyclones		Rainfall	
			2009	20 years ago	2009	20 years ago	2009	20 years ago
Bhoori	Male	39	2.4	4.0	5.0	2.3	1.4	4.5
	Female	16	2.6	4.1	5.0	2.6	1.3	4.2
Tippun	Male	20	2.1	4.4	4.9	2.5	1.5	4.3
	Female	12	2.0	4.5	4.7	2.0	1.5	4.3
Haji Moosa Jat	Male	9	1.7	4.3	5.0	1.9	1.6	4.3
	Female	4	1.75	4.25	5.0	2.0	1.5	4.2
		100						

rainfall at present and 20 years ago. As shown in Table 11.1, the results are quite striking. Males and females in all three villages surveyed strongly agreed that the state of mangroves has deteriorated, that rainfall is less frequent, and that the frequency of cyclones has increased.

In-depth interviews confirmed that the communities are aware of the role of mangroves in providing ecosystem services such as replenishing the fish stock, preventing damage from storms, preventing soil erosion and providing wood and fodder for household consumption. The communities of Bhoori and Tippun, which are living in creeks, responded that the mangrove cover has been substantially reduced over the past 20 years. Both of these communities are now replanting mangroves. One resident reported:

> When I was young, mangroves were rich and dense. The frequency of cyclones was once in a decade. People were happy and there was prosperity. There was wildlife and birds of different kinds would migrate every year. I remember them chirping in the mornings. But things have changed in the past 40 years, there are almost no rains and the frequency of storms and cyclones has increased. Mangrove cover has been reduced and some mangrove species no longer exist. There is more poverty and the fish stock has been drastically reduced. The pressure on fish has increased as all the former farmers [*Jatts*] became fishermen.
>
> (Mohammad Suleman, Tippun, 70)

The survey showed a near unanimous response regarding the lack of rainfall in recent years compared to earlier times. At present there are almost no rains and this is exacerbating the shortage of freshwater and reducing fish stocks and the availability of drinking water. Twenty years ago, the villages were receiving an adequate amount of rain, and freshwater was abundant.

A variety of fish inhabits the coastal waters and creeks, and represents the primary source of livelihood for the local population. Fish, shrimps and crabs are

Table 11.2 Decline in fish catch

Name of fish	Status ten years ago	Present status
Suo	Boat full of the fish was caught	It has almost vanished
Dangra	Boatful was caught	Almost vanished
All	One fishing boat caught about 1,000–2,000 fish	Hardly 500 fish are caught
Paplet	Its catch was 200–300 kg in one trip	One boat only brings 50 fish
Seeri	Its catch was 1,000 kg per fishing trip	Its catch has reduced to only 10 kg per fishing trip
Danthi	Its catch was 100–200 kg per fishing trip.	Its catch is only 10–20 kg per trip
Goli	Its catch was up to 100 kg per fishing trip.	Its catch is only up to 5 kg per trip
Sodi	Its catch was up to 100 kg per fishing trip.	Its catch is only up to 5 kg per trip
Khaga	Its catch was 1,000–2,000 fish per fishing trip	One boat brings hardly 20–50 fish
Palla	Boatful was caught	Completely vanished

Notes
Reasons given: deep sea trawlers, illegal nets and lack of freshwater from the Indus.

Table 11.3 Decline in shrimp catch

Shrimp	Status ten years ago	Present status
Jahira	Its catch was up to 500 kg per fishing trip	Its catch is hardly 5 kg per fishing trip
Tiger	Its catch was up to 100 kg per fishing trip.	Hardly one tiger shrimp is caught per fishing trip

key economic marine resources. Survey responses (Tables 11.2 and 11.3) indicate fish and shrimp stocks have decreased drastically during the last 20 years.

Apart from freshwater reduction, communities are involved in unsustainable fishing practices. Fishermen use banned nets that catch even the juvenile fish, which are considered trash and are used for poultry feed. This activity is reducing the fish stock at an alarming rate. At times there are conflicts in the community when they fish in each other's designated zones. Sea lords and commercial trawlers forcefully occupy some of the channels or creeks and do not allow the local fishermen to harvest in their marked territories. The coastal ecosystem is becoming fragile due to the increase in the number of fishermen, the increase in fishing boats, and an increase in the duration of individual fishing efforts. One villager observed:

The fish stock has declined by more than 50% in recent years. Palla fish which is very expensive has almost vanished. Earlier one fish might weigh 5–6 kilos but now they are around 1 kilo. The use of illegal nets has reduced the fish stock drastically. When we used Thukri [cotton] nets we would catch fewer fish at a time but catch more overall. Now with the Katra nets we catch more fish at a time but less overall. The reason for the decline is that the fish are badly damaged by the nylon nets. Sea lords and big trawlers take all the fish and we are left with almost no fish. The quality of the water has changed and this has changed the taste and size of the fish.

(Yaqoob, Haji Musa Jaat, 60)

There has been a direct loss of income due to declining fish stocks, as shown in Table 11.2. One of the biggest effects of the declining catch has been the growing debt trap due to increased borrowing because of the decline in, and increasing volatility of, the income stream of fishermen. Respondents to the survey indicated that in the past they used to lend money, but now they have become borrowers. Figure 11.2 summarizes the negative changes reported in the survey responses.

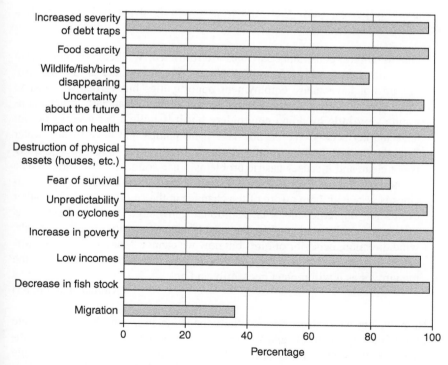

Figure 11.2 Percentage of respondents reporting negative environmental and economic changes.

Migration is not an option for many due to the costs and uncertainties involved. Dollu Yar, one of the residents of Bhoori village said:

> Migration is very limited, even though extreme events have occurred, because we are poor, and have no financial assets and no options. If we were financially strong we could migrate temporarily. The cost of living in urban areas is very high and we cannot afford to live there. In June 2007 we received the news that cyclone was coming and I asked my wife if we should go out of the area. My wife replied, what is the assurance that our lives would be safe if we go somewhere else. If Allah wants to keep us safe we will survive here.
>
> (Dollu Yar, Bhoori, 40)

Almost all the respondents own their houses. Fishing being the only source of livelihood, most of the fishermen own their boats. But villagers who are poor and cannot afford a boat, or had one that was damaged in cyclones, work as helpers. Some communities still have buffaloes and poultry for domestic consumption of milk and eggs. The number of livestock has been drastically reduced compared to 30–40 years ago when freshwater and fodder was available.

Survey responses show that women are entirely dependent on the men. According to one woman:

> Due to cultural constraints our roles are restricted. We help our menfolk in domestic chores, taking care of children, embroidery, and drying the fish. We do not have many employment opportunities but earlier we used to make nets but now they are replaced by nylon nets. Financially we can contribute very little by doing embroidery but it is limited because we do not have market access. We do not have hand pumps and have to buy water from the market. I take care of water consumption and budget it. The water is not clean and it causes gastric problems. I use cotton cloth to filter it. The health facilities are poor and we get expired medicines, the quality of medicines is very bad. I am aware of the changes in the environment but weather events are unpredictable. Our traditional knowledge does not help us as earlier we could predict from the visible signs from the color of clouds, wind direction, behavior of birds but now we cannot. Mangroves are important in fish generation and they protect us from storms. I am replanting the mangroves as it will protect my family and hut.
>
> (Amnah, Tippun, 65)

Respondents were also aware of the connection between changing climate and the frequency of storms and the deterioration of mangrove forests. As indicated earlier, the vast majority of the villagers are illiterate. Those who manage to obtain a moderate amount of education leave the village to work in the cities. However, the lack of formal education should not mask the positive effects of local education from the combination of real-world experience and science-based information campaigns by the WWF and other NGOs. The people of Keti Bunder are well aware of the importance to their future well-being of restoring damaged ecosystems.

11.7 Conclusions: institutions, power and environmental change in Keti Bunder

Our survey confirms these general observations regarding ecosystem services for the poor and the deteriorating state of these ecosystems:

1   Ecosystem functions are directly important for the well-being of the world's poorest. The residents of Keti Bunder depend entirely on the area's fisheries and mangrove ecosystems for their livelihoods. The contention that the GDP of the poor is largely composed of direct ecosystem services is confirmed in Keti Bunder.
2   Coastal ecosystems are under serious threat both from environmental changes and institutional failures. To the extent that Keti Bunder is representative, both of these factors are likely to become more serious in South Asia in the future.
3   Understanding local institutions and institutional failures is the key to formulating effective social and environmental policies.

More specifically, our survey and interviews confirm and extend the findings of previous research in Keti Bunder:

1   A reduction in the health of Indus Delta fisheries from the loss of mangroves and overharvesting due to the use of banned nets.
2   The loss of agricultural land due to increasing salinity.
3   A reduction in freshwater availability due to upstream diversion and salt-water intrusion from rising sea levels.
4   Increased vulnerability to climate events.
5   Increased local conflicts over declining ecosystem functions.

An ominous factor in all these observations is the increased institutional failure arising from migration, ethnic conflicts and changing power relationships. Environmental deterioration has caused occupation switching of one group (*Jaats*) from agriculture to fishing, causing increased pressure on fish stocks from unsustainable fishing techniques. An apparent increase in the number of camels kept by the *Jaats* has caused conflicts over mangroves and exacerbated their destruction. These sorts of resource conflicts among the world's poorest are happening throughout the coastal areas of South Asia and will likely get much worse as climate change disrupts local ecosystems. The implications are sobering not only for the future of the environment but also for social stability worldwide.

Notes

1 The authors would like to acknowledge the assistance of the WWF-Pakistan for providing logistical support in Keti Bunder and access to past surveys of the village. This work was also supported by a grant from the South Asia Network of Economic research Institutes (SANEI). An earlier version of this chapter was presented at the "International workshop on valuation of regulating services of ecosystems," Bangalore, India, 15–16 June 2009. We thank Nilanjan Ghosh, Pushpam Kumar and Michael D. Wood for comments on an earlier version of this chapter.
2 It is useful to distinguish between *stocks* whose *flows* can be called forth at any desired rate (a ton of coal for example) and *funds* whose *services* can only be used at a given rate (solar energy, labor power or ecosystems) (Georgescu-Roegen, 1984).
3 The macroeconomic implications of these examples are disturbing. The loss of ecosystem services can actually be an economic boon by creating jobs where none existed before. The macroeconomy does not operate by the same principles as an individual firm.
4 The following discussion containing general information about Keti Bunder is taken from the following WWF-Pakistan reports: WWF-Pakistan (2005a) and WWF-Pakistan (2006).
5 This research was carried out by the WWF and Emily Woodhouse of the Imperial College, London.

References

Agrawal, A. 2008. The role of local institutions in adaptation to climate change. Paper prepared for the Social Dimensions of Climate Change, World Bank, 5–6 March.

Alongi, D. 2002. Present state and future of the world's mangrove forests. *Environmental Conservation* 29 (3): 331–349.

Anderson, K. and Bows, A. 2008. Reframing the climate change challenge in light of post-2000 emission trends. *Philosophical Transactions of the Royal Society A* 366 (1882): 3863–3882.

Archer, D. 2009. *The Long Thaw*. Princeton, NJ: Princeton University Press.

Banuri, T., Najam, A. and Odeh, N. 2002. *Civic Entrepreneurship: A Civil Society Perspective on Sustainable Development*, vol. 4. Islamabad: Gandhara Academy Press.

Barbier, E.B., Koch, E.W., Silliman, B.R., Hacker, S.D., Wolanski, E., Primavera, J., Granek, E.F., Polasky, S., Aswani, S., Cramer, L.A., Stoms, D.M., Kennedy, C.J., Bael, D., Kappel, C.V., Perillo, G.M.E. and Reed, D.J. 2008. Coastal ecosystems management with non linear ecological functions and values. *Science* 319: 321.

Brock, R. and Kelt, D. 2004. Keystone effects of the endangered Stephens' kangaroo rat. *Biological Conservation* 116 (1): 131–139.

Bromley, D. 1998. Searching for sustainability: The poverty of spontaneous order. In Cleveland, C., Costanza, R. and Stern, D. (eds), *Changing the Nature of Economics*. Washington, DC: Island Press, Chapter 5.

Chichilnisky, G. and Heal, G. 1998. Economic returns from the biosphere. *Nature* 391: 629–630.

Colls, A., Ash, N. and Ikkala, N. 2009. *Ecosystem-based Adaptation: A Natural Response to Climate Change*. Gland, Switzerland: IUCN.

Daly, H. 1985. The circular flow of exchange value and the linear throughput of matter-energy: A case of misplaced concreteness. *Review of Social Economy* 43: 279–297.

Dasgupta, C. 2007. Climate-change challenge for the poor: Part I. YaleGlobal online. Available at: www.yaleglobal.yale.edu/article.print?id=9720.

Dasgupta, P. 2007. Discounting climate change. Mimeo, University of Cambridge. Available at: www.econ.cam.ac.uk/faculty/dasgupta/pub07/stavins_june07.pdf.

Dasgupta, P. 2008. Nature in economics. *Environmental and Resource Economics* 39: 1–7.

Dasgupta, P., Levin, S. and Lubchenco, J. 2000. Economic pathways to ecological sustainability. *BioScience* 50 (4): 339–345.

European Communities. 2008. *The Economics of Ecosystems and Biodiversity*. Wesseling: Welzel-Hardt.

Frey, B. and Stutzer, A. 2002. *Happiness and Economics: How the Economy and Institutions Affect Well-Being*. Princeton, NJ and Oxford: Princeton University Press.

Georgescu-Roegen, N. 1971. *The Entropy Law and the Economic Process*. Cambridge, MA: Harvard University Press.

Georgescu-Roegen, N. 1984. Feasible recipes versus viable technologies. *The Atlantic Economic Journal* 12: 21–30.

Gilbert, N. 2008. A quarter of mammals face extinction. *Nature* 455: 717.

Gowdy, J. 1997. The value of biodiversity. *Land Economics* 73: 25–41.

Gowdy, J. (ed.) 1998. *Limited Wants, Unlimited Means: A Reader on Hunter-Gatherer Economics and the Environment*. Washington, DC: Island Press.

Gowdy, J. 2005. Toward a new welfare foundation for sustainability. *Ecological Economics* 53: 211–222.

Gowdy, J. and Krall, L. 2009. The fate of Nauru and the global financial meltdown. *Conservation Biology* 23 (2): 257–258.

Haq, M. 1997. *Human Development in South Asia*. Karachi: Oxford University Press.

Haywood, A. and Williams, M. 2005. The climate of the future: Clues from three million years ago. *Geology Today* 21: 138–143.

Inglehart, R. 1990. *Cultural Shift in Advanced Industrial Societies*. Princeton, NJ: Princeton University Press.

Intergovernmental Panel on Climate Change. 2007. *Climate Change 2007: The Physical Science Basis*. Contribution of working group I to the Fourth Assessment Report of the Intergovernmental Panel on Climate Change, Geneva, Switzerland. Available at: www. ipcc.ch.

International Union for Conservation of Nature (IUCN) Pakistan. 2003. Poverty in the context of Pakistan. Available at: www.iucn.org/places/pakistan/poverty/poverty.htm.

Jackson, J. 2008. Ecological extinction and evolution in the brave new ocean. *Proceedings of the National Academy of Science* 105: 11458–11465.

Jianchu, X., Shrestha, A., Vaidya, R., Eriksson, M. and Hewitt, K. 2007. The melting Himalayas: Regional challenges and local impacts of climate change on mountain ecosystems and livelihoods. Technical paper, International Centre for International Mountain Development (ICIMOD), Kathmandu, Nepal, June.

Jiang, D., Wang, H., Ding, Z., Lang, X. and Helge, D. 2005. Modeling the Middle Pleistocene climate with a global atmospheric general circulation model. *Journal of Geophysical Research* 110: D14107.

Kahneman, D. and Sugden, R. 2005. Experienced utility as a standard of policy evaluation. *Environmental and Resource Economics* 32: 161–181.

Kallis, G., Martinez-Alier, J. and Norgaard, R. 2009. Paper assets, real debts: An ecological-economic exploration of the global economic crisis. *Critical Perspectives on International Business* 5: 14–25.

Kellert, S. 1996. *The Value of Life: Biological Diversity and Human Society*. Washington, DC: Island Press/Shearwater Books.

Khan, S.R. 2002. Adaptation to climate change in the context of sustainable development and equity: The case of Pakistan. Working paper series 78, Sustainable Development Policy Institute, Islamabad, Pakistan.

Krutilla, J. 1967. Conservation reconsidered. *American Economic Review* 57: 777–786.

McDaniel, C. and Gowdy, J. 1999. *Paradise for Sale: A Parable of Nature*. Berkeley, CA: University of California Press.

McLeod, E. and Salm, R. 2006. Managing mangroves for resilience to climate change. IUCN/Nature Conservancy, Resilience Science Working Group Paper series 2. Available at: www.iucn.org/themes/marine/pubs/pubs.htm.

Mäler, K.-G., Aniyar, S. and Jansson, A. 2008. Accounting for ecosystem services as a way to understand the requirements for sustainable development. *Proceedings of the National Academy of Science* 105 (28): 9501–9506.

Martinez-Alier, J. 1995. The environment as a luxury good or "too poor to be green." *Ecological Economics* 13: 1–10.

Melillo, J. and Sala, O. 2008. Ecosystem services. In Chivian, E. and Bernstein, A. (eds) *Sustaining Life: How Human Health Depends on Biodiversity*. Oxford and New York: Oxford University Press, pp. 75–115.

Millennium Ecosystem Assessment. 2005. *Ecosystems and Human Well-Being: A Framework for Assessment*. Available at: www.millenniumassessment.org/en/Condition.aspx.

Munasinghe, M. 2008. Rising temperatures, rising risks. *Finance and Development* 45 (1): 37–41.

Norton, B. 2005. *Sustainability: A Philosophy of Adaptive Ecosystem Management*. Chicago: University of Chicago Press.

Nunes, P. and van den Bergh, J. 2001. *Ecological Economics* 39: 203–222.

Nussbaum, M. 2000. *Women and Human Development*. Chicago: University of Chicago Press.

Orr, D. 2004. *Earth in Mind: On Education, Environment, and the Human Prospect*. Washington, DC: Island Press.

Rangel, A. 2003. Forward and backward generational goods: Why is social security a good of the environment? *American Economic Review* 93 (3): 813–834.

Rees, G. and Collins, D. 2004. An assessment of the potential impacts of deglaciation on the water resources of the Himalayas. Department for International Development Project No. R7980.

Robinson, G.R., Holt, R.D., Gaines, M.S., Hamburg, S.P., Johnson, M.L., Fitch, H.S. and Martinko, E.A. 1992. Diverse and contrasting effects of habitat fragmentation. *Science* 257: 524–525.

Schneider, S. 2009. The worst case scenario. *Nature* 458: 1104–1105.

Sen, A. 1999. *Development as Freedom*. New York: Anchor Books.

Singh, S.J. 2006. *The Nicobar Islands*. Vienna: Czernin Verlag.

Srinivasan, T., Carey, S., Hallstein, E., Higgins, P., Kerr, A., Koteen, L., Smith, A., Watson, R., Harte, J. and Norgaard, R. 2008. The debt of nations and the distribution of ecological impacts from human activities. *Proceedings of the National Academy of Science of the United States of America* 105 (5): 1768–1773.

Steinbauer, M.J. and Zeidler, J. 2008. climate change in the northern areas of Pakistan: Impacts on glaciers, ecology and livelihoods. Internal Report Version 1.2, WWF-Pakistan.

Stern, N. 2007. *The Economics of Climate Change: The Stern Review*. Cambridge: Cambridge University Press.

Sukhdev, P. and Bishop, J. 2008. The economics of ecosystems and biodiversity (TEEB):

A step towards biodiversity markets? Workshop on Capitalizing on Natural Resources: New Dynamics in Financial Markets. Rüschlikon, Germany, 10 September.

TEEB (The Economics of Ecosystems and Biodiversity). 2008. Interim report. Wesseling: Welzel-Hardt. Available at: http://ec.europa.eu/environment/nature/biodiversity/economics/pdf/teeb_report.pdf.

Tilman, D. and Downing, J. 1994. Biodiversity and stability in grasslands. *Nature* 367: 363–365.

United Nations Development Program. 2007. *Human Development Report 2007/2008: Fighting Climate Change*. New York: UNDP.

Walker, B., Holling, C., Carpenter, S. and Kinzig, A. 2004. Resilience, adaptability and transformability in socio-ecological systems. *Ecology and Society* 9: 5–15.

Wilson, E.O. 1994. *Biophilia.* Cambridge, MA: Harvard University Press.

Womenaid International. 2007. Capability poverty measure (CPM). Available at: www.womenaid.org/press/info/poverty.cpm.html.

Wood, A., Stedman-Edwards, P. and Mang, J. (eds) (2000) *The Root Causes of Biodiversity Loss*. London: Earth Scan.

World Bank. 2006. *Pakistan Strategic Country Environmental Assessment* (2 vols). Washington, DC: South Asia Environment and Social Development Unit.

Worstall, T. 2007. Indian wheat yields. *The Broadsheet*, 17 September. Available at: www.timworstall.com.

WWF-Pakistan. 2005a. Keti Bunder village development plan. WWF Regional Office, Karachi.

WWF-Pakistan. 2005b. Study on knowledge, attitudes and practices of fisherfolk communities about fisheries and mangrove resources. Available at: www.wwfpak.org/pdf/tp_kap_kakapir_village.pdf.

WWF-Pakistan. 2006. Fish marketing chain and economic analysis of indebtedness of fisher-folk of Keti Bunder. Programme Development Division, WWF.

WWF-Pakistan. 2008a. Climate change in the northern areas of Pakistan impact on glaciers, ecology, and livelihoods. Gilgit Conservation and Information Center.

WWF-Pakistan. 2008b. Detailed ecological assessment of fauna including limnology studies at Keti Bunder. Indus For All Program, WWF-Pakistan.

WWF-Pakistan. No date. Satellite remote sensing based forest mapping and monitoring of Keti Bunder. Available at: http://dss-foreverindus.org/Docs/Satellite%20Remote%20Sensing%20Based%20Forest%20Mapping%20and%20Monitoring%20of%20Keti%20Bunder.pdf

12 Valuation of ecosystem services

Methods, opportunities and policy implications

Nicolas Kosoy, Makiko Yashiro, Carlota Molinero and Anantha Duraiappah

12.1 Introduction

In 2005 the Millennium Ecosystem Assessment (MA) reported that 60 per cent of the 24 ecosystem services it assessed were in decline and could be expected to decline further if no immediate action was taken. The MA went on to state that this decline in ecosystem services will be a barrier preventing many countries achieving the Millennium Development Goals. The bottom line is that the world is on an unsustainable path and new models of economic and human development are needed (MA, 2005).

Many reasons were given for the rapid decline in ecosystem services, but the lack of incorporation of the full value (both monetary and non-monetary) of the ecosystem services provided by ecosystems are seldom taken into consideration in policy and decision making. In many instances, the ecosystem services are not exchanged in the market place. This means that there are no prices for these services which, if used, are not valued in any manner. Integrated assessments are useful exercises to help understand the complex relationships between the natural and social systems.

Why are economic valuations needed? In economic terms, externalities, as initially defined by Pigou, are those costs or benefits that remain uncompensated within the economically productive system. They constitute a loss that weakens the system's potential to support socio-economic development. Economists' attempts to achieve efficient levels of resource allocation must internalise these losses. In the case of ecosystem services, it means transferring benefits from positive externality users to providers. In other words, it refers to making the users of forest ecosystem services pay for them. Efforts to value ecosystem services fall within this category of internalising positive externalities. However, benefits and costs may be expressed in different dimensions and units. Some authors suggest that utilitarian values should not guide the decision-making process, but should be constrained by moral and intrinsic rights (Farber *et al.*, 2006). Others reject the hegemony of cost–benefit analysis as an environmental decision-making tool and question the capacity of the preference aggregation procedures that lie at the heart of environmental valuation to provide a genuinely democratic means of establishing the importance of environmental values for society and sustainability policy (O'Connor and Spash, 1999).

We aim to contribute to environmental accounting research. We do this by first reviewing articles on ecosystem service valuation methods and presenting a comparison between orthodox and heterodox value perspectives. Second, this chapter brings economic valuation exercises into the context of sub-global assessments (SGAs) and provides an overview of which methodological approaches are widespread among most SGAs, what are the consequences of adopting such approaches and the opportunities for improvement. While neoclassical economics assumes that values and preferences – tastes in the cultural field – are innate, given, fixed and highly individual in nature, this chapter acknowledges a different perspective, one that recognises values and preferences as social constructions (Vatn, 2004; Sagoff, 1988), similar to how tastes are group-specific and "coordinated" in western societies by a class *habitus* (Bordieu, 1984).

This chapter provides a review of peer-reviewed and non-peer-reviewed valuation exercises around the world. Most case study research was collected from academic and collaborative research initiatives on ecosystem services: eyes4earth from Earth Collective partnership (www.eyes4earth.org/casebase); Sustainable Agriculture and Natural Resource Management Collaborative Research Support Program from Virginia Tech (www.ext.vt.edu/cgi-bin/WebObjects/SANREM.woa/wa/advancedSearch); Payments for Environmental Services Inventory from the Department of Sustainable Development in the Organization of American States (http://ranpa.net/PES/tProjectPES/ShowTProjectPESTablePage.aspx); and the valuation of ecosystem services map from Conservation International (www.consvalmap.org).

12.2 Orthodox ecosystem services valuation studies

The most common methods of valuation of ecosystem services are: contingency valuation; hedonic pricing method (HPM); travel cost method (TCM); market prices and value transfers; and avoided and replacement costs. These can, in turn, be derived from four basic approaches to placing economic values on environmental effects. These are: price-based valuation methods; surrogate market valuation methods; hypothetical market approaches; and cost-based approaches.

Price-based valuation methods, either the direct market prices or their shadow-price versions, are best adopted when the environmental goods and services are transacted in formal markets. The value of the natural capital that provides an input for producing a commodity is the potential rent generated by the resource. This is the total gross revenue derived by the producer minus the total variable cost involved in production. If this is the case, shadow prices are developed. Alternatively, prices of similar goods transacted in the marketplace could be used. However, since these are not perfect substitutes, adjustments need to be made, which may also lead to substantial distortions.

Almost half of the valuation studies concerning biodiversity (17) and those valuing entire ecosystems (11) use price-based valuations. Few water- (7) and soil- (2) related valuations relied on this method for achieving their valuation objective. They relied on market prices and local consumption levels of animals and plants, water and soil. For instance, Knowler *et al.* (2003) specified a production function model for salmon habitat in Canada. The authors estimated the net social benefit from a bio-economic model under habitat-changing conditions – a degraded area provides only C\$0.93 per hectare compared to the C\$2.63 per hectare derived from a protected habitat. However, many ecosystem services are rarely sold and purchased in formal markets, but belong to subsistence economies, with exchanges linked to livelihoods and prices weakly related to consumer surplus. Prices for these goods and services are difficult to find, and perfect substitutes for these "fictitious" commodities do not exist.

Surrogate market valuation techniques are used when there is no formal market to measure an environmental value, but there exists information about a related good or service transacted in the marketplace that can be used to infer the value. Techniques where the value can be derived from other markets include HPM, TCM and the change in productivity (CoP) approach. HPM looks at the differentials in property prices and wages between locations and isolates the proportion of this difference that can be ascribed to the existence or quality of ecosystem goods and services. Travel costs reflect the value that people place on leisure, recreational or tourism aspects of ecosystems. TCM refers to spending, such as on transport, food, equipment, accommodation and time. A demand function is then constructed, relating visitation rates to expenditures made. The CoP method can be used whenever an environmental service or function acts as an input into the production of marketable goods. This technique estimates the changes in output as a result of lost environmental services.

Few water and soil valuation studies (2) use CoP or TCM for valuing the contribution of watershed protection and avoided deforestation in the provision of water flows and improvement of agricultural productivity. However, identifying and measuring the complex ecological linkages can be very difficult, unless data and models exist, which are not common in most of the study areas (Calder, 1999; Kosoy *et al.*, 2007). Several studies regarding biodiversity (5) and entire ecosystems (3) use TCM for valuing the contribution of particular species or ecosystem features to increasing the number of tourist visits to a protected natural area. Verma *et al.* (2001), in their report to the World Bank, use various methodologies to assess the monetary value of Bhoj wetland in India, in particular hedonic prices. Households in front of a lake show an increase of 50 per cent in their property value compared to those without access to this water resource.

In situations where market values cannot be observed or do not exist, rational decisions can be inferred through surveys or direct questions. The most widely used technique of this type is the contingent valuation method (CVM). Contingent valuation techniques infer the value that people place on goods and services by asking them their willingness to pay (WTP) for them (or willingness to accept compensation for their loss) under the hypothetical scenario that these services would be available for purchase.

Eight studies used this technique to elicit the monetary value people placed on wildlife in the context of biodiversity service valuation. Some of this value was linked to eco-tourism and recreation activities. Three studies used WTP in order to monetarily value watershed services, in particular the protection of watershed areas linked to the provision of water quality and quantity, expressed through the willingness of the user to pay an extra water fee. Loomis *et al.* (2000) conducted a study on the willingness to purchase the increase in ecosystem services through a higher water bill in a river catchment in Denver, USA. Respondents were willing to invest $21 per month to restore the river habitat and improve derived ecosystem services, which is then used to inform a farmers conservation easement scheme that is to be implemented in the catchment area. Whole ecosystems were also assessed by means of this technique. In this case, the monetary value of protected areas was assigned by means of individuals' willingness to pay. Ly *et al.* (2006) estimated WTP of recreational visitors to Djoudj National Bird Park in Senegal. This study aimed at valuing the national park and revisited the actual park entrance fees, suggesting a six-fold increase in fees. Revenues would then help improve the park's infrastructure and enhance visitors' experiences. However, CVM requires careful sampling, training of enumerators and long periods of preparation and analysis. The whole process can be very expensive.

The last technique we are considering here is avoided and replacement costs. The former captures people's valuation of ecological services by observing their actual expenditures to prevent its loss, or to defend themselves from the consequence of such a loss. The replacement cost approach examines how much people have to or would pay to restore their damaged environment to its original state.

The number of studies using these techniques is considerably lower compared to the previous methods. Few studies concern entire ecosystems (3) and soil services (2). Biodiversity- (4) and water- (5) related studies have used these techniques slightly more. Zavaleta (2000), for instance, estimates the impact of an invasive plant on the ecosystem services in the United States. The author mainly analyses the costs related to water losses at the municipal, agricultural and hydroelectric-power-generation level. She estimates an annual $127 million to $291 million cost from losing water-related ecosystem services at the national level. It should be noted that these cost-based approaches are based on a number of dubious assumptions: (1) actions are effective and able to perfectly substitute environmental quality; (2) there is complete information, therefore environmental risks are well perceived; and (3) there are no capital constraints.

A common factor running through all the methods described above is the assumption of the individual acting purely as a market agent. This assumption no doubt has merits and is, to a certain extent, true as most of us live in a market-driven society. However, there is merit in also addressing the individual as a citizen who makes choices and takes decision not purely as an individual always maximising her own utility, but as a member of society caring about other individuals' welfare. In this context, the social choice approach advocated by Sen (1995) to value the environment deserves some credit.

Furthermore, the question of who is to be included in the studies estimating the WTP is a critical point. Random sampling or stratified sampling may need to be modified so the various stakeholders are represented in the exercise trying to determine the values of ecosystem services. Appropriate weights may need to be attached so that relative values of the environment are normalised in a manner that makes these differences irrelevant in the final estimation of the value of the environment (ibid.). The same can be said for future generations. Some appropriate method may need to be adopted to reflect future generations' values in the estimation of the value of an environmental asset.

The fact that social discussions and exchanges and their effects on individual valuations can influence the valuation exercise of an environmental asset suggests the need for complementary methodologies to accompany the orthodox techniques described above. There is no doubt that market-driven methodologies do provide useful information on the values of environmental assets. However, there is value in including social approaches to the valuation exercise in order to complement the suite of techniques to get a better understanding of the complexity and full value of the environment.

12.3 Heterodox views on ecosystem services valuation

The neoclassical model rests on the assumption that the absence of markets and the occurrence of externalities lead to over-exploitation of environmental resources. Incentive-based mechanisms should be used to internalise social costs and, therefore, achieve efficient resource allocation. Critical research show that trade-offs arise in every valuation exercise using individual or collective values, monetary or non-monetary units. An analysis of trade-offs also suggests that not only economic efficiency, but equity, sustainability and cultural and ethical values play a significant role in the decision making process (Farber *et al.*, 2006). Moreover, "basic axioms of neoclassical utility theory cannot be reconciled with the current state of knowledge in other relevant disciplines" (Gowdy and Mayumi, 2001: 224). Furthermore, methods that rely on valuations based on individuals to identify optimal natural resource allocations are objectionable on at least two main grounds (Sagoff, 1988): (1) they confuse *oeconomia* with *chrematistics* – they reduce moral principles and values to dollars-and-cents metric in consumer preferences; and (2) moral and social values that pertain to environmental policy are collective action problems and therefore must be negotiated through a deliberative process. In this section we first address the debate concerning social preferences and valuation, and then turn to monetisation and valuation language hegemony.

12.3.1 Social preferences, utility and well-being

Homo economicus' conceptualisation assumes that preferences are given and independent of social conditions. The satisfaction of individual preferences is taken as the appropriate goal of both individuals and society (Zografos and Howarth, 2008). This conceptualisation of human preferences has been challenged on different grounds, which runs from individual to collective, from given and fixed to socially constructed preferences. Alternative perspectives to orthodox valuation draw from deliberation to "outperform, or rather have sounder foundations, than standard economic valuation" (Spash, 2008). Deliberation, then, is a process that allows preferences to be transformed through reflection over available information (Zografos and Howarth, 2008).

A number of approaches are the result of "cross fertilisation" research combining stated-preference methods with elements of deliberative processes.

Nyborg (2000) proposes a formalisation of the distinction between *Homo economicus* and *Homo politicus*, using well-known concepts from neoclassical welfare economics. The author departs from Sagoff's (1988) distinction between the individual's roles as consumer and citizen, and states that certain goods and services such as natural assets cannot be individually valued. Therefore, aggregation of environmental individual preferences will not lead to social well-being. A formalisation of the utility function based on social preferences will assume that individuals, depending on the good to be assessed, will either maximise their own well-being or will maximise social welfare. Following this conceptualisation, CVM then turns the question of environmental valuation into a maximisation of social welfare, which is expected to meet a citizen's views and values of the environment. The issue seems to find resolution based on methodological grounds.

Some studies explore the possibilities of overcoming criticism from non-monetary valuation methods, mainly information processing, object under value, preferences and community- or individual-based values. Alvarez-Farizo *et al.* (2009) combine choice experiment with the citizen's workshop participatory technique as a means to assess the consequences of damage restoration for a simulated nuclear accident. These authors focused on a set of environmental and social impacts in two cities in Spain. They prove that: (1) heterogeneity in responses diminishes with increasing valuation sessions; (2) values change from individually to collectively framed when time and discussion is allowed among valuation exercise participants; and (3) policy advice changes accordingly.

Further improvements to CVM deal with uncertainty and recognise that respondents are hesitant about their own preferences and find it difficult to state a single number. In a study on the value of water quality on the Scottish coastline, the authors support the argument of coherent arbitrariness by proving that respondents engaged in a valuation exercise find it difficult to reveal a single estimate of value, but rather provide a range of acceptable values (Hanley *et al.*, 2007). This has implications for welfare theory and uncertainty of values for public environmental goods. Furthermore, studies concerning CVM claim that missing information and limitations in the respondent's cognitive ability to process the available information are easily interpreted and assessed from a bounded-rationality perspective, leading to optimal decisions (Frör, 2008; Venkatachalam, 2008).

These studies share the aim of using deliberative or other forms of group processes that enable individuals to make judgements over the best use of societal resources; therefore, they claim to obtain a decision directly over the aggregate social value (Spash, 2008). However, they do not challenge the basic premise of economic policy that defines welfare change that arises from an environmental improvement as the sum of monetary values assigned by all individuals affected by an action. Sagoff (2003: 596) shows that "preference satisfaction as a policy goal cannot be justified either in terms of welfare or in terms of choice". This author claims that preference is an artefact of a particular description of choice and therefore should not guide policy analysis. Further criticism is drawn from multi-criteria approaches to decision-making, which state that it should be parametric and based on multiple values rather than on money metric (Gowdy and Seidl, 2004).

12.3.2 Multiple languages of valuation

A competitive equilibrium does not necessarily represent a social optimum. Rational behaviour as assumed by neoclassical welfare models, although theoretically interesting, should not guide policy recommendations (Gowdy and Seidl, 2004). Research on economic behaviour supports the importance of cultural context and group norms as better predictors of behaviour than those depicted in *Homo economicus* (Gowdy *et al.*, 2003).

While Coase (1960) reasoned that the complementary goals of economic efficiency and distributive justice could be effectively decoupled, ecological economists have focused on the need to define and protect the rights of both disempowered groups and future generations (Howarth and Norgaard, 1990). This sets the grounds for rejecting cost–benefit analysis as a hegemonic environmental decision-making tool (O'Connor and Spash, 1999). Moreover, the preference aggregation procedures shown above, which lie at the heart of environmental valuation, should be questioned as legitimate means of establishing the importance of environmental values for society and sustainability policy (ibid.). These two premises have led to the development of multi-criteria analysis either as an alternative decision-making tool to cost–benefit analysis (Munda, 1997) or as an alternative preference aggregation tool (Martínez-Alier *et al.*, 1998). Furthermore, multiple preference orderings would imply that choices made in one context may not be replicated in another.

Environmental value is a group value and should not be sought as an aggregate of individual values (Vatn, 2004). Multi-functionality is a key component of natural systems; externalities in this context also have multiple origins and effects. Therefore, acknowledging the many dimensions of these externalities that are not included in the economically productive system accountings requires defining new tools for moving from individualism to collective solutions. A recent study conducted by Sugimura and Howarth (2008) includes social factors in the assessment of quality for four forest ecosystem services in Japan and proves that social evaluation for valuing forest ecosystem services yields significant differences in forest zoning outcomes. For instance, allocation of areas for wood production is significantly lower (one-third lower) when using social evaluation compared to the usual method. Another example links Patagonian ecosystem processes, goods and services with a qualitative approach to valuation so as to guide decision-making processes regarding conservation and protection initiatives (Martinez-Harms and Gajardo, 2008). The authors estimate the threat level of different pressures and human disturbances in the Patagonian territory and show the unbalanced coverage of the protected area network at the regional scale. The results of this chapter indicate the urgency for re-planning the present distribution of the protected areas if ecosystem services with high conservation value are to be maintained.

Scholars in ecological economics have argued in favour of value-articulating institutions that are capable of integrating multiple values (Vatn, 2005). A case study linking nature conservation and forestry ecosystem services in Finland showed that cultural and local ecological conditions should be included when formulating environmental policy recommendations so as to enable the creation of new rules for financial, voluntary and temporal conservation practices (Palo-niemi and Vilja, 2009).

12.4 Economic valuation of ecosystem services in sub-global assessments

This section presents the findings of eight SGAs and their use of economic valuation to inform policy processes. These assessments covered a diverse range of services, from regulating and provisioning to cultural ecosystem services. SGAs were introduced by the MA primarily as a tool to generate information on the state of ecosystems and the changes in the delivery of ecosystem services and their impacts on human well-being on different scales, perspectives and stakeholders. The MA conceptual framework defines an assessment as "a social process to bring the findings of science to bear on the needs of decision-makers" (MA, 2005). The process is thus as important as the quality of the end product in determining the effectiveness of an assessment (Cash and Clark, 2001). Furthermore, SGAs have the potential to generate policy-relevant information at the local, national and regional level that can be used by the appropriate policy makers as well as other relevant stakeholders at these respective levels in their decision making.

More than 30 SGAs have been undertaken around the world. Under the MA, 18 SGAs were approved and an additional 15 had an associated status. Today, five SGAs are taking place and three more are about to start. Assessments at sub-global scales are needed because ecosystems are highly differentiated in space and time, and because sound management requires careful local planning and action. Many assessments concerning the environment rely on monetary valuation for acknowledging and weighing the importance of natural resources in human production.

The economic value of cultural ecosystem services such as recreation services was estimated by using CVM and surrogate markets (e.g. mainly WTP and TCM), and helped to identify the potential economic gains from the tourism sector in financing natural reserves. However, as mentioned above, the use of these methods does not necessarily capture the value of cultural ecosystem services for non-commoditised assets. For instance, the value of culture-related biodiversity ecosystem services in the context of rural and indigenous communities is not expressed through formal or informal markets, but through traditional institutions that articulate, manage and regulate the use and distribution of benefits derived from these services. Therefore, policy recommendations based on CVM and TCM may be misleading, and might promote, for instance, the use of tariffs that overstate the importance of monetary values in these non-market contexts. Participatory CVM, such as those currently under development by heterodox economists, may offer an opportunity to deliberate on the value of cultural ecosystem services allowing a channel of communication for non-monetary experienced values.

Provisioning services were widely studied in the SGAs, particularly referring to food and fibre provisioning, timber and non-timber forest products, and fisheries. Emphasis was given to extraction levels of these environmental goods and their economic value to local and national economies through market prices. However, little emphasis was given to linking natural production and extraction of these goods; therefore, although information points towards a depletion of these resources, limited policy recommendations are being made towards achieving sustainable management of these provisioning services. Lack of information seems the ultimate reason for delivering weak recommendations at the policy- and decision-making level. Economic valuation studies simply highlight the level of contribution of these ecosystem services to the economies; however, they fail to address the institutional and ecological framework that promotes or deters the degradation of these services. Traditional market price approaches to provisioning services that consider ecological limits allowing for re-stocking and social rules that govern provisioning service exploitation rates may provide more robust policy than those policies based on demand and supply curves and self-regulatory approaches (Fisher *et al.*, 2008).

Regulating services were also studied in almost all eight SGAs reviewed, in particular water-related ecosystem services. Water flows captured most of the attention of these assessments. Analyses on the total flow in relation to withdrawal rates allowed for the estimation of future scenarios. These, in turn, allowed policy recommendations regarding the volume of water that should remain in the water systems so as to secure actual and future uses. Water quality was another service receiving extensive focus in the SGAs. Relationships between land-use changes and drinking water provision were analysed for the case of the city of Sao Paulo. Economic benefits were not fully addressed in either cases – it just highlighted the importance of maintaining the water flows and the water quality, but no methodological nor practical approaches were made to estimate the economic contribution of watershed-regulating services in rural nor urban contexts. Also, links between land-use changes and water were made but no evidence was presented, leading to general recommendations and limited policy action. Soil stabilisation and pollutant reduction were also targeted by the SGAs. Links were established between urban sprawl pollutant reduction and soil erosion, and recommendations were directed towards protecting forest cover in high-slope areas. However, the economic implications of preserving forest cover for maintaining the soils and reducing the level of pollutants from water sewage were not estimated.

The use of economic valuation in SGAs to provide information to decision makers regarding environmental issues seems to have been limited. Economic valuation of cultural and provisioning services is more widespread; however, the translation of such findings to the decision-making arena is not yet clear. Figures are used more as a tool for showing the importance of these ecosystem services to the overall economy rather than to guide the decision-making process in the quest for equitable and efficient policy instruments addressing environmental degradation. It is with regards to regulating ecosystem services that economic valuation is urgently needed, and it is in this particular area that little progress has been made. Although regulating ecosystem services have been studied in many SGAs, their contribution to the economic process is not systematically addressed, even less so in the decision-making process.

12.5 More limitations in ecosystem services valuation and final remarks

The importance of economic valuation studies on ecosystem services has been shown throughout this chapter. The pitfalls of the different valuation methods were highlighted when addressing ecosystem services. However, another important issue that was addressed throughout this chapter is the classification of ecosystem services. The definition that has been widely recognised is the one developed by the MA (2005), which states that ecosystem services are "the benefits people obtain from ecosystems". According to the MA, there are four different types of ecosystem service: (1) provisioning services, which are the products obtained from ecosystems such as food, timber and fresh water; (2) regulating services, which are the benefits obtained from the regulation of ecosystem services, such as air quality regulation and water regulation; (3) cultural services, which are the non-material benefits people obtain from ecosystems, such as aesthetic values and cultural heritage values; and (4) supporting services, which are the services necessary for the production of other services such as soil formation and nutrient cycling. While this categorisation has contributed significantly to an improved understanding of the links between different services provided by ecosystems and various constituents of human well-being, when applied for economic valuation, this classification of ecosystem services may cause some confusion and could lead to double counting of some of the services.

Boyd and Banzhaf (2007) and Fisher *et al.* (2008) argue that this double counting occurs due to the fact that some of the ecosystem services are "intermediate services" (e.g. nutrient cycling) that are needed for the "final services" (e.g. clean water provision) to bring benefits (e.g. drinking water) to human welfare. Therefore, for example, if the value of nutrient cycling (supporting services under the MA definition) and clean water provision (provisioning services under the MA definition) were individually valued, this will lead to double counting, as the intermediate services – in this case, nutrient cycling – are embedded in the measurement of the value of the final service – clean water provision. Drawing on the work of Boyd and Banzhaf (2007), Fisher *et al.* (2008) suggest the separation of ecosystem services into intermediate and final services and benefits, proposing that only the benefits generated by the final services should be aggregated in accounting and valuation exercises, in order to avoid double counting.

Finally – and back to valuation issues – we demonstrate that economic valuation of ecosystem services in the context of SGAs, although important, is not yet fully articulated in guiding policy action. It is, then time to ask whether SGA practitioners are aware of the usefulness of valuation techniques, or if the academic community is able to bridge the gap between research findings and policy making? To our understanding, it is neither the role of SGA practitioners to devise valuation methods nor the role of scientists to deliver policy recommendations, but it is the role of both to respond to the current environmental crisis by making use of the best information available. Regulating ecosystem services provides us with a unique opportunity to devise new methods for economic valuation, adjust old ones, and find new ways of communicating research findings to policy makers. The nature of these services requires the participation of many different stakeholders, with special attention paid to the above-mentioned heterodox valuation methods. These participatory valuation approaches may then facilitate the interaction between policy makers and decision makers, and the scientific community.

References

Alvarez-Farizo, B., Gil, J.M. and Howarth, B.J. 2009. Impacts from restoration strategies: Assessment through valuation workshops. *Ecological Economics* 68 (3): 787–797.

Bourdieu, P. (1984 [1979]) *Distinction: A Social Critique of the Judgement of Taste.* Trans. R. Nice. London: Routledge.

Boyd, J. and Banzhaf, S. 2007. What are ecosystem services? The need for standardized environmental accounting units. *Ecological Economics* 63: 616–626.

Calder, I.R. 1999. *The Blue Revolution: Land Use and Integrated Water Resources Management.* London: Earthscan.

Cash, D. and Clark, W.C. 2001. From science to policy: Assessing the assessment process. Faculty research working paper series, John F. Kennedy School of Government, Harvard University.

Coase, R. 1960. The problem of social cost. *Journal of Law and Economics* 3: 1–44.

Farber, S., Costanza, R., Childers, D., Erickson, J., Gross, K., Grove, M., Hopkinson, C., Kahn, J., Pincetl, S., Troy, A., Warren, P. and Wilson, M. 2006. Linking ecology and economics for ecosystem managment. *Bioscience* 56 (2): 121–133.

Fisher, B., Turner, K., Zylstra, M., Brouwer, R., de Groot, R., Farber, S., Ferraro, P., Green, R., Hadley, D., Harlow, J., Jefferiss, P., Kirkby, C., Morling, P., Mowatt, S., Naidoo, R., Paavola, J., Strassburg, B., Yu, D. and Balmford, A. 2008. Ecosystem services and economic theory: Integration for policy-relevant research. *Ecological Applications* 18 (8): 2050–2067.

Frör, O. 2008. Bounded rationality in contingent valuation: Empirical evidence using cognitive psychology. *Ecological Economics* 68(1–2): 570–581.

Gowdy, J.M. and Mayumi, K. 2001. Reformulating the foundations of consumer choice theory and environmental valuation. *Ecological Economics* 39 (2): 223–237.

Gowdy, J.M and Seidl, Irmi. 2004. Economic man and selfish genes: The implications of group selection for economic valuation and policy. *Journal of Socio-economics* 33 (3): 343–358.

Gowdy, J., Iorgulescu, R. and Onyeiwu, S. 2003. Fairness and retaliation in a rural Nigerian village. *Journal of Economic Behavior and Organization* 52 (4): 469–479.

Hanley, N., Kristrom, B. and Shogren, J. 2007. Coherent arbitrariness: On value uncertainty for environmental goods. *Land Economics* 85 (1): 41.

Howarth, R.B. and Norgaard, R.B. 1990. Intergenerational resource rights, efficiency, and social optimality. *Land Economics* 66: 1–11.

Kosoy, N., Martinez-Tuna, M., Muradian, R. and Martinez-Alier, J. 2007. Payments for environmental services in watersheds: Insights from a comparative study of three cases in Central America. *Ecological Economics* 61(2–3): 446–455.

Knowler, D., MacGregor, B., Bradford, M. and Peterman, R. 2003. Valuing freshwater salmon habitat on the west coast of Canada. *Journal of Environmental Management* 69: 261–273.

Loomis, J., Kent, P., Strange, L., Fausch, K. and Covich, A. 2000. Measuring the total economic value of restoring ecosystem services in an impaired river basin: Results from a contingent valuation survey. *Ecological Economics* 33: 103–117.

Ly, O., Bishop, J., Moran, D. and Dansokho, M. 2006. Estimating the value of ecotourism in the Djoudj National Bird Park in Senegal. Gland, Switzerland: World Conservation Union.

MA. 2005. *Millenium Ecosystem Assessment: Findings of the Condition and Trend Working Group*. Washington, DC: Island Press.

Martínez-Alier, J., Munda, G. and O'Neill, J. 1998. Weak comparability of values as a foundation for ecological economics. *Ecological Economics* 26 (3): 277–286.

Martínez-Harms, M.J. and Gajardo, R. 2008. Ecosystem value in the Western Patagonia protected areas. *Journal for Nature Conservation* 16 (2): 72–87.

Munda, G. 1997. Environmental economics, ecological economics, and the concept of sustainable development. *Environmental Values* 6 (2): 213–233.

Nyborg, K. 2000. Homo Economicus and Homo Politicus: Interpretation and aggregation of environmental values. *Journal of Economic Behavior and Organization* 42 (3): 305–322.

O'Connor, M. and Spash, C.L. 1999. *Valuation and the Environment: Theory, Method and Practice*. Cheltenham: Edward Elgar.

Paloniemi, R. and Vilja, V. 2009. Changing ecological and cultural states and preferences of nature conservation policy: The case of nature values trade in South-Western Finland. *Journal of Rural Studies* 25 (1): 87–97.

Sagoff, M. 1988. *The Economy of the Earth*. New York: Cambridge University Press.

Sagoff, M. 1998. Aggregation and deliberation in valuing environmental public goods: A look beyond contingent pricing. *Ecological Economics* 24 (2): 213–230.

Sagoff, M. 2003. On the relation between preference and choice. *Journal of Socio-economics* 31 (6): 587–598.

Sen, A. 1995. Rationality and social choice. *American Economic Review* 85(1): 1–24.

Spash, Clive L. 2008. Deliberative monetary valuation (DMV) and the evidence for a new value theory. *Land Economics* 84 (3): 469–488.

Sugimura, K. and Howard, T.E. 2008. Incorporating social factors to improve the Japanese forest zoning process. *Forest Policy and Economics* 10: 161–173.

Vatn, A. 2004. Environmental valuation and rationality. *Land Economics* 80 (1): 1–18.

Vatn, A. 2005. *Institutions and the Environment*. Cheltenham: Edward Elgar.

Venkatachalam, L. 2008. Behavioral economics for environmental policy. *Ecological Economics* 67 (4): 640–645.

Verma, M., Bakshi, N. and Nair, R. 2001. Economic valuation of Bhoj wetland for sustainable use. Project report of the Environmental Management Capacity Building Technical Assistance Project Implemented by the Ministry of Environment and Forest and Coordinated by EERC Implementation Cell at IGIDR, Mumbai, India. Available at: http://earthmind.net/values/docs/valuation-wtland-bhoj.pdf.

Zavaleta, E. 2000. The economic value of controlling an invasive shrub. *Ambio* 29: 8.

Zografos, C. and Howarth, R.B. (eds). 2008. *Deliberative Ecological Economics*. Oxford: Oxford University Press.

13 Valuation of regulating services

Key issues and future perspectives

Pushpam Kumar and Michael D. Wood

13.1 Nuances and imperatives in the valuation of regulating services

Valuation of ecosystem services helps in mapping the contribution of ecosystem services to human well-being. It also brings conservation closer to the decision-making process. All ecosystems can be considered as capital stock. Through their ecological production function, analogous to the engineering production function in production economics, they provide ecosystem services. Forests providing groundwater augmentation and carbon sequestration, mountains yielding hydrological services and wetlands providing bioremediation and water storage, are all examples of ecosystem services that are beneficial to society through enabling production and consumption processes. Various market- and non-market-based valuation methods capture these ecosystem services in monetary terms, enabling them to be incorporated in the 'values' box. There are direct benefits of ecosystems known as intrinsic values or bequest values that directly enter into the 'values' box. Formation of values will be influenced by how robust and accurate the valuation methodologies are in capturing the services of the ecological production functions. For example, decision-making criteria, like cost–benefit analysis or the multi-criteria method, depend upon values estimated using valuation methods. These decision-making criteria influence choice and subsequently impact on the condition and trend of the ecosystem under consideration. In effect, value determines choice and choice impacts the fate of ecosystems and their services. Thus, valuation of ecosystems plays a pivotal role in designing the appropriate response option(s).

Valuation of the ecosystem services makes the stakeholders accountable for conservation and management in a more efficient way than otherwise. As the chapters in Part I demonstrate, defining the purpose for which valuation is to be undertaken and determining the appropriate classification of ecosystem services are the first milestones in valuation. In addition, the temporal and spatial dimensions of ecosystem goods and services must also be delineated in order to define the scope and boundaries of valuation.

Successful valuation requires a joint effort between natural scientists and economists. This is reflected in the various chapters of this book and in the expertise of the book editors. The whole process of applying valuation tools to ecosystem services is essentially interdisciplinary in nature. Practitioners in the valuation of ecosystem services must break the disciplinary boundaries because valuation is a problem-solving strategy and a problem is a problem; it does not respect the boundary of any particular discipline. Economists must learn from and interact with natural scientists if they wish to apply valuation tools meaningfully. For example, economists wishing to estimate ecological production functions may need to interact with limnologists (wetland), plan taxonomists (biodiversity), hydrologists (water recharge) and many other similar professionals who are typically outside of the economics discipline. Likewise, natural scientists must learn from economists to understand the concepts and information requirements for valuation in order to provide the necessary biophysical data to underpin the valuation exercise. An interdisciplinary approach combining ecological information with economic methods yields the most robust results in valuation and the methodological paradigm should be fluid enough to embrace assumptions of other disciplines like ecological and physical sciences.

Understanding the ecological production function through collaborative effort with ecologists provides the necessary information on issues critical to undertaking the valuation exercise, including:

1   the initial condition of the ecosystem and the corresponding ecological production function;
2   drivers of change, their impacts on the ecosystem and the resultant effects on the flow of ecosystem services;
3   measurement of ecosystem services in quantifiable units;
4   additional perturbations creating changes in the flow(s) of ecosystem services (basically marginal change in ecosystem benefits as a response to marginal change in drivers);
5   the ecological scale of change over relevant temporal scales;
6   identification of the 'gainers' and 'losers' in the process of ecosystem change.

From Parts I and II, it emerges that value and valuation tools are multiple and their application depends on the decision-making context, as well as the data and expertise that are available. Some of the valuation tools used for regulating services are summarized in Table 13.1.

However, many of the techniques based on behavioral models are based on a normative version of economics and do not convey the way in which the individual or society is actually valuing the ecosystem service under consideration. Here, one can observe the distinction between those who want to value ecosystem services by asking what people would do and those who would actually observe what people have done (as emphasized by Simpson in Chapter 4 of this book). Methods based on stated preference, like contingent valuation method (CVM), choice experiments (CE) or contingent ranking, tend to ask what people would do and this may entail numerous sources of bias which

Table 13.1 Application of some of the major economic valuation techniques available for use in the valuation of regulating services

Methodology	Approach	Applications
Change in productivity	Trace impact of change in environmental services on produced goods	Any impact that affects produced goods (e.g. declines in soil quality affecting agricultural production)
Cost of illness, human capital	Trace impact of change in environmental services on morbidity and mortality	Any impact that affects health (e.g. air or water pollution)
Replacement cost	Use cost of replacing the lost good or service	Any loss of goods or services (e.g. previously clean water that now has to be purified using a technological solution)
Travel cost method	Derive demand curve from data on actual travel costs	Recreation, tourism
Hedonic prices	Extract effect of environmental factors on price of goods that include those factors	Air quality, scenic beauty, cultural benefits (e.g. the higher market value of waterfront property, or houses next to green spaces)
Contingent valuation	Ask respondents directly their willingness to pay for a specified service	Any service (e.g. willingness to pay to keep a local forest intact)
Choice modeling	Ask respondents to choose their preferred option from a set of alternatives with particular attributes	Any service
Benefits transfer	Use results obtained in one context in a different context	Any service for which suitable comparison studies are available

detract from the credibility of the valuation exercise in the eyes of decision makers.

13.2 Challenges in valuation of regulating services

Several issues pertinent to valuation of ecosystem services and application to decision making have emerged, especially with a better understanding of the mechanisms of ecosystem functioning. The relevance of the state of ecosystem functioning has not been given adequate emphasis in the derivation of ecosystem values, thereby rendering the values of little worth, especially when one is examining issues related to sustainability.

In order to provide a meaningful scarcity indicator of ecosystem values and functions, economic valuation should account for the state of the ecosystem.

Though ecosystems can recuperate from some shocks and disturbances through an inherent property of resilience, there are several circumstances under which the ecosystem shifts to an entirely new state of equilibrium (Holling, 2001; Naeem *et al.*, 2009). Ecosystem goods and services, by definition, are public in nature, meaning that several benefits accrue to society as a whole, in addition to the benefits provided to individuals (Daily, 1997; Heal, 2000). Valuation methodologies such as contingent valuation utilize individual preferences as the basis of deriving values that are subsequently used for resource allocation of goods which are largely public in character. While methodologies for deriving values with economic efficiency as the goal are comparatively well developed, integrating equity and sustainability requires a better understanding of the functional relationships between various parameters and phenomena responsible for generating the ecosystem services in the first place and the social processes governing the mechanism of value formation. Discourse-based valuation is one such approach (Wilson and Howarth, 2002).

In the discussion of valuation of ecosystem services that contribute to human well-being and societal welfare, assumptions regarding rational economic agents, well-functioning markets, consistent preferences, ecosystems and their services, and future projections are all critical. However, these assumptions are far from resolved and need serious attention if the value is to be comprehensive and acceptable to all stakeholders. In the past, assumptions of economic theory have maintained distance from behavioral science, especially psychology. Economists, whether dealing with the issues of valuation or forecasting, seem to be functioning independent of the psychological dimension, even though this psychological dimension is quintessential to the entire exercise of economic analysis of ecosystems (Kumar and Kumar, 2008)

Some of the key messages emerging from the analysis are:

1   Market and non-market valuation methods for valuation of ecosystem services can capture some of the 'out-of-market' services.
2   Valuation does not intend to establish the importance of an ecosystem for humans; it is intended to help decision makers in a situation of trade-off or where there are alternate courses of action.
3   Valuation of ecosystem services has to be context- and ecosystem-specific and guided by the perception of beneficiaries.
4   Total valuation should be evaluated for whole catchments, landscapes and mapping units, while marginality valuation should be used for incremental changes in ecosystem services as a consequence of measured pressure on the ecosystem in consideration.
5   Increasingly, focus should be on the valuation of marginal changes of an ecosystem rather the total economic value of the ecosystem.
6   The initial condition and state of the ecosystem must be defined when estimating the value of ecosystem services.
7   Valuation should be done for ecosystem services assuming they are independent of each other.

8 Establishing property rights for the ecosystem is critically important for valuation.

9 While doing valuation, issues of irreversibility and resilience must be kept in mind.

10 Clear-cut biophysical linkages and relationships not only facilitate the valuation exercise, but help to ensure its credibility in the domain of public policy.

11 Uncertainty is one of the key challenges in valuation of ecosystem services, and sensitivity analysis is therefore helpful when communicating the results of valuation exercises to decision makers.

12 Participatory exercises that utilize representative samples ensure broad participation and embed outcomes in institutional processes prove helpful in informing decision-making processes.

13 Valuation has the potential to clear the clouds of conflicting goals in terms of political, social and economic feasibility of policies (but it should be seen as one of a range of tools in that area available for this purpose).

14 In the context of sectoral and project policies, valuation of ecosystem services will strengthen the environmental impact assessment and make the appraisal criteria more acceptable, transparent and credible.

Valuation is only one element in the effort to improve the management of ecosystems and their services. Economic valuation may help to inform management decisions, but only if decision makers are aware of the overall objectives and limitations of valuation. The main objective of valuation of ecosystem services is to indicate the overall economic efficiency of the various competing uses of a particular ecosystem. That is, the underlying assumption is that ecosystem resources should be allocated to those uses that yield an overall net gain to society, as measured through valuation in terms of the economic benefit of each use adjusted by its costs.

While valuation of regulating services is certainly difficult, the benefits make the exercise worthwhile. The case studies presented in Part II of this book demonstrate how some of the standard economic methodologies can be applied to the valuation of regulating services such as watershed services, carbon sequestration by forest, pollination, corals and storm protection by mangroves.

We sincerely hope that this book helps to clarify some of the doubt and uncertainty regarding the valuation of regulating services. Innovative methodologies in this field have started to emerge (e.g. Daily *et al.*, 2008), and we anticipate that in coming years there will be much further discussion on this topic as methodologies and understanding continue to evolve. This is a highly active area of interdisciplinary research with far-reaching social and environmental implications.

References

Daily, G.C. (ed.) (1997) Nature's Services: Societal Dependence on Natural Ecosystems. Washington, DC: Island Press.

Daily, G.C., Stephen Polasky, Joshua Goldstein, Peter M. Kareiva, Harold A. Mooney, Liba Pejchar, Taylor H. Ricketts, James Salzman and Robert Shallenberger (2008) Ecosystem services in decision making: Time to deliver. *Frontiers in Ecology and Environment* 7 (1), 21–28.

Heal, G. (2000) Valuing ecosystem services. *Ecosystems* 3, 24–30.

Holling, C.S. (2001) Understanding the complexity of economic, ecological and social systems. *Ecosystems* 4, 390–405.

Kumar, M. and P. Kumar (2008) Valuation of ecosystem services: A psycho-cultural perspective. *Ecological Economics* 64, 808–819.

Naeem, S., D.E. Bunker, A. Hector, M. Loreau and C. Perrings (2009) *Biodiversity, Ecosystem Functioning, and Human Well Being*. Oxford: Oxford University Press.

Wilson, M.A. and R.B. Howarth (2002) Discourse based valuation of ecosystem services: Establishing fair outcomes through group deliberation. *Ecological Economics* 41, 431–443.

Index

Note: Page numbers in **bold** denote tables. Those in *italic* denote figures or illustrations.

For Product Safety Concerns and Information please contact our EU
representative GPSR@taylorandfrancis.com
Taylor & Francis Verlag GmbH, Kaufingerstraße 24, 80331 München, Germany

www.ingramcontent.com/pod-product-compliance
Ingram Content Group UK Ltd.
Pitfield, Milton Keynes, MK11 3LW, UK
UKHW021616240425
457818UK00018B/587